MW01051951

LAWYERING FROM THE INSIDE OUT

Law is a varied, powerful, and highly rewarding profession. Studies show, however, that lawyers have higher rates of alcoholism, divorce, and even suicide than the general population. Stress creates these poor outcomes, including the stress of dealing with other people's problems all day, the stress of spending excessive amounts of time at work, and the stress of being disconnected to what is most meaningful in life. Through mindfulness and emotional intelligence training, lawyers can improve focus, get more work done in less time, improve their interpersonal skills, and seek and find work that will make their lives most meaningful. This book is designed to help law students and lawyers of all experience levels find a sustainable and meaningful life in the field of law. This book includes journaling and other interactive exercises that can help lawyers find peace, focus, meaning, and happiness over a lifetime of practicing law.

Nathalie Martin is the Frederick M. Hart Chair in Consumer and Clinical Law at University of New Mexico School of Law, where she teaches commercial and consumer law, as well as mindfulness and professional development. As a long-time yoga and meditation practitioner and teacher, Nathalie is part of a growing movement to teach mindfulness and emotional intelligence in the law school classroom. This movement makes explicit that the interpersonal side of lawyering is critical and that many lawyers need help finding purpose or meaning in their work. Nathalie is the author of dozens of books and articles, including *Yoga for Lawyers: Mind-Body Techniques to Feel Better All the Time* (2015, with Hallie Love).

Lawyering from the Inside Out

LEARNING PROFESSIONAL DEVELOPMENT THROUGH MINDFULNESS AND EMOTIONAL INTELLIGENCE

NATHALIE MARTIN

University of New Mexico School of Law

With

JOSHUA ALT

KENDALL KEREW

JENNIFER LAWS

Illustrations by

PAMELA "ZEN" MILLER

CAMBRIDGE
UNIVERSITY PRESS

CAMBRIDGE
UNIVERSITY PRESS

University Printing House, Cambridge CB2 8BS, United Kingdom

One Liberty Plaza, 20th Floor, New York, NY 10006, USA

477 Williamstown Road, Port Melbourne, VIC 3207, Australia

314–321, 3rd Floor, Plot 3, Splendor Forum, Jasola District Centre,
New Delhi – 110025, India

79 Anson Road, #06–04/06, Singapore 079906

Cambridge University Press is part of the University of Cambridge.

It furthers the University's mission by disseminating knowledge in the pursuit of
education, learning, and research at the highest international levels of excellence.

www.cambridge.org
Information on this title: www.cambridge.org/9781107147478
DOI: 10.1017/9781316556139
© Nathalie Martin 2018

First published 2018

Printed in the United States of America by Sheridan Books, Inc.

A catalogue record for this publication is available from the British Library.

Library of Congress Cataloging-in-Publication Data
NAMES: Martin, Nathalie, 1961– author. | Alt, Joshua | Kerew, Kendall | Laws, Jennifer L. |
Miller, Pamela Zen, illustrator.
TITLE: Lawyering from the inside out : learning professional development through
mindfulness and emotional intelligence / Nathalie Martin, University of New Mexico
School of Law , with Joshua Alt, Kendall Kerew, Jennifer Laws ; illustrations by Pamela
"Zen" Miller.
DESCRIPTION: Cambridge, United Kingdom ; New York, NY, USA : Cambridge
University Press, 2018. | Includes bibliographical references and index.
IDENTIFIERS: LCCN 2018018691 | ISBN 9781107147478 (hardback)
SUBJECTS: LCSH: Practice of law – Psychological aspects – United States. | Mindfulness
(Psychology) | Emotional intelligence.
CLASSIFICATION: LCC KF300 .M37 2018 | DDC 340.023–dc23
LC record available at https://lccn.loc.gov/2018018691

ISBN 978-1-107-14747-8 Hardback
ISBN 978-1-316-60196-9 Paperback

To my parents for deeply enriching my life and demonstrating how short and precious life can be, and to Hyime Paley and Saul Kent. I am grateful for both of you.

Contents

Figures

Contributors

Joshua Alt is a newly minted graduate of the University of New Mexico School of Law with a deep interest in mindfulness and emotional intelligence. He practices criminal law.

Kendall Kerew is a Clinical Assistant Professor and Director of the Externship Program at Georgia State University College of Law in Atlanta, Georgia. She received the College of Law's David J. Maleski Award for Teaching Excellence in 2017 and the Black Law Student Association's Bernadette Hartsfield Faculty Award in 2016. Professor Kerew's previous textbook contribution is Chapter 17, *Writing for Practice* in LEARNING FROM PRACTICE: A TEXT FOR EXPERIENTIAL LEGAL EDUCATION (WORTHAM, SCHERR, MAURER, AND BROOKS EDS., 3rd EDN. 2016).

Jennifer L. Laws is a member of the University of New Mexico Law Library faculty, where she is the E-Resources and Scholarly Communication Coordinator. Her most recent publication is *A Legal History of the Civil War and Reconstruction: A Nation of Rights by Laura F. Edwards*, 108 LAW LIBR. J. 292 (2016).

Foreword

I am astonished how effortlessly Nathalie Martin names, clarifies, and explores the perplexing, disorienting legal – yet deeply human – dilemmas we encounter, in such clear and simple language. Obviously an excellent teacher, her classroom acumen naturally carries over into an easy elegance throughout her writing, which makes this an eminently readable book.

She speaks with fierce wisdom and a refreshing depth of understanding. She examines those places where, following a legal calling, one invariably finds our most noble, universally accepted truths – justice, fairness, guaranteed access to "one's day in court," a fundamental equality before the law – directly clashing, at times violently, with the sloppy, uncooperative "facts" of "real life." These painful realizations can disrupt, challenge, and even ridicule our more hopeful expectations that *anything* we are called upon to defend equitably or represent as true will ever be an "easy" case.

Still – she honors the pain and confusion of being a lawyer in a world of exponential complexity, and fearlessly, yet mercifully, attends to this ever-changing rule of law in the world, as it intersects with the more personal, intimately tender gifts and challenges we encounter in our own inner and outer lives.

Can the arc of our inner life bend toward justice?

Martin does not shrink from addressing this question. As the world increasingly demands we function as part of an efficient legal machine – churning out more opinions, convictions, closed cases – what if our humanity (especially those irrational, intuitive, quiet knowings of the heart; things that both slow us down and invaluably aid in our *discerning more accurately* what is authentic, right, and true) ultimately helps us build a more just and honorable world? What if these emotional, sensitive, invisible knowings, our "human inefficiencies," are demonstrably the most valuable tools in our toolbox? How can we honor the spirit, rather than merely the letter, of the law if we lose our ability to hear those still, small voices of our own spirit, speaking clearly and reliably within us in every moment?

Nathalie Martin makes a compelling case that to be of service to the law, to justice, to right action, we need more information – readily available to us all – that we are sadly taught to ignore, silence, and disregard, in service of increasing the speed and efficiency of the legal machine. She and her colleagues refuse to shrink from the very real, however subtle, implications of accepting this call, of following this vocation, of practicing the law, as a fully awake and accountable human being.

If anyone ever wonders, "How do I improve my skills as a lawyer? Where can I find good company to examine these deeper personal and collective challenges I face every day? How do I feel more comfortable, more assured, more gently easy, as I listen carefully for the next, right thing in each moment?" I cannot imagine a more comprehensive, more elegant, more beautifully thoughtful place to begin that inner pilgrimage than in these pages.

Lawyering from the Inside Out is a rich, reliable companion. Nathalie Martin has offered us all a most exquisite gift.

Wayne Muller
Author of many books and founder of Bread for the Journey; The Center for Living Sabbath; In Common – A Refuge for Telling the Truth; and Learning through Difficult Conversations

Acknowledgments

With universal gratitude but especially for my amazing husband Stewart Paley, who read every word, my colleagues Cheryl Burbank, Cindy Nee, Chad Covey, Marlene Valdez, David Stout, Frederick Hart, Rob Schwartz, and Jenny Moore, my co-authors, Joshua Alt, Jennifer Laws, and Kendall Kerew, for Ben Jacobs, Peter Huang, Pamela Foohey, Todd Petersen, Neil Hamilton, Jerry Organ, Randy Kiser, Ocean Tama, Clark Freshman, Susan Brooks, my cousins Philip and Stephen Haines, my editors Matthew Gallagher, Lisa Sinclair, and Llinos Edwards, my yoga teacher Kali Om, and my two deans, Alfred Mathewson and Sergio Pareja. These pages came together in many beautiful and inspiring places over the past several years, including the home of Dottie Davis in the Jemez Mountains, Ravenshores of Southern Oregon, Ak'bol Retreat Center in Amergris Cay, Belize, the Wild Horse Guest House in Durango Colorado, and the shores of Juneau, Alaska and British Columbia, Canada. I am especially grateful for my remarkable students, who inspire and motivate me every day. You are my teachers.

Introduction

Nathalie Martin

Welcome to legal education and all that a law school education has to offer. There is virtually nothing as eye-opening or personally fulfilling as finding ways to help solve society's problems, which is one thing lawyers do. Studying law is challenging in all of the right ways. It is intellectually stimulating, socially valued, useful in everyday life, and meaningful on multiple levels. It also opens doors in ways few other educational opportunities do. The fact that you are studying law makes you one of the fortunate few.

This book is designed to help you make the very best use of your legal education, and to help you develop your professional identity as a lawyer through mindfulness and emotional intelligence practices. Some might find it frivolous to study professional development, mindfulness, and emotional intelligence in law school, particularly compared to the study of contracts or torts. However, teaching professional development in law school is a trend that is hitting law schools by storm. While law was not the first field to jump on the bandwagon, the importance of teaching value-driven purpose, as well as personal well-being, is now well-recognized in law, medicine, and all of the professions.[1] This subject matter is incredibly important to your future, and by the end of this book, we think you will understand the significance of the subject matters covered here.

Mindfulness means learning to live in the present moment and to do just one thing at a time. For lawyers, mindfulness exercises can help in three fundamental ways. On the most superficial level, these practices can reduce stress. On the next level of practical utility, these practices can help us keep calm, stay focused, and, as a result, increase productivity. On the most meaningful level, mindfulness practices can help us find our life work and our purpose here on earth. The practices are simple but the results can be life-changing.

[1] Peter Huang and Corie Rosen, *The Zombie Lawyer Apocalypse*, 42 Pepperdine Law Review 727, 763 (2015).

Some exercises ask you to practice being still, and others request that you be actively reflective. All are designed to help with one of these fundamental goals: calm, focus, and purpose.

Beginning with the goal of a calm state of mind, it helps to acknowledge that being an attorney can be one of the most rewarding endeavors in life, but also one of the most stressful. Lawyers have a higher than average rate of job-related stress, substance abuse, and divorce. Stress reduction is more than a nice idea. It is a lawyer survival technique. Calm people are happier and healthier. Calm lawyers also get better outcomes for their clients.

Regarding focus, a calm mind allows one to think better. Some studies show that IQ increases when the mind is calm. Decision-making is also better when one is calm. Attorneys are valued for their intellect and their ability to solve complex problems, but are also charged with helping people through some of the most difficult and challenging experiences of their lives. To achieve these goals, it helps to be calm, cool, and collected. As lawyers, we are asked to facilitate many changes in society, yet are rarely trained in the mindset needed to accomplish the things asked of us, whether this means writing briefs and memos, negotiating a deal between two countries, writing a complex multilateral contract, dealing with a contentious divorce, or writing policies to be used by the entire US military system. This book fills in some of this missing law school curricula.

Regarding finding each of our own unique purposes in life, a quiet mind and active self-reflection can help us discover what we are passionate about. Self-awareness is a trait that we all value in others. The American Bar Association, the professional legal association that accredits law schools and lawyers, now recognizes the benefits of training lawyers in self-reflection.[2] Thus, it is time for American law schools to formally incorporate self-reflection in the curriculum. This book provides a curriculum for this self-refection, and allows students to begin creating a meaningful, sustainable, lifelong career for themselves while in law school.

As lawyers, everything we do is for someone else, never for ourselves. Law is a service profession. Without service, we don't exist. As such, self-reflection and good interpersonal skills are of paramount importance in this profession. Lawyers with good interpersonal skills have a competitive advantage in the marketplace. Legal jobs that require sound judgment and excellent interpersonal skills can never be outsourced to artificial intelligence or an overseas attorney. If you can learn to

---

[2] *See ABA Standard Learning Outcomes Interpretation* 302–1, stating that "for the purposes of Standard 302(d), other professional skills are determined by the law school and may include skills such as, interviewing, counseling, negotiation, fact development and analysis, trial practice, document drafting, conflict resolution, organization and management of legal work, collaboration, cultural competency, and self-evaluation."

develop good interpersonal skills, there will always be a place for you in the world of law. Self-awareness is the gateway to developing strong interpersonal skills.

This book is designed to help you become a happy and healthy lawyer for life, by giving you tools to help law become a compelling, rewarding, sustainable profession for you. Through this book, we hope to help you find meaning in your work, by showing you various methods for getting to know yourself, your strengths, and your deepest professional desires. We also hope to help you strengthen your resilience, increase your emotional intelligence, and help you learn to swim with the currents of life rather than against them. If lawyers and law students can reduce stress, think more carefully about what they do and why, and approach their careers in thought-ful and directed ways, they can be more effective professionally and happier personally.

While you are free to use it any way you like, this book was originally written based upon a fourteen-week, one-hour, one-credit, law school class that I and others at my law school teach in the first semester. This class, called Practicum, is referenced frequently throughout this book.

FEATURES OF THIS BOOK

In various places, we ask you to pause in two ways. First, we ask you to pause briefly and think about something. We call each of these pauses a Little Pause. Second, we ask you to pause, take a bit more time, and, typically, write about something. We call each of these a Law Pause. Both types of pause will help you gain meaning from this book and from your own ideas.

Journaling through the Law Pauses is the primary self-reflection technique used in this book. These journaling exercises help you find your strengths, learn new skills, identify meaningful work, increase the likelihood of success in the profession, and increase your work and life satisfaction.

This book also contains visual aids, such as textboxes, photos, and illustrations, for emphasis, as well as mindful breathing exercises and a few simple meditation techniques.

This book proceeds in three parts. The first part helps you learn to nurture yourself and develop your own strategies for becoming your best. The second part builds on the first, using what you learned about self-care to help you get along better with others and thus enhance your career and your life. The third part helps you direct your life with greater meaning and purpose. Throughout all three parts, we ask you to do a series of self-exploration exercises, designed to help you make the most of your life as a lawyer. We ask that you not waste your one life, or as poet Mary Oliver would ask, "Tell me, what is it you plan to do with your one wild and precious life?"[3]

---

[3] Mary Oliver, Selected Poems (Beacon Press 1992).

[handwritten margin notes: "Little Pause", "Law Pause"]

Finally a word about self-help books, including this one. None of us can become better at being someone else, only at being our true selves. This book never seeks to change you, but only to help you find out who you are and what fuels you. This helps you and it helps me, not to mention everyone else alive. In the words of screenwriter Barnet Bain, "the more inspired and innovative you are, the better off the world is."[4]

---

[4]   BARNET BAIN, THE BOOK OF DOING AND BEING: REDISCOVERING CREATIVITY IN LIFE, LOVE, AND WORK xvii (ATRIA 2015).

PART I

Nurturing Your Best Self

1

Gaining Self-Awareness

Nathalie Martin

Tear down this house. For under it lies a treasure far greater than you could ever imagine. Tear down this house, for a hundred thousand new houses can be built from the transparent yellow carnelian buried under it.

Rumi

You can certainly become a lawyer without becoming more familiar with yourself. People have been doing it for centuries. There is no doubt, however, that self-awareness is a trait we all value in others.

Today, many people expect their lawyers to be more interpersonally skilled than perhaps in the past. Rather than mere legal technicians, people expect lawyers to listen and act with humility, compassion, and an understanding of the human condition. New American Bar Association rules suggest that lawyers be trained in self-reflection, as well as interpersonal awareness and skill, yet most law schools still do not train lawyers in these essential skills. Lawyers with these skills will always be in high demand. This is because self-aware lawyers are better at resolving conflict, which is one of our main jobs in society.

William Ury of the Harvard Program on Negotiation and Harvard Negotiation Project calls the process of mindful self-awareness "getting to yes with yourself." In his book by the same name, he explains the many benefits of mindful self-awareness:

> The process of getting to "yes with yourself" not only makes it easier to *resolve* conflicts, but it also actually helps *prevent* conflicts from arising in the first place. By not reacting, by staying calm, and grounded, you will avoid being provoked and will be less likely to take attacks personally. You are far less likely to say or do things you will later regret. With an attitude of sincere respect and a genuine willingness to help address the needs of others, you will be able to resolve matters long before they

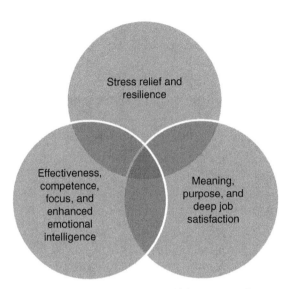

FIGURE 1.1 Venn diagram of ways in which mindfulness can enhance your life, created by author, Nathalie Martin.

escalate into serious disputes. You will get along naturally with others with a minimum of conflict.[1]

This book, on the subject of attorney professional development through mindfulness and emotional intelligence, is designed to help you accomplish these goals and others. Through the practices outlined in these pages, we hope to help you reach the state described by Ury above. We also hope to help you experience less stress, become more focused, and eventually experience deep job satisfaction.

Figure 1.1 shows the overlapping ways in which mindfulness can enhance your life, from the entry-level use of mindfulness for self-care and stress reduction, to the highly useful improvements in function, focus, and emotional intelligence, to the highest and most meaningful benefit of mindfulness, to help you find meaning and purpose in your work and your life.

As Tal Ben-Shahar explains in his book, *Happier*, finding work that combines your unique strengths with what gives you meaning and pleasure will make you happier.[2] Figure 1.2 shows the three things that help us create the most happiness in our lives.

As it turns out, happy people are more successful in life than non-happy people, yet even without that success silver lining, happiness is obviously desirable in and of itself. We all want to be happy. We also all have the right to choose a path for

[1]   WILLIAM URY, GETTING TO YES WITH YOURSELF 174 (HARPER ONE 2015).
[2]   TAL BEN-SHAHAR, HAPPIER: LEARN THE SECRETS TO DAILY JOY AND LASTING FULFILMENT 102 (MCGRAW-HILL EDUCATION 2007).

FIGURE 1.2 Tal Ben-Shahar's three things that create happiness at work and in life, created by author, Nathalie Martin.

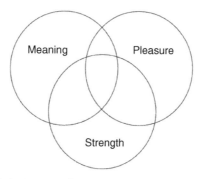

FIGURE 1.3 Tal Ben-Shahar's Venn diagram of the things that create happiness at work and in life, created by author, Nathalie Martin.

ourselves that makes us happy and fulfilled.[3] Figure 1.3 shows the synergy between Ben-Shahar's combination of strengths, meaning, and pleasure.[4]

Finding work that combines our strengths with the things that bring us pleasure and meaning is possible when we carefully identify things that fall into each of these categories.

LAW PAUSE

Make a list of things in each category: strengths, meaning, and pleasure. See where the three categories overlap. Then create your own three-circle Venn diagram and insert categories from each list into each circle, seeing where the listed items overlap. Including these items in your life work will make life more fulfilling. While you are at it, make a fourth list of things you simply cannot live without in life.[5]

This exercise will help you determine what to look for in your future work. Your job is out there. You only need to know enough about yourself to find it.

One thing that makes most people happy is creative work. Thankfully, law practice involves a great deal of creativity.[6] In many ways, the creative opportunities

[3] *Ibid.* at 142.   [4] *Ibid.* at 104.   [5] *Ibid.* at 108.
[6] *Ibid.* at 155 (discussing the connection between flow and creativity).

for attorneys are greater than ever before in history, especially for well-educated, emotionally intelligent, self-aware lawyers. We all have the choice to make our lives as meaningful as possible. As freelance screenwriter, film producer, and creativity scholar Barnet Bain explains:

> No matter what your vocation, you come to realize that *life* is a freelance affair and you no longer take anything for granted, whether it's a paycheck, a marriage vow, or your health and well-being. You discover that none of these is outside of you. You can't put them in a vault to accumulate interest and guarantee a particular future. Everything that matters to you comes from an inner reservoir that is always available in the present moment.
>
> When you know that your whole life is a creative act, you begin to take responsibility for it. And claiming 100 percent responsibility makes everything crystal clear. You can see that each one of us is a freelancer, regardless of job title. You know each of us is the writer and director of our own unforgettable story.
>
> That knowing is a fundamental shift – a transformation. It happens when you are intimate enough with your past to be able to create an original framework that is yours alone, one that is as distinctive to you as your fingerprints. Living from the inside out, every facet of your life is freelance, designed by your own hand. You are a free agent. *You are free.*[7]

We start in this chapter with self-exploration and awareness. Chapters 2–8 continue with lessons in self-growth, protection, and regulation. From there, in Chapters 9–15, we discuss how to build interpersonal skills and get along better with others for both personal and professional benefit, and finally in Chapters 16–18, we discuss how to find and sustain the most meaningful life you can.

You will find a compilation of research on many topics here. You might not think that some of these topics *need* to be researched. For example, who knew that there was an International Listening Association, as well as an American Institute of Stress. There is even a Center for Appreciative Inquiry. Imagine the business cards of the executives who head and work at these organizations. It is surprising how many books have been written on topics such as emotional intelligence, mindfulness, resilience, positive psychology, receiving and getting feedback, decision-making, life coaching, finding purpose in life, and so on and so on. We have read many of these books in order to share the best of what they say, but you may also want to read some of them yourself.

In reading these self-help books, we have noticed two overriding themes. First, the authors write about what interests them. Second, and less obvious, many of these authors have struggled with the problems about which they write. In the same way that dancers suffer for their art, many of these extremely accomplished people chose their subject because they were looking for answers to their own problems.

For example, Martin Seligman was named a father of modern positive psychology after publishing a book called *Learned Optimism*. Seligman claims to be a "pessimist

---

[7] Barnet Bain, The Book of Doing and Being: Rediscovering Creativity in Life, Love, and Work xii (Atria 2015).

by nature."[8] Susan M. Heathfield struggled with receiving feedback, so she learned what she needed to know and wrote *Receiving Feedback with Grace and Dignity*.[9] Jack Kornfield teaches loving-kindness meditations, and in one of his lectures he recounts a fight with a girlfriend right before leading a large retreat meditation. He recalls telling the huge group to "think of someone you love and bring them into your heart," while thinking, "that was so wrong of her, I can't wait to call her right back and give her a piece of my mind," then saying to the group "feel that love in your heart," and thinking "I am going to let her have it, etc." We are all human, we all have something to learn, and like most things in life, getting there is half the fun. Just as these authors struggle, so do I. I am still working on every topic covered in this book. I struggle to meditate and put others above myself. In other words, I too am human. I also chose my subject, and continue to study these topics because the study helps me. I hope it will help you too.

Several authors have contributed to this book, so except for chapters with single authorship, references to "I" and "we" are clarified within brackets. Scattered throughout these pages I have also shared my students' stories, with permission, from the Practicum class that all 1Ls take at the University of New Mexico School of Law. We are thrilled that you are using this book and that you have chosen law as a profession. Lawyers are among society's most influential servants.

GETTING TO KNOW YOURSELF

We'll start our exploration of you with a few probing questions.

What am I Doing in Law School Anyway?

Have you thought much about why you want to become a lawyer? Not how you decided, but why you made that decision?

LAW PAUSE

See if you can articulate that reason in a paragraph now.

Why *do you* want to become a lawyer? "I am not quite sure" is a fine answer. It is also fine if you already know your passion within the law. If your answer is, "Because I want to make lots of money," you may want to reconsider this whole endeavor or at the very least, find another reason to become a lawyer. There are many other ways to make money and most of them are much easier than becoming a lawyer. Most

---

[8]   Martin E. P. Seligman, Authentic Happiness: Using the New Positive Psychology to Realize Your Potential for Lasting Fulfillment 24 (Atria Paperback 2004).

[9]   Susan M. Heathfield, *Receive Feedback With Grace and Dignity*, available at http://humanresources .about.com/cs/communication/ht/receivefeedback.htm.

lawyers deal with humanity day in and day out, all day every day, 24/7, and not merely *any* people but people with problems with the law.

Law is a service profession and we serve other people. If you don't particularly care for other human beings, you'll need either to develop that people-pleasing skill, or work in one of the rare legal fields where contact with other people is limited, such as one where you mostly draft documents. Either way, there will always be other people to serve, and in most situations you will have no choice but to deal with them.

Do not worry at all if you are not quite sure what kind of law you'd like to practice. You will find your way. Randi McGinn, journalist turned trial lawyer and author of the book, *Changing Laws, Changing Lives*, attended law school to get more publishers to read and publish her freelance journalism stories, and to improve her notoriety and her chances of being published in national news outlets, not to become a lawyer. Nevertheless, she became a highly successful and inspiring trial attorney. She offers this advice:

> For those of you who are adrift and not yet sure what you want to do in life, the good news is sometimes, by continuing to stumble forward, you find the thing you were always meant to do.[10]

In this book, we help you stumble intentionally and help you find that thing you were always meant to do, sooner rather than later.

What are Your Peak Experiences, Key Strengths, and Core Values?

Whatever your ultimate occupational plan, it will help you to know what really matters to you and what you are good at. Figuring out what matters most to you is sometimes accomplished by identifying your core values. This may or may not be helpful in devising a vocational plan. For example, I feel strongly about equality and would like to see the entire world become more equitable. That does not mean my job needs primarily and directly to promote equality. I like to solve complicated problems, learn new things, write, and spend a fair amount of time alone. I figured this out by describing a few of my peak experiences in a journal and by picking my core values from a list similar to the one provided below. You will now get an opportunity to do the same, after a bit of instruction.

A peak experience is one that makes you feel totally alive and engaged in what you are doing, and in flow, a state in which time flies and you fully engage in whatever it is you are experiencing at the moment.[11]

In his book *The Creative Lawyer*, attorney and executive coach Michael Melcher describes peak experiences as those that allow you to align your deepest values with experiences that you long for: things like creativity, fun, fame, spirituality, financial

---

[10] RANDI MCGINN, CHANGING LAWS, CHANGING LIVES 6 (TRIAL GUIDES LLC 2014).

[11] MIHALY CSIKSZENTMIHALYI, FLOW: THE PSYCHOLOGY OF OPTIMAL EXPERIENCE 1–5 (HARPER & ROW 1990).

gain, etc. He has produced a long list of statements that may guide you to some of these experiences.[12] You can finish this sentence any way you like, but Melcher offers a few possibilities below.[13]

I feel most alive when
- I am spending time with my spouse.
- I am learning something new.
- I am in nature.
- I am part of a team.
- I am running a deal.
- I am being an advocate.
- I am writing something good.
- I am by myself.
- I am helping someone.
- I am cashing my paycheck.
- I am seeing my kids.
- I am playing with my dogs.

Peak experiences can occur in a few moments or over years. You may not realize these experiences *are* peak experiences until they are over and you feel a sense of deep accomplishment or fulfillment.

LAW PAUSE

Try identifying a few of these peak experiences from your life, including any prior work life. Use these prompts from Melcher's book, *The Creative Lawyer*, if they help you.[14] Otherwise, write about whatever you like.

1. An experience I'm proud of is when I _____.
2. One of my biggest work or school accomplishments was when I _____.
3. My family and friends think it is great that I _____.
4. A colleague, client, family member, or friend once complimented me in a way that really meant something. He or she said _____.
5. Something in my personal life that is as important to me as my work is

_____.

Now, write the story behind one or two of your peak experiences. Do not identify any particular values right now – simply write about what happened, how you felt, what was positive about it, what skills you used, and the feedback or validation you felt.

---

[12] MICHAEL MELCHER, THE CREATIVE LAWYER 29–30 (2ND EDN. AMERICAN BAR ASSOCIATION 2014).
[13] *Ibid.* at 29–30.   [14] *Ibid.* at 32–33.

After you are done, read what you wrote. See if any core values pop out. Pay attention to any themes.

While we do not typically provide two Law Pauses in a row, we suggest one more very useful self-awareness technique. Please go to the Authentic Happiness Questionnaire Center, University of Pennsylvania, available at www.authentichappiness.sas.upenn .edu/testcenter. You will need to create an account by entering a username and password.

Please take the VIA character strengths test found at www.authentichappiness.sas .upenn.edu/questionnaires/survey-character-strengths, as well as one or two other self-awareness tests. These other tests measure overall happiness, optimism, forgiveness, gratitude, positive and negative affect, work–life balance, compassion, and even meaning in life.

Record the results in your journal, along with a few of your reactions to those results.

The VIA character strength test is particularly useful in helping you find meaningful work.[15] As the VIA Institute for Character explains on its website:

> VIA's work is about the core or essence of who we are as humans – our character strengths. These positive, core characteristics of our personality are different from strengths of talent (innate abilities), strengths of interest (what we like to do), strengths of skill (proficiencies we develop), and strengths of resources (external supports).
>
> While each of these areas of strength are important, it is character strengths that provide a pathway for developing each of these areas. For example, we use perseverance and self-regulation to pursue a talent in music or sport, hope in developing a new skill for work, curiosity as we explore our interest areas, and gratitude and kindness when we are tapping our resources. Also, it is our strengths of character that we have to turn to when we lose resources, talents, and skills, or when we lose interest in something.[16]

By using this particular test to identify what is most important to you, you can focus on and mindfully use those character strengths throughout your week.

LEARNING TO BE STILL TO CURB ANXIETY AND STRESS

Sometimes we need to learn to be still. Law professor Peter H. Huang is a long-time proponent of mindfulness practices and has done much to help like-minded law

---

[15] *The VIA Survey*, VIA INSTITUTE ON CHARACTER, available at www.viacharacter.org/www/Character-Strengths-Survey.

[16] FAQs, VIA INSTITUTE ON CHARACTER, available at www.viacharacter.org/www/About-Institute /FAQs.

professors organize and offer mindfulness curricula to law students around the country. Huang's article on good lawyer decision-making contains the following quote from Chief Justice Stephen Breyer of the US Supreme Court. According to Huang, Justice Breyer told CNN contributor Amanda Enyati that he pauses for ten to fifteen minutes twice daily:

> I don't know that what I do is meditation, or even whether it has a name. For 10 or 15 minutes twice a day I sit peacefully. I relax and think about nothing or as little as possible. And that is what I've done for a couple of years ... And really I started because it's good for my health. My wife said this would be good for your blood pressure and she was right. It really works.
>
> I read once that the practice of law is like attempting to drink water from a fire hose. And if you are under stress, meditation – or whatever you choose to call it – helps. Very often I find myself in circumstances that may be considered stressful, say in oral arguments where I have to concentrate very hard for extended periods. If I come back at lunchtime, I sit for 15 minutes and perhaps another 15 minutes later. Doing this makes me feel more peaceful, focused and better able to do my work.[17]

Without other people, we would be out of work. People need lawyers and we need them back. Many people experience anxiety when they need access to the legal system, and lawyers are the primary pathway through which people manage the legal system. As a lawyer, you *are* their access, their voice. People may even confuse you *with* the legal system, concluding that you are part of the problem rather than the solution. People can sometimes pass their stress to you, which is one reason it is important to learn early how to take care of yourself and protect yourself.

ELEVATING THE NEEDS OF OTHERS ABOVE OUR OWN AND DEALING WITH LIFE'S DICHOTOMIES

One thing students find immediately frustrating about law school is that there is usually no fixed answer to the questions asked by the professor. It always depends. The reason we teach in this way is that learning to be a lawyer involves learning how to apply rules of law to facts that are unique in each individual case. This means that the answer changes along with the facts. Facts drive the result, not the rule of law by itself.

The principles discussed in this book might create similar frustration for different reasons. First, we will try to train you to put others above yourself, given that law is a service profession. Putting others above ourselves, however, is an unpleasant task. Moreover, who wants to be told that they *need to* put others above themselves? Even

---

[17] Peter H. Huang, *How Improving Decision-making's Mindfulness can Improve Legal Ethics's Professionalism*, 21 J. L. BUS. & ETHICS 35, 55 (2015).

Mother Teresa did not want to be told what to do. People, especially Americans, value their autonomy.

Second, as with the frustrating cases in which the results seem to change with the facts, there are few absolutes in the study of professional development through mindfulness and emotional intelligence. You will be asked to balance opposite ideas in your life. We do not ask, for example, that you live in the present moment all day, but rather that you mix being in the present with planning for the future. We ask that you make a point *not* to work hard *all* the time, but rather that you balance work and play. We also ask that you *not* be in your head all the time, but also sometimes actively use your body. Here are a few of the dichotomies we will work with in these pages:

1. Living in the present versus preparing for the future.
2. Accepting things as they are versus doing something to fight injustice.
3. Refusing to judge others versus calling out reprehensible acts.
4. Being still versus being active.
5. Being calm versus getting things done.
6. Practicing non-attachment versus caring enough to achieve your goals.

We need to balance the principles in these dichotomies to live our best, most fulfilling lives. Just as we can't appreciate, or even have, good without evil, hot without cold, or darkness without light, we can perform better when our dichotomies live in balance.

A FEW RULES TO LIVE BY

Before we get to the heart of the subjects covered in this book, we share a few tips that will make life easier for you and help you swim with rather than against the currents of your life in law school and as a lawyer. These tips are some favorite things we learned in the process of writing this book.

Make Every Day the Ideal Day

If we could share just one tip that could make your life easier it is this one, modified from Talane Miedaner's book, *Coach Yourself to Success.*[18] Give yourself something to look forward to every day. Better yet, plan out and have the ideal day. Write down what would make a day truly wonderful, try it for one day, and then see how many of the elements of the perfect day you can incorporate into your everyday life.

Miedaner tells the story of Marjorie, a successful woman who was having trouble getting out of bed in the morning. Miedaner told Marjorie to plan the perfect

---

[18]   Talane Miedaner, Coach Yourself to Success 28–29 (McGraw-Hill 2000).

morning. Marjorie did so. She planned to awaken, meditate, go for a walk in the woods, shower, and have a fresh-baked muffin and coffee while on her veranda writing in her journal. Marjorie discovered two things through this exercise: one, she really needed her own downtime in the morning, and two, to her delight she could fit many of the elements of the perfect morning into her everyday routine.

Consider writing down in vivid detail what your best morning would look like, and when you get a chance, try it out. How much of that best morning, or evening for that matter, can you bring to your day today? You can extend this principle and plan an entire ideal day. I wake up and tell myself, "today will be the ideal day." Much of the time, it is the ideal day, because I planned and built in as many elements of the ideal day as I could.

Balance Hard Work with Silence, Solitude, and Easy Transitions

In this book, and in the life that follows your reading of it, you will be asked to swim with rather than against the stream. To help with that, try to do one thing at a time. I love nature and frequently draw my inspiration from it. I love to birdwatch and to watch other forms of nature. But consider the movie, *The Big Year*, which is about how driven and crazy some birdwatchers can be. However, to see the most wildlife, you need to stop moving, sit back down, and observe life.

Recently, I was up in the Jemez Mountains near my home in New Mexico, walking my dog. While playing with my phone in order to take a picture, I saw two beautiful deer not far away, but only as they were fleeing away. Why was I not paying attention? I could have approached slowly and watched them for a long, long time.

It is important to work hard, but why not make it as easy as possible to work hard? In other words, plan for life to be easy. If you need to get something done, plan a reward for afterwards, and go with the flow, literally. Do not fight yourself. Get out of your own way and do it. Let things do their own work. Then go for a walk, or do whatever other sweet, peaceful reward you planned for yourself. Go easy and get it done, no big deal. Swim with the current.

For creativity, you need space in your mind. Stop and pause, smell the roses. Go ahead and work hard. Just don't work yourself into a frenzy or pay such close attention to the trees that you miss the woods. Note the transitions between tasks, thoughts, and breaths. Take a minute to pause in the transitions, to be present, and at rest.

Giving the People Around You Your Present Attention

Cell phones bring you closer to people far way, but further away from those people right near you. Can you recall the last time you dilly-dallied with your cell phone when you were with other people? When was the last time you found yourself in the presence of one person while emailing or texting another? Dr. James A. Roberts

"It keeps me from looking at my phone every two seconds."

FIGURE 1.4 *New Yorker* Cartoon "It keeps me from looking at my phone every two seconds," Image I.D. no. TCB-138227, licensed from *The Cartoon Bank, a feature of Condé Nast Collection.*

wrote an entire book on phone addiction called *Too Much of a Good Thing*, and Suffolk Law Professor Lisle Baker and Harvard Medical School Professor Daniel Brown dedicated seventy pages to a law review article entitled *The Lost Art of Paying Attention.*[19]

Most of us are addicted to our personal technology to one degree or another, as Figure 1.4 depicts. Would you like to make more money and be much happier? If so, you can decide to train yourself *not* to use technology while in the presence of others. Unplugging may sound unrealistic. We can hear the protests (or even better since you are about to become a lawyer, the protestations)[20] now. The profession requires us to be on call and at the ready. This may well be true but the profession also requires us to be present while with other human beings. If you would like to improve your chance of success in the profession, consider weaning yourself off

[19] R. Lisle Baker and Daniel P. Brown, *On Engagement: Learning to Pay Attention*, 36 U. Alr. L. R. 338–39 (2014).

[20] This is a joke about lawyers using big words. If a shorter, easier to understand word works just as well, use it. You are a communicator and a wordsmith.

the habit of dishonoring others in this way. If you need more time with technology, spend more time alone, but consider giving others your full attention and you will become uniquely valued in society.

Keep a journal for one day of all the times you used technology in the presence of others. What triggered these events? Boredom? Fear? A truly pressing situation or deadline? Sharing pictures with others at social events? On the whole, did these techno-interactions enhance or detract from your engagement with others?

Then for another full day, try not to use technology in the presence of others. Keep a journal and keep track of all the times you wanted to reach for technology and decided not to do so. What triggered your desire to reach for technology? Did taking a break from technology enhance or detract from your personal interactions?

We will practice this exercise again in Chapter 6, with the help of a phone application, so we will see then how well these new habits have stuck with you.

Make the Decision to Take Good Care of Yourself and Get to Know Yourself

There is no question that being an attorney is a public job with a public face. Nevertheless, like most of life, it is an inside job. Knowing about yourself and how you operate will help you succeed in your career and do so using less of your personal time and while having more positive experiences. Consider making the decision to have fun while learning about yourself, and allowing that learning to continue throughout your life.

CONCLUSION

We conclude with a final exercise to help you get out of your own way. Having read many self-help books in preparation to write this one, I know it is annoying to ask people to dedicate 30–40 minutes a day to a task. This is even truer for time-stretched law students. I will not suggest you do one thing every day for the duration of this book, but I will ask that you try one of these four things daily. A little mindfulness goes a long way, especially if you do not currently exercise, meditate, do yoga, or keep a journal. I like to do more than one, so if you like it, add more. These opportunities to pause will make your brain work better. You will unquestionably get that time back in enhanced productivity. You can think of these as human capital investments with a positive rate of return.

Spend ten minutes doing one of these daily practices:

- Exercise vigorously. Run, jog, or otherwise tire your physical body out. If you already exercise, pick something else.
- Practice yoga, qigong, or tai chi.
- Journal out three notebook pages of gobbledy-gook writing (nothing you or anyone else ever needs to read) as suggested by Julia Cameron in her book, *The Artist's Way*.
- Pray in any tradition you choose with an open heart. Try not to ask for anything but to simply be grateful.
- If you like to read ahead or if you already meditate, meditate using one of the techniques found in Chapters 2, 8, and 9, or on the internet.

2

Introduction to Mindfulness Techniques

Nathalie Martin

Later in this book, we tell you more about how, why, and for how long people have been using calming techniques like meditation and yoga to improve their lives. These techniques are sprinkled throughout this book, and in Chapter 8 we review the history and development of mindfulness, as well as some of the many mindfulness techniques you might find useful. Here we give you a taste.

WHY BE MINDFUL?

Being mindful and practicing simple mindfulness techniques, even in small doses, can strengthen your intellect, improve your resolve, and improve your interpersonal skills. Mindfulness techniques can also help you relieve stress. Although being an attorney is not an easy job, it can be very rewarding. The difficulties of the job are part of what make the work of an attorney meaningful. As Tal Ben-Shahar explains in his book, *Happier*, we are happiest when we work in jobs that combine our strengths with what we find pleasurable and meaningful.[1] We also grow deeply and steadily through adversity. As Ben-Shahar explains, "we are designed for the climb."[2]

Adversity happens to us and those around us every day, yet we survive and often thrive. Part of what helps me survive and thrive is the practices of mindfulness. I have been practicing the techniques shared in this book, in one form or another, for a long time. While I still get upset, hurt, and even depressed sometimes, and while my own life ebbs and flows with the same sort of problems as everyone else, I have been able to ride the currents a little easier because of these techniques, and also get more done, more effectively, because of the way mindfulness techniques improve focus and flow.

---

[1] TAL BEN-SHAHAR, HAPPIER: LEARN THE SECRETS TO DAILY JOY AND LASTING FULFILLMENT 103–104 (McGRAW-HILL EDUCATION 2007).
[2] *Ibid.* at 22.

FIGURE 2.1 Keep Calm and Lawyer On, created by author, Nathalie Martin.

MODERN VIEWS ON MINDFULNESS MUDDY THE WATER

Admittedly, mindfulness is now in vogue, almost to the point where it means nothing. Everyone is now talking about mindfulness, including the *New York Times*, the *Wall Street Journal*, *Time Magazine*, and many other publications. When the subject of mindfulness first went mainstream, this seemed to be a great development. As mindfulness has flourished as a topic of conversation, it has also lost some of its meaning. Magazines feature the obligatory "Ten steps to making you happier and more mindful." Popular culture makes mindfulness sound new, complex, and difficult, when it is none of the above. Yes, it can be hard to focus on one thing at a time, but not impossible. In some ways it is the simplest thing in the world. We just need to reprogram ourselves to value single-mindedness.

Modern views on mindfulness also make mindfulness seem fake and faddish. I especially dislike it when people charge money for mindfulness. Mindfulness does not cost money. There is no need to purchase costly apps, monthly subscriptions, and so on, any more than you need the costly vitamins sold in infomercials. If a free or inexpensive app will motivate you the way exercise clothes might, great (I love the chimes on my Samadhi meditation app), but you don't need to buy anything.

EASY MINDFULNESS

This breath counting exercise is simple and a great way to take a break from life's "stuff" and "to do lists," and get back to yourself. The trick is to actually do it. As we discuss later, if sustained over a long period, this exercise can also make you smarter and more focused.

LAW PAUSE

Sit up straight in a quiet place, any place. It can even be a park bench, a classroom chair, or a car. Put your phone on "do not disturb," set your timer for six minutes, and calm down. Let out all the breath. Let any thoughts or worries go right out with that preparatory breath. Inhale deeply and when you exhale count in your head "one."

Keep breathing and counting on exhale until you reach five. Then start over, one, two, three, four, five, on the exhale. Keep going for six minutes. Stay focused on your breath. If another thought arises, which might happen even though you are counting, acknowledge that thought and let it go, bringing your attention back to your own sweet breath.

How do you feel? Write it down.

Moving from Law Pause to Daily Practice: Mindful Moments Throughout Your Day

Try the five-count technique again, when you are standing around or waiting in line today a few times. Tomorrow, sit for another six minutes. Notice subtle changes in your thought processes as you dabble a bit here and there. Get out of your own way and let things be. It takes far less time to create a mindful moment than you'll lose sticking with your existing thinking when you are otherwise doing nothing. Some of this downtime thinking consists of a negative feedback loop in which you ruminate on the past (often regrets) and the future (often worries), rather than the present. Bringing your mind to the present moment, at least some of the time, clears the mind and prepares it for whatever comes next.

THE LOST ART OF PAYING ATTENTION

One of the main benefits of mindfulness is that it can help you learn to focus on one thing at a time. This may be the most important skill you can learn as a lawyer. In their article, *On Engagement: Learning to Pay Attention*, Lisle Baker and Daniel Brown tell this story:

> [Malcolm] Smith, a Democrat, was the New York State Senate Majority Leader who famously fiddled with his BlackBerry, checking e-mails, while billionaire Thomas Golisano, a major independent political player in New York, was trying to talk to him. Golisano, who had made a special trip to Albany to meet with Smith, was furious.
>
> "When I travel 250 miles to make a case on how to save the state a lot of money and the guy comes into his office and starts playing with his BlackBerry, I was miffed," he told reporters.
>
> As a response, Mr. Golisano "went to the Republicans and told them he'd be happy to unseat Smith, perhaps in the hopes of having him replaced with someone who could pay attention for a few minutes." Golisano was successful, and Smith was unseated.[3]

---

[3] R. Lisle Baker and Daniel P. Brown, *On Engagement: Learning to Pay Attention*, 36 U. Alr. L. R. 338–39 (2014) (citing Paul Hammerness et al., Organize your Mind Organize your Life: Train Your Brain to Get More Done in Less Time, at xv–xvii (MIRA 2011)). Baker and Brown also report on a neurosurgeon who made personal phone calls during an operation, a nurse who checked airfares during surgery, and "a poll showing that half of technicians running bypass machines had admitted texting during a procedure." *See*. p. 339 (quoting Matt Richtel, *As Doctors Use More Devices, Potential for Distraction Grows*, New York Times, Dec. 14, 2011).

In other words, politician Malcolm Smith lost his job for playing with technology rather than paying attention to the live human being (who happened to be a billionaire) in front of him. Smith was doing more than one thing at once. He was not living in the present. Rather, he was giving up the present in hopes of creating a more interesting future. This cost him his job.

If you have trouble staying off your phone during meetings, take notes. This will give your hands something to do and avoid the embarrassment of looking like you are not paying attention.

MULTITASKING ROBS US OF CALM, FOCUS, AND LIFE DIRECTION

Many studies show that multitasking is ineffective. Multitasking doesn't even save us time. Researchers at Stanford University found that while multitasking, people had more difficulty organizing their thoughts and filtering out irrelevant information than non-multitaskers, and were slower at switching from one task to another. This was equally true of people who thought they were particularly gifted at multitasking.[4] These Stanford researchers found that multitasking reduces efficiency because the brain can only focus on one thing at a time.

FIGURE 2.2 Perilous Multitasking, created by illustrator, Pamela "Zen" Miller.

---

[4] Travis Bradberry, *Multitasking Damages Your Brain and Career, New Studies Suggest*, TALENTSMART, Aug. 10, 2014, available at www.forbes.com/sites/travisbradberry/2014/10/08/multitasking-damages-your-brain-and-career-new-studies-suggest/#213c58442c16.

In addition to slowing us down, multitasking can lower our IQs. A study at the University of London found that participants who multitasked during cognitive tasks experienced IQ score declines that were similar to what they'd expect if they had smoked marijuana or stayed up all night. The study found that multitasking lowered IQ by an average of fifteen points. Lawyers need to teach themselves to focus on one task at a time.

Why is multitasking so appealing, then? Popular culture sees multitasking as smart. Many superheroes and characters in movies seem to be able to multitask. Technology also makes it easy to *think* we are doing several things at once, which in turn makes us feel like we are accomplishing a lot.

Multitasking, busyness, and being in constant psychic motion serve another tempting purpose. Busyness protects us from ourselves and our deeper thoughts. Being in constant mental motion allows us to run away from ourselves, which is comforting if we are a little afraid of what is inside there. And let's be honest, who isn't?

There could be some things about ourselves we'd rather not find out. I know this feeling very well, as do most human beings. What is in there is less scary than you think, however, and finding out will help rather than hurt you.

LAW PAUSE

Think of someone you know who will do almost anything to avoid being alone with his or herself, and his or her thoughts in a calm setting. What do you attribute this to?

These several layers of activity create layers of armor between our external selves and our internal selves. Busyness with no breaks to consider what is going on inside of us and around us causes us to live in a sort of trance.

HOW TO AVOID LIVING IN A TRANCE

Consider this observation by French philosopher Anaïs Nin:

> You live like this, sheltered, in a delicate world, and you believe you are living. Then you read a book . . . or you take a trip . . . and you discover that you are not living, that you are hibernating. The symptoms of hibernating are easily detectable: first, restlessness. The second symptom (when hibernating becomes dangerous and might degenerate into death): absence of pleasure. That is all. It appears like an innocuous illness. Monotony, boredom, death. Millions live like this (or die like this) without knowing it. They work in offices. They drive a car. They picnic with their families. They raise children. And then some shock treatment takes place, a person, a book, a song, and it awakens them and saves them from death.

Where are you now? Awake or asleep, alive or dead? Let today be the day you live in the present, even for a short time.

Little Pause: Pause and breathe. What are you thinking about? How do you feel?

As Jon Kabat-Zinn, founder of the modern mindfulness movement, says, life happens not in months or years, but moment to moment, in a series of moments. When you stop and note a bird flying by, or glimpse a flower as you pass by, you are living in that moment. When you spend most of your time thinking about the past (again, usually regrets) or the future (worrying), you are giving up the present moment, a moment you can never get back. The idea is not to *always live* in the present, but to balance our planning about the future and regrets about the past, with time where we are right now.

Planning is great and you will need to do a lot of planning in your life. Set aside time to plan and the rest of the time, live in the present. Catch at least some of those moments. Don't lose them. Eleanor Roosevelt purportedly said it best when she said, "Yesterday is history, tomorrow is a mystery, but today is a gift and that is why we call it the present."

Little Pause: Look around and notice something in your surroundings that you have never noticed before. Now what are you thinking about?

LETTING GO OF EXCESS STRESS

One purpose of this book is to help you manage stress. Some stress can be motivating, especially if you rename it as energy and use it that way. Too much stress, however, can debilitate us. Like a few other professions, a lawyer's work is stressful by nature. Our work can entail difficult clients and adverse parties, arguing, and fighting for justice or a client's interests. While the public might question how difficult it really is to do a job involving mostly writing and talking, lawyers and law students often face adversity.

Lawyers also have a troubling track record for dealing with these problems in healthy ways. In 2014, CNN published a disturbing article noting that lawyers are 3.6 times more likely than average to experience depression.[5] This statistic helps us understand another troubling statistic: lawyers are fourth on the list of professions most likely to commit suicide.[6] The CNN article suggests that the seeds of this depressive effect are sown not once lawyers encounter clients, but long before that, in law school.[7] According to a study by Dr. Andy Benjamin, approximately 40 percent of students experience depression by the time they graduate, before they even apply for the bar.[8]

---

[5] Rosa Flores and Rose Marie Arce, *Why are Lawyers Killing Themselves?* CNN.COM, Jan. 20, 2014, available at www.cnn.com/2014/01/19/us/lawyer-suicides/.
[6] *Ibid.*   [7] *Ibid.*   [8] *Ibid.*

In some ways, however, the CNN article barely scratches the surface. Two professors recently completed a study examining the effects of law school on law students in more detail, finding that before law school, law students were *no more* depressed or anxious than the rest of society.[9] During law school, however, these distressing signs of mental trauma start to emerge and grow alarmingly among many students. Professors Sheldon and Krieger did extensive empirical work and found that law school itself has a negative effect on students, reducing subjective well-being and intrinsic motivation (which are signs of a well-balanced, healthy psychological disposition).[10] This decline in well-being during law school need not happen, particularly if you are aware of the risks and take to heart the recommendations found in this book. There are many ways to counteract these historically harmful law practices, and nearly everyone in the profession now recognizes the need to do just that.

A LITTLE SCIENCE ABOUT STRESS

As the studies above and many others show, mindfulness is best known for its capacity to reduce stress. Thus, we end this chapter with a few words about the brain science of stress. Some stress can be motivating but most lawyers have much more stress in their lives than they need. In prehistoric days it was necessary to be able to run from saber-toothed tigers and other dangers. Life depended on being able to run from danger and engage all possible strength and power to do so.[11]

Today, we utilize this biological flight, fight, or freeze response on much smaller stressors that are not life or death. In fact, there is a constant barrage of stimuli that can seem stressful, including driving in traffic, dealing with difficult colleagues, responding to emails and texts nonstop, and other little life annoyances. Then there are the bigger things we face in society today, such as sexism, violence, racism, homelessness, and even mass death, things cavemen could not even have imagined. All activate our flight or fight response, but the flight or fight response does not help with modern life stressors.

Neutralizing the flight or fight response caused by stress can improve our mental and physical health. Stress causes many minor health risks, such as sleeplessness, weight gain, and reduction in overall health. It weakens the immune system so that all other health threats are exacerbated, and can then lead to major health problems such as heart attacks, cancer, and disabling accidents. Fortunately we can reverse

[9] Kennon Sheldon and Larry Krieger, *Does Legal Education Have Undermining Effects on Law Students? Evaluating Changes in Motivation, Values, and Well-Being*, 22 BEHAV. SCI. LAW, 261–86 (2004).
[10] *Ibid.* at 267–68.
[11] RICK HANSON, BUDDHA'S BRAIN: THE PRACTICAL NEUROSCIENCE OF HAPPINESS, LOVE & WISDOM 40–41 (NEW HARBINGER PUBLICATIONS 2009).

these negative results through our own mindful behaviors and thought processes, one brain cell at a time.

Neuroscientist Alex Korb gives a great example of how anxiety wastes time in his book, *The Upward Spiral, Using Neuroscience to Reverse the Course of Depression, One Small Change at a Time.*[12] He worked himself into a lather over a dinner party he was throwing, when he realized he needed to shower and clean his apartment in addition to making the food. His anxiety cost him an extra twenty minutes in wasted time and also caused him to miss a call from his guests saying they'd be half an hour late. Without the anxiety attack, he would have had more than enough time.[13]

Our brains do these things but we do not have to let it happen. As Korb explains, the emotional part of the brain is the limbic system, which is responsible for excitement, fear, anxiety, memory, and desire.[14] It has four distinct regions: the hypothalamus, the amygdala, the hippocampus, and the cingulate cortex. The hypothalamus regulates and controls the body's stress response, and activates flight, fight, or freeze mode. The amygdala is located close to the hypothalamus and regulates anxiety, fear, and other negative emotions.[15] For example, depressed people have high amygdala activity, so reducing amygdala activity can help relieve anxiety and depression. The hippocampus is near the amygdala. It turns short-term memories into long-term memories. Because the hippocampus responds strongly to even minimal negative stimuli, it is like a canary in a coal mine.[16] Finally, the cingulate cortex controls attention and concentration. As the above story illustrates, stress also affects the function of the cingulate cortex by interfering with concentration.[17]

Stress is experienced first in the hypothalamus, which creates the flight, fight, or freeze response described above. Thus, calming the hypothalamus is a worthy goal.[18] Additionally, when the amygdala is triggered, fear and anxiety result. In addition, the hippocampus has trouble turning short-term memories into long-term memories, and the effects on the cingulate cortex result in difficulty concentrating.[19]

Being anxious is the brain's natural reaction to perceived danger, so try not to be too hard on yourself for being anxious. Just watch out if it seems chronic. Constant anxiety is bad for your brain and impedes clear thinking, as we have seen.[20]

Tips on Allaying Anxiety, Sadness, and Depression

As we have seen, anxiety activates the fear circuit, the same neural circuitry that keeps us out of danger from saber-toothed tigers.[21] This fear circuit can be mediated by

[12] ALEX KORB, THE UPWARD SPIRAL: USING NEUROSCIENCE TO REVERSE THE COURSE OF DEPRESSION, ONE SMALL CHANGE AT A TIME 33–34 (NEW HARBINGER PUBLICATIONS 2015).
[13] *Ibid.* [14] *Ibid.* at 20. [15] *Ibid.* [16] *Ibid.* [17] *Ibid.* [18] *Ibid.* at 21. [19] *Ibid.* at 22. [20] *Ibid.* at 41–42. [21] *Ibid.* at 39–41.

calming and placating the amygdala and the hippocampus.[22] Korb provides useful advice for doing this in order to tamp down anxiety. To help achieve this, he suggests we develop mindful, conscious awareness of the anxiety as it comes up. Name it "anxiety." Note the triggers. Note where this anxiety came from.[23] Move toward mindful acceptance that anxiety will happen, which will help you see it, name it, and calm it.[24] Next, try to focus on the present moment, just as we have been talking about.[25] Worry is never in the present tense. It is always about something that happened or might happen in the future.[26] Staying present and self-examining the triggers of emotion activates the prefrontal circuits, which can in turn calm the limbic system.

To really tamp down anxiety and immediately calm the prefrontal cortex, Korb suggests we put our emotions into words.[27] He suggests we feel the emotions without attaching emotional reactivity to them. Just feel them and write it down.[28] Use your journal for this.

LAW PAUSE

Take Korb's advice. Next time you experience anxiety, fully feel that anxiety and then name it in your journal. Don't judge it or react emotionally, just write about the experience for what it is.

It is amazing what we can do to actually improve our brain's function, not to mention make life a little easier. You might recognize this exercise as mindfulness in action. As Korb explains, all mindfulness activities cut off worry and anxiety at the source.[29]

While Korb writes mostly about helping relieve clinical depression, his tips are also useful for allaying anxiety and sadness, both of which, if left unchecked, can lead to clinical depression. Here are a few more of his anxiety, sadness, and depression-busting tips:

1. **Move Your Body.** Moving your body will create new neurons in the hippocampus and relieve negative emotions. Hate exercise? Call it something else. Just get outside and move for some other reason, to see a friend, watch a sporting event, watch birds, or whatever it takes. Do not just sit there. Go outside. Bring a friend for accountability.[30] Connect body movement with a long-term goal.[31] Remember that exercise improves sleep.[32]

2. **Do Yoga.** Getting more specific on suggestion number one above, Korb suggests that yoga in particular can provide your body with immediate biofeedback, giving the brain useful and calming information about how the mind and body are connecting.[33] Yoga can also help open the front body (avoid slumping) and stand up straighter, which improves mood.[34]

---

[22] *Ibid.* at 39–41.   [23] *Ibid.* at 42.   [24] *Ibid.*   [25] *Ibid.* at 45.   [26] *Ibid.*   [27] *Ibid.* at 46.
[28] *Ibid.*   [29] *Ibid.*   [30] *Ibid.* at 81.   [31] *Ibid.* at 83.   [32] *Ibid.* at 83.   [33] *Ibid.* at 138.
[34] *Ibid.* at 143–44.

3. **Breathe and Relax.** Breathe and relax, whatever that takes. It helps with brain function.[35]
4. **Fight Perfection.** Accept that you will not be prefect. It is the human condition. As Korb says, "It is better to do something only partly right than to do nothing at all."[36] If you are out there making mistakes, it means you are out there doing something. Way to go!
5. **Develop Long-term Goals.** Long-term goals create good habits and fire up the brain in all the right ways.[37]

Since the brain is the lawyer's most important tool, we need to protect it from harm, in the ways suggested by Korb. Try to incorporate as many of his suggestions into your life as you can, and for starters, try this breathing exercise.

Little Pause: Take and count ten long deep breaths in and out, and really sigh it out on the exhale. Make it loud and fun. Count them and keep your focus on these breaths. As other thoughts arise, acknowledge them and let them go, bringing your attention back to your own sweet breath.

How do you feel? Practice this throughout your day today and continue thereafter if it helps you.

As alluded to above, we can turn the stress that remains into our friends. Think of stress as a motivating energy that will get you through those really important tasks. Reframing stress in this way can make stress work for you rather than allowing stress to control you. Once the big event is passed, come back down and enjoy some calm energy.

CONCLUSIONS ABOUT AN INTRODUCTION TO MINDFULNESS

For a while, Google was paying people 20 percent of their salary to spend time in a mindfulness and emotional intelligence class similar to the one described in parts of this book. Right now, some companies are actually paying employees bonuses to unplug from technology during vacations.[38] Companies do these things because mindfulness training helps employees and improves the bottom line. These practices help employees deal with the scarcity of time and peace of mind. In their book, *Scarcity*,[39] Sendhil Mullainathan and Eldar Shafir discuss managing scarcity of all kinds. It seems that we are all short on something. For some it is money, for others time, for still others space, love, attention, confidence, and so on.

---

[35] *Ibid.* at 147–49.   [36] *Ibid.* at 94.   [37] *Ibid.* at 115.

[38] Brigid Schulte, *No Vacation Nation? One Company Gives Workers $7,500 to Unplug and Get Away*, WASHINGTON POST, Oct. 23, 2014, available at www.washingtonpost.com/news/local/wp/2014/10/23/no-vacation-nation-one-company-gives-workers-7500-to-unplug-and-get-away/.

[39] SENDHIL MULLAINATHAN AND ELDAR SHAFIR, SCARCITY, WHY HAVING TOO LITTLE MEANS SO MUCH (TIME BOOKS, HENRY HOLT & COMPANY LLC 2013).

Mullainathan and Shafir have studied scarcity in numerous contexts for many years, finding that scarcity, or a shortage of something significant, causes us all harm to varying degrees in a variety of ways. For all forms of scarcity, whether it is time, money, or confidence, we tend to fixate on the problem or issue that is at the forefront of our mind. This focus can give us a "focus dividend."[40] A great example is the incredible productivity you achieve when you are under a tight but still realistic deadline.

Scarcity also has less favorable side effects. It can cause tunnel vision, so we only see the immediate or most pressing needs, thus overlooking things that are pretty important but in the future. We can call this a tunnel tax.[41] Scarcity's most damaging side effect is that it uses up very precious bandwidth or mindspace.[42] Scarcity occupies the mind in ways that interfere with peace of mind.[43] When the scarcity is money, researchers have found that people in poverty or with deep financial problems literally cannot think straight. They perform worse in tests at school, including college,[44] they cannot concentrate at work, they yell at their kids and exhibit other poor parenting skills. They also suffer diminished self-control, as well as the ultimate scarcity tax: they cannot sleep.[45]

In the context of your most likely scarcity, time, Mullainathan and Shafir provide a helpful tip:

> Imagine two students, Felix and Oscar. Felix spends a good amount of time on work due at the end of each week and turns in his assignments on time. He is busy but relaxed. Oscar, on the other hand, who is equally talented, and taking the same classes, is crunched for time. He is working more hours, feels hurried, and rushes to turn in his assignments late every week. What makes Oscar so much busier? He is not taking more classes, he is not a less productive person. Instead, Oscar is simply one step behind: he is working on last week's assignments. Unlike Felix, for whom the material is vivid because he just heard the lecture, Oscar takes extra time reminding himself what the class did last week, and trying to keep it apart from (yet not forget) this morning's lecture. Oscar works harder but gets no more work done. Oscar is one step behind.[46]

The same thing happens to people who are behind with money, but let's stay focused on the time crunch. Can you think of a way to fix this problem of always being behind due to the scarcity of time? Would it have helped Oscar to pause, engage in some calm, mindful breathing, and focus on his week's schedule and priorities? How would it have helped Oscar to be more effective, efficient, and engaged, if he had paused and planned a bit?

To prepare for the next chapter on managing energy not time, please try this activity.

---

[40] *Ibid.* at 141. [41] *Ibid.* at 35–38, 119–21. [42] *Ibid.* at 157 [43] *Ibid.* at 125. [44] *Ibid.* at 157.
[45] *Ibid.* at 160. [46] *Ibid.* at 125.

LAW PAUSE

Give yourself a limited amount (in hours) of time to catch up or better yet, get ahead, in something you need to do. When I say a limited time, I mean for example, three hours, but you pick the amount of time you have and catch up on just one thing. Briefly write down the plan, then do it. If it is not done perfectly, it is fine. It won't be, but you need to have a very explicit schedule with breaks and stick to it. As the next chapter explains in detail, breaks provide the fuel and the mental and emotional space needed to continue and finish strongly.

In any case, what is not done by the end of the time allotted is not done, and that is how it is. You'll just need to take your break and finish it later as best you can in the least amount of time possible. You'll become more efficient with time, and we have some ideas for that in the next chapter, but, at least for now, you have caught up or are ahead in at least one thing.

3

Managing Energy, Time, and Physical Space for Happy and Healthy Efficiency

Joshua Alt and Nathalie Martin

Law has become commoditized over the past few decades, meaning it has become much more competitive and like a business. Perhaps it is fitting then that the most recent research on optimal energy for maximum professional productivity comes from the *Harvard Business Review*. While historically we have focused on "time management" when attempting to become more productive, the modern trend is to focus on managing energy instead. In their article entitled "Managing your Energy Not your Time," originally published in the *Harvard Business Review*, authors Tony Schwartz and Catherine McCarthy draw on "four main wellsprings in human beings: the body, emotions, mind, and spirit."[1] We discuss this article and its ramifications for lawyers at some length in this chapter, as well as some other sources. We also discuss traditional time management techniques and productive physical workspaces, all to help you become more efficient, effective, and happy.

INTRODUCTION TO MASTERING OUR ENERGY STORES

Time is Time

We each have a finite amount of time, and time passes even if we do not "use" it. An hour will pass as quickly as an hour passes. We may perceive the flow of time differently based on how we are working (or not), but an hour is still an hour.

How quickly we act or work, or what we get done, is not determined by the hour itself. We are not machines. We don't just go 60 miles per hour, every hour, day by day, month by month, and year by year. How quickly we work, and what we actually get done, depends upon many things, including skill at the required task, available resources, deadlines, motivation, interest, other projects, etc.

---

[1] Tony Schwartz and Catherine McCarthy, *Manage Your Energy, Not Your Time*, HARVARD BUSINESS REVIEW, Oct. 2007, available at https://hbr.org/2007/10/manage-your-energy-not-your-time.

No matter what, there are always impediments to working at our best. Sometimes, these impediments do not slow us but at other times, they drag us down. What accounts for this difference? How can we succeed in one instance but not the other, despite the impediments? The answer lies in how much energy we have.

We are Whole Beings

What happens to us one day could affect the next day, even the rest of our lives. Many external or controllable factors can also affect our ability to work, including whether we exercise, eat well, and get enough sleep. If we are conscious of our energy reserves, we can spend our energy appropriately or plan for more breaks. As I (Joshua) recall:

> Many times when I did not get enough sleep, I worked horribly. I couldn't seem to muster enough energy for long enough. Instead of taking a break, I would try to push through. It never worked out. I was able to work much better when I spaced out my work, taking breaks at strategic times, and never trying to work harder than my energy levels would allow.

Little Pause: Can you think of a time when you managed your energy levels well? How about when you didn't manage them so well? What was the difference between the two times and the effect on you?

ADOPT SOME POSITIVE MANTRAS

We will all face problems in our lives and we will all make mistakes. If you tend to get nervous speaking in public or being around people you don't know, try to reframe your need to do these things as opportunities for growth while at the same time appreciating yourself for exactly who you are. From Professor Heidi Brown's book, *The Introverted Lawyer*, heed this advice:

- Perfection is boring; be yourself.
- You care about what you have to say and you care about people.
- You have a different and interesting perspective.
- You like yourself; not everyone needs to like you.
- If people are not listening to you, or ignore or talk over you, it's their loss; let them be.
- If you feel drained during or after speaking, this may be normal for you. It is OK.
- You work on yourself every day; you are putting your best self forward.[2]

---

[2] Heidi Brown, The Introverted Lawyer 95 (ABA Publishing 2017).

MANAGING ENERGY, NOT TIME

According to Schwartz and McCarthy, the key to being happy and efficient is learning to use and restore four "wellsprings." If we do not make choices that keep the body, mind, emotions, and spirit in good shape, we run out of energy and find unhealthy ways to cope.

We eventually need to figure out how to know when *not* to work, how to know when we are "done." While this recognition can be considered part of achieving general work–life balance, ideally we do not have lives that are dissected into two separate parts, work and life. For our purposes here, work is when you are actively doing the job for which you are employed (lawyer, policeman, teacher, pundit, etc.), and life is what you do with yourself when you are not at work (activities, relationships, etc.).

We say ideally because lawyers have a reputation and a tendency to let work take over life, often resulting in a heavier reliance on drugs and alcohol than we find among non-lawyers. Many of us do things that others might find odd, not to mention destructive, such as drinking coffee all day, eating whatever we can find at our desks, and then collapsing in front of a television or computer with an unhealthy dinner and wine or martinis.

LAW PAUSE

Keep track of the following for two or three days: time spent with family and friends, during breaks between work such as ten minutes here and fifteen minutes there, television, web surfing and other entertainment, sports, fitness, praying, meditating, and other "downtime." Take the time to write down what you do that's *not* work. The list need not be exhaustive, but it should be fairly detailed.

What did you learn about yourself? How long is your list? As I (Joshua) explain:

> When I wrote out my list, I found that I was not doing all the things that I wanted to do outside of work and school (since I was still a law student at the time). I wasn't spending enough time talking to my wife while not distracted. I played games on my phone far too much. I was not eating breakfast that often, if at all, and I sure as hell did not drink enough water. I was good at spending time with my wife when we went out to eat or to shop, pretty much any time. I was good at playing with my pets. I was good at playing games and working out.

For the time being, take note of the things you've written down. Think about how much of your time you dedicate to work or school, and how much time you dedicate to non-work or non-school activities. Do you find yourself working when you shouldn't be? Think of a time when work crept into your mind while you were at home relaxing, and you couldn't get it out of your mind. Did you start working? Did it decrease the quality of time you spent outside of work? Take note, and look at where and how your time is spent. Then look at where you'd like it to be spent. Without judgment, see if your reality and your wishes can possibly mesh.

The First Wellspring: Physical Energy

One aspect of energy is the body or physical energy.[3] Lawyers and law students may be among the more intelligent members of society, but we are not necessarily smart about everything. Too many of us operate mostly from the head up, despite the mind and body being connected. We each need a healthy body to fuel a healthy mind.

Exercise
Studies show that exercise makes our brains work better. More specifically, the body needs both regular cardiovascular exercise and regular strength training exercise. Some lawyers like interval training because it is intense, fast, and efficient. Would you expect anything less from lawyers? On the other end of the spectrum, yoga can be a wonderful way to get in shape with some emotional, intellectual, and spiritual benefits mixed in.

As far as exercise goes, it doesn't matter what you choose as long as you commit to yourself to do something and stick to it. If you are not very fit or motivated to exercise, try walking. Consider doing a written contract with yourself to get a certain amount of exercise each day. Schedule this time and keep track of it until it becomes a habit. You'll be surprised how much writing this down will help you get it done.

Food
As for food, healthier food will unquestionably help you think better. I (Professor Martin) love to gorge on junk food, but I also know it is not good for me. As a compromise, I let myself gorge on junk food once in a while, but do it mindfully, knowing it is not nutrition, it is harmful, and doing this might need to be countered with extra exercise (which, by the way, I don't really like).

At the UNM School of Law, breakfast for many students consists of what you can forage for free in the forum. Typically, these free food offerings consist of donuts and pizza rather than fruits and vegetables. Also, when stress begins to take over, some students stop eating entirely or binge on anything in sight. Law students can be running on fumes by the end of the semester, both nutritionally and financially, and the resulting poor nutrition can affect final exam results, and overall health and happiness.

Whatever you have done with and to your body in the past, you can make the decision to change that right now. Schwartz and McCarthy recount a story in which a busy manager shifted his eating habits to smaller meals and light snacks every three hours instead of two big meals a day.[4] By consuming higher quality food throughout

[3] Tony Schwartz and Catherine McCarthy, *Manage Your Energy, Not Your Time*, HARVARD BUSINESS REVIEW, Oct. 2007, available at https://hbr.org/2007/10/manage-your-energy-not-your-time.
[4] *Ibid.*

the day, the manager became more consistently effective and efficient, not to mention happier.

Rituals or Positive Habits

Schwartz and McCarthy use the word "ritual" to describe things we do consistently and purposefully, better enabling us to make good choices. Although the word ritual also has some negative connotations,[5] we will use this word to describe the process through which we can schedule and carve out health and fitness commitments without having to give these healthy habits too much thought. Like taking a particular route to work, a healthy breakfast and a scheduled exercise plan can become routines without having to think about them, a real help when it comes to willpower. We can plan ahead and take the uncertainty out.

Once the physical side of building energy is taken care of, we can start to think about the other wellsprings.

The Second Wellspring: Emotional Energy

Schwartz and McCarthy refer to emotional energy as the quality of energy.[6] Take a minute to consider the quality of various types of emotional energy. Consider an emotion, say "anger," and consider how anger affects your energy. While angry, you might be aggressive, tense, argumentative, and even violent, perhaps even slamming a door or throwing something onto the ground.[7]

The quality and even quantity of energy used when angry is vastly different from the quality and quantity of energy we use when we are happy. Happiness isn't tense, argumentative, or aggressive. After a happy thought, we are often energized, while after an angry one, we are often tired. Surprisingly, it is generally easier to be happy than it is to be angry when we consider how those emotions affect us.[8] We say "surprisingly" because it is amazing how few people actually choose happiness.

---

[5]   UNM Law Professor David Stout dislikes the word ritual. As he explains:

> I have this conception of a ritual as a practice that has lost it meaning over time and, therefore, as become routinized through ritual. I think of the Catholic Mass for example, or in my own Protestant experience the ritualized communion. Wearing of the green on St. Patrick's Day is not only a ritual completely devoid of its antecedent meaning, but commercialized to boot. To some degree mindfulness is the antidote to ritual in the sense that we focus on the moment and therefore maybe find the meaning in the immediacy of the experience. It is a tough word to replace – somehow the idea of a meaningful recurrent practice is more along the lines of how I would like to conceive of "it."

[6]   Tony Schwartz and Catherine McCarthy, *Manage Your Energy, Not Your Time*, Harvard Business Review, Oct. 2007, available at https://hbr.org/2007/10/manage-your-energy-not-your-time.

[7]   Emotions can be represented by colors, and perhaps we could equate anger with the color red.

[8]   *Ibid.* When our bodies are not receiving energy, we tend to shift into a fight or flight mode. This happens a lot when people aren't eating enough. The colloquialism is "hangry," or hungry anger. Similarly, not getting enough sleep makes us grumpy. Being sleepy is not fun. There isn't enough energy to really perform. This also affects our mood.

Of course, negative emotions are inevitable. Someone or something will eventually come along and cause us to feel anger, resentment,[9] sadness, depression, or maybe even hate. As discussed in other parts of this book, however, we need not dwell on these difficult experiences. We can accept that these emotions will come. We can even get to a point where we can simply watch them come and go. By knowing that we will experience negative emotions, we can prepare for them.

Schwartz and McCarthy offer us three practices to help neutralize negative emotions, all of which are discussed in different contexts in other parts of this book. We include them here as well to demonstrate how these techniques affect the subject of this chapter, energy and productivity:

1. **Breath:** Buy some sweet time through deep abdominal breathing. Inhaling and exhaling slowly for a certain number of counts induces relaxation and recovery, and turns off the fight or flight response.[10] Please give this a try right now. This exercise is slightly different from the breath counting exercise in Chapter 2. Start by inhaling for six counts, holding for three counts, exhaling for six counts, holding for three counts, repeat. Train yourself to practice deep breathing as soon as you feel a negative emotion, even a slight one. This practice, as well as the five count breathing we learned in Chapter 2, work well in traffic, while speaking in public, or during performance reviews.

2. **Show Gratitude:** Show your appreciation to other people,[11] a practice that is as beneficial to the giver as to the receiver.[12] Take the time to write a note, send an email, or approach others in the hallway to tell them how much you appreciate them. Be as specific as possible.[13] This gratitude "practice" forces us to really think about the ways others have positively impacted our lives, which in turn increases dopamine in the brain and makes us feel good. Again, gratitude helps the giver as much or more than the receiver.[14]

3. **Rewrite Your Story:** See if you can look at a negative situation from a different perspective and change the story you tell yourself.[15] Often, people in conflict cast themselves in the role of victim, blaming others or external circumstances for all their difficulties.[16] If we change the way we view situations, then the emotions we feel toward those situations will also change. Schwartz and McCarthy use what they call a "three lens" technique to help us view situations differently:

   a. With the *reverse lens*, for example, people ask themselves, "What would I – or if it is a conflict with another person, the other person in this conflict – say about it in retrospect, and in what ways might that be true?"[17]

---

[9]   *See ibid.*, particularly the section in the article entitled *Letting Go of Resentment.*
[10] *Ibid.* Schwartz and McCarthy explain that smokers tend to smoke in response to stress because of the deep breathing involved in inhaling and exhaling.
[11] *Ibid.*   [12] *Ibid.*   [13] *Ibid.* (stating that the "more detailed and specific, the higher the impact").
[14] *Ibid.*   [15] *Ibid.*   [16] *Ibid.*   [17] *Ibid.*

b. With the *long lens* they ask, "How will I most likely view this situation in six months?"[18]
c. With the *wide lens* they ask themselves, "Regardless of the outcome of this issue, how can I grow and learn from it?"[19]

After practicing this technique, I (Joshua) recall:

> This practice reminds me of something my mother used to tell me whenever I felt defeated. She used to say, "Son, you can sit there and call yourself a victim and play that game. Or, you can overcome the hardship. It's your choice. Are you going to be a *victim* or a *victor?*"

LAW PAUSE

Apply the three lens approach to a recent disappointment or challenge, and write about it, including your reaction to the approach. Did this help you feel better about the situation?

The Third Wellspring: The Focused Mind

As we discussed in the last chapter, Schwartz and McCarthy note that despite our abiding belief that multitasking is normal, we all have difficulty effectively switching attention from one task to another.[20] Shifting attention from a task, even temporarily such as to check email, voice mail, or text messaging, "increases the amount of time necessary to finish the primary task by as much as 25%."[21] In today's techno-world, we are in a constant state of interruption. Even as we write this paragraph, emails are popping onto our devices, and it takes every cell in our bodies not to look as they come in.

Why is this? Are we trying to save time later? This is a fallacy. Is ego part of it? Do we want everyone to think we are working 24/7? Working harder than they are? Why not instead make the choice to show people that you are managing your energy well, living in the present moment, and giving each task its own priority?

Whether it is email, text messages, or social media notifications, Schwartz and McCarthy suggest two interrelated pieces of advice to avoid time loss through "switching."

1. Develop rituals to keep you on task.
2. Work in chunks of time called "ultradian sprints," which is a fancy phrase for 90–120 minute fully focused work periods, followed by a true break.

---

[18] *Ibid.* [19] *Ibid.* [20] *Ibid.* [21] *Ibid.* (calling this switching time).

Developing rituals takes a bit more thought, though it is fun. Perhaps you can find a quiet room away from email or other devices. You should definitely have a ritual for turning off your phone and other electronics, for a period of time.

LAW PAUSE

Think of and then write about a ritual you can use to unplug.

For example, if you need to write but not research, which will become very common throughout your career, turn off your internet; perhaps, you can check email just two or three times a day, and turn the phone on "do not disturb," or only allow emergency calls to get through.

For a drastic example, I (Professor Martin) edited this chapter while on the Oregon Coast where I had no television or phone service and could only get phone calls by driving into town. I noted how much fuller life is and how much more peaceful it is when the phone never rings. While this may sound a bit drastic, perhaps you could try a 24-hour media and technology "fast." Whatever you choose, find rituals that work for you, and remember to take those breaks.

The Fourth Wellspring: Spiritual Energy

Spiritual energy, in many ways, is the most critical wellspring because this form of energy makes us happy and that happiness keeps us motivated. Spiritual energy comes from living life with purpose. When we believe that we are living with purpose, in line with our core beliefs, our lives are more positive.[22] Schwartz and McCarthy discuss developing spiritual practices last because it is easier to learn to develop rituals around physical and emotional energy than around amorphous and controversial ideas such as spiritual energy or core beliefs.[23]

To develop rituals around our core beliefs and access the energy of the human spirit, Schwartz and McCarthy suggest that we clarify priorities and establish accompanying rituals in three categories:

1. Doing what we do best and enjoy most at work;
2. Consciously allocating time and energy to the areas of their lives – work, family, health, service to others – we deem most important; and
3. Living our core values in our daily lives through our behavior.[24]

As articulated in Chapter 1 and again in Chapter 16, you can determine where your strengths lie by reflecting on a time when you were in flow, when everything clicked and you worked efficiently and effectively with minimal effort.[25] What made it so easy? What were you doing at the time? Was this you at your best? Remember that

---

[22] *Ibid.*   [23] *Ibid.*   [24] *Ibid.*   [25] *Ibid.*

while what you do best and what you enjoy most are not always identical, one can help the other.

> Devoting time to what's important to us can be difficult because we don't necessarily even know what the important things are. We do what comes our way and what seems easiest. Like many things in life, however, if we put in the up-front planning time to discover what is important to us, we can live a much easier, happier, more successful life.

LAW PAUSE

To pay more attention to what is truly most important to you, start with a list. Write down what is important to you and why. Then, develop a ritual around it. If you love being outdoors, set aside time every week to go for a hike or walk around the park. If you enjoy spending time with your spouse, schedule a date, recreation, movie night, or whatever you like. Take the time to devote time to what's important to you.

TIME MANAGEMENT

Having said all of that about managing energy rather than time, in reality you need to manage both. You will start by managing your energy and then by managing your time.

Jar of Stones Analogy

One way to think about time management is to picture a jar and on the side some large stones, medium-sized stones, pebbles, and sand. Imagine that you need to fit all of the stones, pebbles, and sand in the jar. Due to the size and shape of the jar, if you put the sand and pebbles in the jar first, not all of the large and medium-sized stones will fit.

Imagine that the large stones are the highest priorities you have, the things that matter most to you. Put those in the jar first. Next add the medium-sized stones, which represent the next most important things in your life. Now working around those, add the pebbles, or not very important tasks, and finally fill in with the sand, which represents tasks that are very low in priority. If you put those large important tasks in first, everything will fit, or if something doesn't fit, it will be something unimportant.

LAW PAUSE

Make a list of your big stones, medium-sized stones, pebbles, and sand. Now schedule a week of tasks, using the sizes of the stones to prioritize tasks. Put the items into your journal.

Practical Time Management

The easiest way to manage your time is to make a weekly calendar and schedule in all of the things you need to do, including studying for two hours for each one hour of law school class time, exercising, spending time with family and friends, and even grocery shopping.

Once you have done this, you will likely feel less stressed, and you may even recognize that there is still time in a day to do things other than law school. Attending law school takes up about as much time as a hefty full-time job, but no more, assuming you stay focused and healthy using the techniques outlined in this chapter and the rest of this book.

In his book, *The Creative Lawyer*, Michael Melcher suggests some outstanding time management techniques, including the following:[26]

1. Set maximum rather than minimum times to do the task. Don't say, "I have to work on my resume for at least 45 minutes." Rather, say, "I will work on this resume for up to 45 minutes and that is it. It will have to be good enough."

   I (Professor Martin) have been using this technique for over thirty years in both private practice and in academia, allocating time for projects at the beginning of the day and letting myself spend only that amount of time on that one task and no more. If I can't do the task in that amount of time, it will have to be good enough. That's it.

2. In *The Artist's Way*, Julia Cameron suggests that you give yourself permission to do an OK job but not a great job on some things. Make sure these things are not law school assignments but other tasks in life, such as cleaning the house or organizing a closet. According to Cameron, "anything worth doing, is worth doing poorly." This is a wonderful way to make sure the perfect does not become the enemy of the good, and the little tasks that don't matter much don't take over your whole life!

3. Divide tasks into tiny steps so they do not overwhelm.

4. Do the worst task for fifteen minutes. Anyone can do anything for fifteen minutes.

5. You may also find Gretchen Rubin's "virtual prison" idea beneficial. Pick a day and use that day to complete your most boring tasks at one time. Say to yourself, "Yes, this is boring, but it is OK. I am in prison and I have no choice."[27]

6. On some tasks, embrace the beginner in you. Acknowledge and accept your low level of competence on these tasks, and then, simply do your best. Accept that others are better at this particular thing and feel the freedom that comes from having low expectations of yourself. Also, let others do some of these things rather than you. I could get used to this!

[26] Michael Melcher, The Creative Lawyer 183–84 (2nd Edn. American Bar Association 2014).
[27] *Ibid.* at 184.

7. If you have to do something high level in a big rush, do the opposite. Know you are NOT a beginner. Remind yourself of how incredibly competent you have been at other similar tasks. Use that great past experience to catapult you into achieving this one too!

8. Pick one "must do" for the day and do not leave until it is done. Better yet, if your schedule allows, do it first and set a noon deadline.

9. Always do the things that are hardest for you (based upon your personality and your energy flow) at the time of day that you have the most energy.

10. Rank your priorities for the day and set out the time each will take in parenthesis right next to the task. I (Professor Martin) even do this for long-term projects such as this book, writing down the number of hours and even the number of pages for each section or chapter or sub-chapter. Once I started doing this, all tasks seemed doable.

Now, I do have a question about lists. Is it ever OK to live *off* list? Is it ever OK to say that today, for the next several hours, or for whatever time I pick, I am just going to do what comes naturally and I am not going to force myself to get anything at all done? This is a question my husband Stewart asked when we were both suffering from health and personal problems. Generally, Stewart and I never stop moving and do not relax unless forced through a practice or routine of sorts, so it was a fascinating question.

Living off-list sometimes is not only permitted but required, if you are to operate at your highest level. Try to have some unplanned time, or permit unplanned time, and then try not to fill it with errands. Of course if every day was empty and you had no responsibility and no purpose, that probably would not sit well either. We are seeking balance between purpose, efficiency, interest, joy, and, yes, space, so you can think your best.

By managing our energy, rather than merely the amount of time that we have, we can all be more efficient and effective in every aspect of our lives. Focus on filling the four reservoirs of energy: physical, emotional, mental, and spiritual. If you manage to do so, you will find yourself living life with more ease.

MANAGING PHYSICAL SPACE

By now you know that small changes in attitude and mindset can yield big changes in overall happiness, satisfaction, and personal fulfillment. Just as a ritual to keep your mind clear and your spirits up can bring great rewards, so too can making small changes in your work environment. Physical space can be a mirror for emotional space and life in general, so make yours mirror those things you want to bring into your life.

Very small changes matter. Most people prefer to work in a clean space. A few photos and a picture of a nice view, if not a real view of nature, can go a long way, as can rearranging furniture, as discussed below. If you already have an office at work, you can use all of these principles there, but even if you don't, you can create a workspace anywhere. Having a designated space to work gets the creative juices flowing whenever you are there. Having a brief mindfulness ritual to use as you sit down to work is also very helpful. For example, at my (Professor Martin's) office and on my home computer, as the Microsoft four color icon moves and forms, I sit quietly and breathe. I have found that I do this without thinking, even when I am stressed out, and it calms me right down. You have to wait for the program to start working anyway, so why not? As you take breaks in the work, come back to the ritual as a way to come back to center. My icon ritual takes less than a minute.

The Science on the Mindful Workspace

Just as your mindset matters, science confirms that our physical space also affects our efficiency and our overall well-being. According to psychology and neuroscience studies, the way your workspace looks can significantly affect your productivity.[28] Having the freedom to choose the way your workspace looks has an empowering effect and has been linked with improved productivity. When Londoners in one study were allowed to put plants and art in their office in whatever way they liked, productivity increased by 32 percent.[29] Employees also identified more with their employer, a sign of increased commitment to the team effort.[30] A personal touch matters, so display a few items that express who you are in order to stay connected and motivated. Even a cork board with a few photos can be motivating and increase productivity.

For example, a 2011 study of undergraduates showed that people rated curvy, rounded environments as more beautiful than straight-edged rectilinear environments.[31] Moreover, rounded spaces triggered more activity in brain regions associated with reward and aesthetic appreciation. If you are designing a workspace, use curved rather than sharp-edged furniture.[32] Curved furniture promotes positive emotions, creativity, and productivity. Another big benefit boost to creativity is high ceilings, so if you are able to choose a space with high ceilings, do it.[33]

Specific Office Tips

Whether you're working at home, at school, or in an office, clean up the clutter for more productivity. Your desk need not be super-neat, but remove things you do not need to create space for your ideas.[34] Also, assuming you have your own workspace,

---

[28]   Christian Jarrett, *The Perfect Workspace (According to Science)*, 99U, available at http://99u.com /articles/17437/the-perfect-workspace-according-to-science.
[29]   *Ibid.*   [30]   *Ibid.*   [31]   *Ibid.*   [32]   *Ibid.*   [33]   *Ibid.*
[34]   On the other hand, a bunch of studies recently found that messy desks are the mark of more creative people, so the goods are not yet in on this one. *Ibid.*

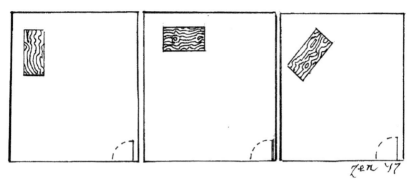

FIGURE 3.1 Your Desk in the Power Position, created by illustrator, Pamela "Zen" Miller.

spend a little time thinking about your décor. Supposedly, the color of your accessories, walls, and even the light in your lightbulbs can affect creativity and productivity. Color has a big impact on your psychological and physical well-being. Soft yellow, sandstone, pale gold, pale orange, pale green, and blue-green are good office colors. Adding white will increase clarity and mental focus. Browns and earth tones will ground and stabilize the office, but they don't stimulate the mind. These shades actually lower productivity and perhaps even your IQ, according to a two-year US public health study of public buildings.[35] Accessories in red and green are especially motivating, according to the same study.[36]

Artwork and greenery can increase healing, comfort, empowerment, and productivity.[37] Fresh air makes us work better too, as does natural light, so work near a window if possible. A nice view is also terrific though we know this is not possible for everyone. I (Professor Martin) have from time to time set up home offices in dark corners, only to abandon them in favor of the kitchen table or my bed, both of which face glass doors.

Think closely about where to put your furniture. Start by putting your office desk either along the northwest wall or as far away from the door as possible, or both, as pictured in Figure 3.1. This is known as the power position, meaning you can see the door and most of the room from your desk. Figure 3.1 shows some possibilities that will all work.

Also, when in a meeting, say in a common room or conference room, the person seated farthest from the door will have the most power.[38] If you sit too close to the door, you will be distracted by daily/petty details, and if you sit with your back to the

[35] MICHAEL F. ROIZEN AND MEHMET C. OZ, YOU: STRESS LESS 53 (SIMON AND SCHUSTER 2011).
[36] *Ibid.*   [37] *Ibid.*
[38] *Feng Shui Office: The Six Most Important Things You Need to Know about Feng Shui in Your Office*, FENG SHUI AND BEYOND, available at www.feng-shui-and-beyond.com/feng-shui-office.html.

door, some say you will suffer from backstabbing and office politics, and other behind the scenes antics.[39]

Remember that meetings are not always about you, and you don't always run the show, or even want to run the show. Sometimes you will intentionally *not* want to be in the limelight or the center of attention, for example, when you are too busy to do any more projects and work will be assigned at the meeting. In meetings where I (Professor Martin) do not want to be asked to do a lot of follow-up or to participate much in the decisions or conversation, I purposely avoid the power seat. I sit in the middle, making it easier to listen to others. You will always want to sit in the power seat in your own office or workspace, however.

If you share an office, avoid sitting back to back or face to face. Both positions purportedly create conflict.[40] If you can, create a small barrier between workspaces with a plant, photo or other object. Concentrate on acoustical privacy by keeping conversations low or using headphones.[41]

In any office, soften sharp corners with plants, as these sharp objects are said to cause irritability, discomfort, and even disease. Plus, they hurt when you hip-check them. Also, keep aisles wide enough to allow energy to move through effortlessly. Make sure to use subtle colors in an open office plan. Bright, vivid colors are too active in a large bustling room, but are great in a private office.

Make sure all main and closet doors open and close fully, and make absolutely sure there is always room for more, so that more abundance – material or otherwise – can come into your life. Empty wastebaskets often and get rid of broken or damaged things to keep all the energy flowing positively. These tips will help you feel in control, inspired, productive, and powerful and can enhance your creativity, discipline, and success.

Add something in your office that you can touch or look at to reduce stress. There is a reason why stress balls that you squish with your hands are so popular at lawyer conferences. Stress in the office can dominate and throw you off track.[42] Avoiding harsh lighting or lots of glare is also helpful, because these cause irritability and fatigue.

LAW PAUSE

Take a few minutes this week to incorporate as many of the suggestions found here as you like. As you sit down in the workspace after making these changes, note any subtle changes in your outlook or your output.

---

[39]   Sally Painter, *How Do You Determine the Appropriate Feng Shui for an Office,* LOVE TO KNOW, available at http://feng-shui.lovetoknow.com/How_Do_You_Determine_the_Appropriate_Feng_Shui_for_an_Office.

[40]   *Ibid.*   [41]   *Ibid.*   [42]   *Ibid.*

Conclusions About the Mindful Office Space

You will likely spend a great deal of your time on earth working, hopefully on things that inspire and move you. Why not do this work in a place that speaks to you? The tips above are easy to incorporate and should pay for themselves in enhanced productivity and happiness. No matter what, taking these types of small steps to increase your work and career satisfaction is a worthwhile investment in your well-being.

4

The Lawyer in Society: Popular Culture Images of Lawyers and Your Self-Image

Nathalie Martin and Jennifer Laws

This chapter asks you to examine your personal role in the profession through the lens of society's perceptions of attorneys. We ask that you place a vivid image of yourself as a lawyer front and center in your mind, and then read about lawyer jokes and images of lawyers in books, television, and movies. We then return to your own view of yourself to think about your professional identity formation in the law. We study the media and the jokes to see how we can work together to dispel negative images of our profession. As you no doubt know, lawyer jokes and negative images in the media are incredibly prevalent. Indeed, when hearing that we are writing a book about mindful lawyering, many people assume it is a joke about an oxymoron.

Lawyer jokes and media images of lawyers may not be totally accurate, but they do provide a window into the public's perception of our profession. While these jokes and television and movie roles may be funny or entertaining on some level, they portray lawyers in a way that perpetuates deeply negative stereotypes. Many of these jokes also have an ounce of truth in them. As a profession, we need to look at ourselves, our training, and our practices to see what can be done to change not only our collective image, but our actions. The goal of this chapter is to lead you on the path toward creating this necessary change in the profession. In this chapter, we examine the roles of lawyers in society from the perception of the general public, so you can imagine and find your place in that world. First, however, we ask you to visualize yourself as a lawyer.

YOUR PLACE IN THE LAW

Your Image of Yourself

LAW PAUSE

Think about what people said when you told them you were going to become a lawyer. Write a few sentences about the themes of these reactions.

Lawyers in Society

Little Pause: Think of your favorite positive image of a lawyer in society. Now think of a negative one. Muse for a moment about where these images come from.

PERCEPTIONS OF LAWYERS THROUGHOUT THE AGES

One of the oldest images our society associates with the law is Blind Justice, or Justitia, shown in Figure 4.1.

In Roman times, Justitia appeared wearing her blindfold. By the medieval era her blindfold was gone. Over the course of the sixteenth and seventeenth centuries, the blindfold returned,[1] but we do not know why. Does the blindfold represent Justitia's blindness to outcomes of legal decisions (good or bad)? Is it representative of her blindness to class and social status, emphasizing that her justice is fair and impartial? We also don't know what role lawyers played in the dispensing of her justice at that time and throughout history.

LAWYER AS THE BUTT OF JOKES

Lawyer jokes are seen as a big problem in our profession. For example, as we briefly mentioned in Chapter 1, law schools are accredited by an organization known as the American Bar Association or the ABA. The ABA was founded August 21, 1878, to set academic standards for law schools, create model ethical codes related to the legal profession, to provide ongoing advocacy and education for and about lawyers, and to promote a positive image of lawyers in society. The ABA now has over 400,000 members. One of the ABA's recent activities was designed to combat images of lawyers as snakes, vultures, and greedy ambulance chasers found in lawyer jokes.[2] Back in 1993, the ABA spent $700,000 on an attorney image-improvement campaign, and in 2015, the ABA's Law Practice Division adopted a formal National Love Your Lawyer Day. This process is no joke. Here's an excerpt from the resolution:

> WHEREAS, Lawyers have consistently been the target of verbal bashing, deroga-tory portrayals and literature is rife with lawyer bashing dating back hundreds of years; and
>
> WHEREAS, A 2013 Pew Research Center survey found lawyers last among ten professional categories for "contributions to society;" and

---

[1] MICHAEL ASIMOW AND SHANNON MADER, LAW AND POPULAR CULTURE: A COURSE BOOK 8 (PETER LANG 2004).

[2] Malcolm Kushner, *Lawyer Jokes: The Image of Lawyers Is No Joke, But Maybe It Should Be: In a world of sound bites where people get their news from late-night comedy shows, telling positive lawyer jokes may be more effective than you'd think*, Feb. 8, 2016, available at www.Callawyer.Com/2016/02/Lawyer-Jokes-The-Image-Of-Lawyers-Is-No-Joke-But-Maybe-It-Should-Be/.

FIGURE 4.1 Justitia or Lady Justice, created by illustrator, Pamela "Zen" Miller.

WHEREAS, According to a 2014 Gallup survey, the public perception of lawyers on honesty and ethics is an unsatisfactory 21%; and

WHEREAS, The portrayal of lawyers in American popular culture, including on television and cinema, is largely negative, which promotes a negative stereotype of lawyers in society; and

WHEREAS, National Love Your Lawyer Day was initiated in 2001 by the American Lawyers Public Image Association as a day to celebrate lawyers for their many positive contributions, and to encourage the public to view lawyers in a more favorable light; and

WHEREAS, National Love Your Lawyer Day is celebrated annually on the first Friday of November; and

WHEREAS, The American Bar Association has as its mission to uphold the honor of the profession of law and to this end should promote a positive public image of lawyers in the nation; and

WHEREAS, The American Bar Association Law Practice Division desires to promote a positive public image of lawyers by celebrating National Love Your Lawyer Day . . .[3]

As this resolution demonstrates, jokes and other media can affect the public's perception of us, but what are these perceptions, and how can they be changed?

LAW PAUSE

Write down your favorite lawyer joke. What makes this joke funny? Be very specific, even if it ruins the joke.

Now write about this: under what circumstances would this and other law jokes no longer be funny?

Lawyer jokes portray lawyers in the worst possible light, typically as caricatures of greed and dishonesty. The themes of these jokes show that a large segment of US society seems to have rejected the notion that lawyers are fair and impartial servants of Justitia, instead opting for the image of deceitful, greedy, self-absorbed participants in a system blind to the public good.[4] A few lawyer jokes demonstrate this point:

1. What's the difference between a good lawyer and a bad lawyer?
A bad lawyer can let a case drag out for several years. A good lawyer can make it last even longer.[5]

2. Santa Claus, the tooth fairy, an honest lawyer and an old drunk are walking down the street together when they simultaneously spot a hundred dollar bill. Who gets it?
The old drunk, of course – the other three are fantasy creatures.[6]

---

[3] You can find the whole resolution at www.americanbar.org/content/dam/aba/images/abanews/ LoveYourLawyerDay.pdf.
[4] Popular culture as that phrase is used here means works produced and marketed for consumption by popular audiences rather than the elite.
[5] *World's best (and worst) lawyer jokes*, LAWYERS WEEKLY, available at: www.lawyersweekly.com.au/folk law/6045-world-s-best-and-worst-lawyer-jokes.
[6] *Ibid.*

FIGURE 4.2 Lawyer as Shark, created by illustrator, Pamela "Zen" Miller.

3. What do you call six thousand lawyers at the bottom of the sea?
A good start.[7]

4. What's the difference between a dead snake lying in the road and a dead lawyer lying in the road?
There are skid marks in front of the snake.[8]

This one only works for male lawyers but here goes:

5. What does a lawyer get when you give him Viagra?
Taller.[9]

Finally, we offer a visual in Figure 4.2 that seems to say it all and then some.

Little Pause: Now conjure up an image of a good lawyer. What attributes does this person have?

THE FALL OF LAWYERS IN THE MEDIA

Here we briefly review some lawyer characters found in books, movies, and television. These images reflect how public opinion of lawyers has fallen steadily since the 1960s.[10] While lawyers have always been portrayed in media as a mix of good and bad, negative images now far exceed positive ones.[11] According to an ABA Section of Litigation study in 2002, Americans have only slightly more confidence in the legal profession than in the media, far below the confidence in doctors, judges, and the judicial system in general. Those polled described lawyers as "greedy, manipulative, and corrupt,"[12] a perception often reflected in

7 MARC GALANTER, LOWERING THE BAR: LAWYER JOKES AND LEGAL CULTURE 213 (THE UNIVERSITY OF WISCONSIN PRESS 2005).
8 *Ibid.* at 196.
9 *World's best (and worst) lawyer jokes*, LAWYERS WEEKLY, available at: www.lawyersweekly.com.au/folklaw/6045-world-s-best-and-worst-lawyer-jokes.
10 MICHAEL ASIMOW AND SHANNON MADER, LAW AND POPULAR CULTURE: A COURSE BOOK 52 (PETER LANG 2004).
11 *Ibid.*
12 American Bar Association (ABA) Section of Litigation. *Public Perceptions of Lawyers: Consumer Research Findings* 4, 2002, available at www.americanbar.org/content/dam/aba/migrated/marketresearch/PublicDocuments/public_perception_of_lawyers_2002.authcheckdam.pdf.

film, television, and jokes. While we can't be sure that negative portrayals of attorneys in popular culture have negatively influenced public opinion of the legal profession, we do know that the images resonate because they reflect some version of reality.[13] We also know that these images are sometimes exaggerated for the sake of drama and while we can't say for certain that these images are hurting lawyers, they certainly aren't helping us.

Two empirical studies, one from 1995[14] and the other from 2001,[15] offer further insight into that feedback loop. The 1995 study compared heavy watchers of *L.A. Law*, a television legal drama series that was broadcast on NBC from 1986 to 1994, to those who almost never watched. *L.A. Law* featured legal cases about hot topic issues of the time, such as capital punishment, abortion, racism, gay rights, sexual harassment, and domestic violence. The show also focused heavily on the personal and sexual lives of the employees of McKenzie, Brackman, Chaney, and Kuzak. The study showed that heavy watchers perceived lawyers as more powerful and with better character, more physically attractive and more sociable than the non-watchers.[16] Some people even believe that the interesting cases and lavish surroundings portrayed in *L.A. Law* were responsible for a surge of applications to law school.[17]

The 2001 study compared watchers of *Judge Judy*, a reality court show that premiered in 1996, to those who didn't watch. Judge Judith Sheindlin has been credited with introducing a "tough" adjudication approach into the courtroom, which has led to several television imitators. Eighty-three percent of those who regularly watched *Judge Judy* thought the judge in real cases should ask questions during the trial and be aggressive with litigants; 74 percent of frequent *Judge Judy* watchers thought that a judge's silence means the judge believes a witness's answer to a question.[18] These studies show that television and film portrayals of attorneys affect real perceptions of the legal profession.

Depictions of attorneys in US films and television have been extreme in many cases – lawyer as hero, lawyer as villain (or at least highly unethical), and sometimes lawyer as fool. Back in the 1950s and 1960s, in the days of Atticus Finch from the novel *To Kill a Mockingbird*, and television's premier criminal defense lawyer *Perry Mason*, lawyers were portrayed predominantly as heroes. Since that time, the scale seems to be tilting toward negative views of lawyers, such as those portrayed as more

---

[13] MICHAEL ASIMOW AND SHANNON MADER, LAW AND POPULAR CULTURE: A COURSE BOOK 54 (PETER LANG 2004).

[14] Michael Pfau et al., *Television Viewing and Public Perceptions of Attorneys*, 21 HUMAN COMMUNICATION RESEARCH 307–30 (1995).

[15] Kimberlaine Podlas, *Please Adjust Your Signal: How Television's Syndicated Courtrooms Bias Our Juror Citizenry*, 39 AM. BUS. L. J. 1, 1–24 (2001).

[16] Michael Pfau et al., *Television Viewing and Public Perceptions of Attorneys*, 21 HUMAN COMMUNICATION RESEARCH 307–30 (1995).

[17] MICHAEL ASIMOW AND SHANNON MADER, LAW AND POPULAR CULTURE: A COURSE BOOK 101 (PETER LANG 2004).

[18] Kimberlaine Podlas, *Please Adjust Your Signal: How Television's Syndicated Courtrooms Bias Our Juror Citizenry*, 39 AM. BUS. L. J. 1, 1–24 (2001).

interested in their sex lives than their cases (think Jack McCoy, from *L.A. Law*), those that are broken, crooked, and scheming (think alcoholic ambulance chaser Frank Galvin in the 1982 movie *The Verdict*; Annalise Keating in current television show *How to Get Away with Murder*; or Saul Goodman in the 2008–2013 hit *Breaking Bad*), to those that are just plain losers (think the unnamed attorney in the 2005 to present television show *It's Always Sunny in Philadelphia*). Perhaps you can recount some of the attorney images you have encountered in your favorite movies and television shows.

What do all of these media and real-life images of lawyers say about our role as lawyers in society? What do the jokes say about our profession? It is curious that lawyers are such a popular source of negative entertainment, but it is not a coincidence. The media mocks lawyers because of what lawyers do. Again, art imitates life and not vice versa. The question is how we can change those real-life behaviors so they no longer reflect lawyer reality.

LAW PAUSE

Write a journal entry describing what you personally can do to counter the negative images of lawyers in society through your own life and service.

REVERSING NEGATIVE IMAGES THROUGH RIGHT ACTION AND SERVICE

Recall the lawyer jokes and the resulting National Love Your Lawyer Day – as it turns out, the lawyer who created this special day got the idea after hearing a nasty lawyer joke. Author Malcolm Kushner, an attorney who is also now a humor consultant and the author of *Comebacks for Lawyer Jokes*, suggests we can change law jokes and some of the public perceptions flowing from them by telling jokes that portray lawyers not as rich, greedy, or arrogant, but as they are at their most positive.[19]

Here are few of Kushner's examples and their intended messages. To show that lawyers can be beloved, heroic figures:

1. How many lawyers does it take to change a light bulb?
None, if the lawyers are Abraham Lincoln, Mahatma Gandhi, or Nelson Mandela. Then the light comes from within.

To show that lawyers serve the public good:

2. How many public interest lawyers does it take to change a light bulb?

---

[19] Malcolm Kushner, *Lawyer Jokes: The Image of Lawyers Is No Joke, But Maybe It Should Be: In a world of sound bites where people get their news from late-night comedy shows, telling positive lawyer jokes may be more effective than you'd think*, Feb. 8, 2016, available at www.Callawyer.Com/2016/02/Lawyer-Jokes-The-Image-Of-Lawyers-Is-No-Joke-But-Maybe-It-Should-Be/.

Two. One to change the bulb and one to shine it on corruption.

3. What do pro bono lawyers charge that poor people have and rich people need?
Nothing.

To show that many lawyers are not rich and choose a career of self-sacrifice:

4. What's the difference between a legal aid lawyer and a picnic table?
A picnic table can support a family of four.

5. What's the difference between a well-paid legal aid lawyer and the Invisible Man?
You've got more chance of seeing the Invisible Man.

6. What are McDonald's employees now asking public interest lawyers?
Can you afford fries with that?

Kushner believes that by telling the alternate story even in humor, we can, over time, contribute to a change in public perceptions of lawyers.[20]

Throughout your career, you will also have many years to inform the public through your actions. After all, there is a reason why negative lawyer jokes and media depictions resonate with the public. Many people have had bad experiences with lawyers in the past. We can improve lawyer images through our deeds and service.

PICTURING THE LAWYER YOU WILL BE

LAW PAUSE

Write a list of traits you hope to exhibit as a lawyer. Print out the list and tape it to your computer.

Now visualize yourself going to work, in the clothes and the car, and picture as vividly as you possibly can what you actually do at your job, what tasks you undertake, what is annoying, what you love, what gets you out of bed in the morning. Write it all down.

Now think back to your peak experiences from Chapter 1. What has made you really happy in the past? What makes you immerse yourself in your work or projects to such a degree that you lose total track of time? At what times in your life have you felt most alive, most needed, most fulfilled?

Write a two or three paragraph essay answering some of these questions. Include a synthesis of your picture of yourself through your peak experiences.

In the coming chapters, we will explore how to begin making your new vision of yourself as a professional a reality. First, we will explore what skills lawyers need. Then we will explore how your own professional identity will develop.

---

[20]   *Ibid.*

5

Lawyer Skill Sets: What We Have, What We Need

Nathalie Martin

In the last chapter we discussed some of the negative traits attributed to lawyers in society, including dishonesty, greed, and narcissism. Through these images we know what people *dislike* in attorneys, but what attributes and skills are actually *valued* in lawyers? What are clients and legal employers looking for in their young attorneys?

This chapter describes these most desirable lawyer skills using empirical research on the subject of which skills are most valued by clients and legal employers. For context, this chapter first describes a few typical law jobs. It then briefly describes the history of legal education, which helps explain why the skills we learn in law school are not necessarily the ones most valued by clients and legal employers. The bottom line is that trustworthy, empathetic people are more successful, so collegiality and good communication skills are paramount.

ONE LEGAL TRAINING, MANY DIFFERENT KINDS OF LAWYERS

When my friend Ocean wakes up in the morning, he gets his kids ready for school, then puts on a suit and goes to his job working as in-house counsel for a bank. His job is to negotiate contracts with all different types of vendors, from the photocopy vendor to multimillion-dollar financial institutions that hold billions of dollars' worth of collateral. Every week he gets to use the knowledge we discussed in our 1L Contracts class. He also helps steer the bank through a complex federal and state regulatory landscape that is constantly shifting. To do a good job, he has to remember that good lawyers don't panic – staying calm and grounded is a helpful attribute. It is rewarding and not too terribly stressful.

When my friend Jenny gets up, she throws on jeans and sweater, gets her son off to school, and then sets off to direct the non-profit she formed. Her job

FIGURE 5.1 Collegial Lawyers, created by illustrator, Pamela "Zen" Miller.

involves raising money, hiring and training attorneys and paralegals, and educating the public about the plight of undocumented people living in the US. Jenny knows she is doing important work and feels great about her contributions to society.

When my friend Julie gets up, she puts on casual clothes if she is spending the day in her office, or a great suit if she is going to trial. Either way, she braves LA traffic to drive to her job at the Los Angeles County District Attorney's Office, where she prosecutes child prostitute pimps. She described with glee a recent case in which the leader of a child prostitute ring took the stand in his own case and told the jury how nice he was to his under-aged prostitutes, buying them gifts etc. She said it was "delicious" to watch the way he incriminated himself.

These descriptions barely scratch the surface of the wide variety of law jobs out there. These jobs are as different from one another as the people who perform them, and each job requires its own skill set. Some skills are necessary for all law jobs, however, and all lawyers can improve in these areas.

LAW PAUSE

Think about the best lawyers you know or have seen in the media or read about in books. What makes them successful? Make a list of the top ten skills you think every lawyer needs.

A BRIEF HISTORY OF LEGAL EDUCATION

By now, you might be curious about how legal education developed the way that it has. Why, for example, do professors use the case book method where you read appellate cases nonstop, the silly hypotheticals where the answer always changes even though the legal rules do not, and that off-putting and demeaning "Socratic" method in which people are called on in class without their permission? Why are whole classes organized around legal opinions that often make no sense, are incomplete, and are frequently written in language that the average person cannot understand? You might wonder why we don't simply teach you the legal rules and move on. You might also wonder why we never ask how the people in the cases feel or what it must be like to wait three, five, or seven years for one's case to go to trial.

There are good answers to these questions. Legal education experienced a major paradigm shift in the 1870s when Harvard Law School's Dean, Christopher Columbus Langdell, moved legal education from a law school as "trade school" model, to a more analytical and academic model. Before Langdell completely disrupted legal education with these controversial innovations, lawyers were trained by practicing lawyers in the technicalities of legal practice. Langdell took the training of future legal professionals out of the hands of the practicing bar and bench, at least at Harvard, by hiring academics – not practitioners – to teach law. In so doing, he transformed teaching methods in law school from traditional lectures to a teaching method using real cases and hypothetical problem-solving techniques. This innovation was thought to increase academic rigor and improve the thinking and analytical skills of lawyers.

It is not completely clear if this shift was beneficial to society. In many ways, this system takes thinking and feeling individuals and turns them into people who, rather than thinking and feeling like a human being who serves other human beings, are taught instead to think "like lawyers." Karl Llewellyn, a legal realist and father of American commercial law, describes the results of Langdell's new model, back in 1930, as follows:

> The first year . . . aims to drill into you the more essential techniques of handling cases. It lays the foundation simultaneously for law school and law practice. It aims, in the old phrase, to get you . . . "thinking like a lawyer." The hardest job of the first year is to lop off your common sense, to knock your ethics into temporary

anesthesia. Your view of social policy, your sense of justice – to knock these out of you along with woozy thinking, along with ideas all fuzzed along their edges. You are to acquire the ability to think precisely, to analyze coldly, to work within a body of materials that is given, to see, to see only and manipulate the machinery of the law.[1]

This process is what the Carnegie Foundation for the Advancement of Teaching's 2007 report entitled *Educating Lawyers: Preparation for the Profession of Law* (hereinafter the Carnegie Report) calls a temporary moral lobotomy,[2] but I am not sure how temporary it actually is. After watching students move through the law school system for two decades, too many students seem more like real human beings on day one than on graduation day. Other scholars and legal educators agree that the effects of law school teaching methods could be lasting and damaging, as Professor Llewelyn goes on:

> It is not easy thus to turn human beings into lawyers. Neither is it safe. For a mere legal machine is a social danger. Indeed, a mere legal machine is not even a good lawyer. It lacks insight and judgment. It lacks the power to draw into hunching that body of intangibles that lie in social experience.[3]

Almost ninety years after Llewelyn's statements, in an article entitled *The Zombie Lawyer Apocalypse*, legal scholars Peter Huang and Corie Rosen liken law school training to a zombie apocalypse:

> [M]onsters recently released into our midst, are roaming the fair streets of our city. They appear each morning and again at each day's end, carrying briefcases and book bags, riding bicycles, walking, or, most ominously, taking the local trains. It is up to us to discover their origins and the best means for dispatching them.
> This Zombie Apocalypse, as those who read the papers already know, has now reached dangerous proportions. Some have referred to its creeping nature as "insidious" or "spooky." No matter what they call it, all who speak of it do so with a note of terror. In the kind of twist so typical of horror tales, the apocalypse has targeted only a single segment of the population. Researchers are hard at work trying to discover how and why this apocalypse has zombified only those among us possessed of a special set of skills and educational experiences. Yes, Dear Reader. You already know which members of our society we speak of, and the knowledge may send a ripple of fear shivering down your spine. The Zombie Lawyer Apocalypse has targeted those who most want to engage our business, political, and public sectors. We are talking, of course, about law students and lawyers.[4]

---

[1] Karl N. Llewellyn, The Bramble Bush 116 (Oxford University Press 1930).
[2] William Sullivan et al., Educating lawyers: Preparation for the Profession of Law 78 (Jossey-Bass 2007).
[3] Karl L. Llewellyn, The Bramble Bush 116–17 (Oxford University Press 1930).
[4] Peter Huang and Corie Rosen, *The Zombie Lawyer Apocalypse*, 42 Pepperdine Law Review 727, 728 (2015).

In this article, Huang and Rosen draw parallels between the zombie state of being –
that of being mindless, thoughtless, and devoid of hope – and the state of
legal culture and legal education today. They note that while not all law students
have 'turned,' a fair number have, as evidenced by a life of dispirited, disengaged,
mindless, herd mentality, and a life without meaning. They review the causes
of lawyer zombification, which include a demoralizing mode of education, a de-
emphasis on fairness and justice, and a disconnect between how the subject matter
of law is taught and most student's core values. They also propose some solutions to
the ongoing problem, including the following:

> As an institution, we are in a position to produce, not zombies, but fully realized
> human beings who care about accomplishment and relationships, about meaning
> and not only money, and about themselves, their peers, and the broader world
> around them.
>
> If we are to stem the tide of law student and lawyer depression and emerge as
> victors in the battle of the Zombie Lawyer Apocalypse, we must . . . begin to change
> the way we engage with one another and with our institutions. We must move away
> from a culture of dehumanizing competition and away from the notion that the
> legal discipline is a purely instrumental one, devoid of human emotion, engage-
> ment, and ideas.
>
> Instead, we must embrace the tenets of mindfulness, ethical decisionmaking, and
> positive psychology in order to build a profession and professional education system
> that encourages individuals and organizations to flourish . . . When individuals
> flourish, health, productivity, and peace follow. If we can shift the culture of the
> legal profession and the legal academy and begin to work toward flourishing, then
> we can end the Zombie Lawyer Apocalypse and breathe life back into those who
> have been harmed by the profession.[5]

What Huang and Rosen are suggesting is part of one of the biggest revolutions in
legal education, one that changes the profession from the inside out, to one
that values interpersonal skills at the same or a higher level than other attorney
attributes.

A REVOLUTION IN LEGAL EDUCATION

But recognizing what the Carnegie Report refers to as the importance of
"the intangibles that lie in social experience" took time. Eighty years after
Llewelyn's observations, the Carnegie Report chronicled the limitations of the
current legal education system. At around the same time, the Holloran Center for
Ethical Leadership in the Professions was formed in order to help law schools begin
training students in these interpersonal skills. Up to this point, there were "few
published studies of what clients want and few published studies of what legal

---

[5] *Ibid.* at 770–71.

employers want. Both lawyers and law professors have historically believed that they are 'experts' who know what both clients and students need and want."[6]

In the years that followed, several impressive empirical studies have proven Llewelyn's point that the standard law school curriculum dehumanizes the practice of law. We review a few of these studies and historical moments in this new movement in legal education here, before returning to the question of how we can improve legal education, and how you can prepare yourself to be the best lawyer you can be.

The Formation of the Holloran Center in 2006

The formation of the Holloran Center at St. Thomas School of Law in St. Paul, Minnesota, has changed the focus of legal education at many law schools around the country. The Holloran Center was formed in 2006 to research the changing roles of lawyers and lawyer training in society. Its specific mission was to help the next generation of lawyers form professional identities with a moral core of responsibility and service to others, and to provide innovative interdisciplinary research, curriculum development, and programs focusing holistically on helping students become ethical leaders in their communities.

The Holloran Center has published numerous studies on what legal employers want from young lawyers, some of which are discussed below, but here we simply note the historical shift in thinking that began when the Holloran Center was formed. The Holloran Center has also hosted a series of very successful conferences and workshops to spread the word about this new legal movement to dozens of law schools around the country.

The Holloran Center's activities have helped let the cat out of the bag. Lawyers need to focus more on service to clients and to society, in all fields of law. Moreover, lawyers need to be trained in the human side of law.

Schultz and Zedeck Shake Up Legal Education in 2011

In 2011, legal innovators Marjorie Shultz and Sheldon Zedeck further shook up legal education when they published the results of a multiyear empirical study in which they interviewed lawyers around the nation about what makes a good lawyer.[7] To predict who would be an effective lawyer, Shultz and Zedeck conducted hundreds of individual and group interviews with lawyers, law faculty, law students,

---

[6] Neil Hamilton, *Professional-Identity/Professional-Formation/Professionalism Learning Outcomes: What Can We Learn About Assessment from Medical Education?*, 13 ST. THOMAS L. REV., App. C, p. 2 (2017, forthcoming, draft on file with author).

[7] Marjorie M. Shultz and Sheldon Zedeck, *Predicting Lawyer Effectiveness: Broadening the Basis for Law School Admission Decisions*, 36 LAW & SOC. INQUIRY 620, 621–30 (2011).

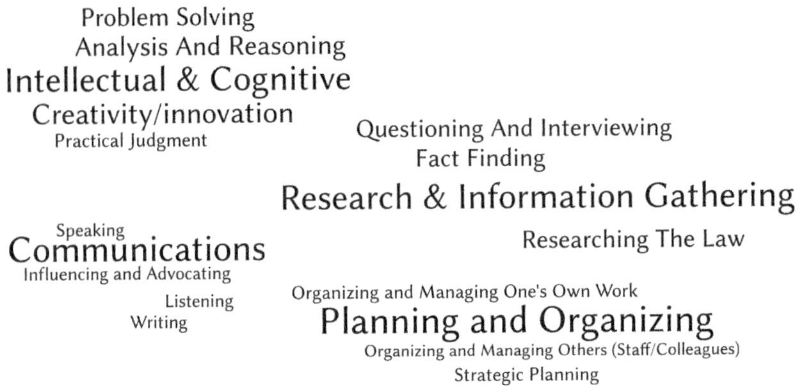

Problem Solving
Analysis And Reasoning
Intellectual & Cognitive
Creativity/innovation
Practical Judgment
Questioning And Interviewing
Fact Finding
Research & Information Gathering
Speaking
Communications
Influencing and Advocating
Researching The Law
Listening
Writing
Organizing and Managing One's Own Work
Planning and Organizing
Organizing and Managing Others (Staff/Colleagues)
Strategic Planning

FIGURE 5.2 Shultz and Zedeck Traits of a Good Lawyer Part 1, created by author, Nathalie Martin.

Able to See the World Through the Eyes of Others
Conflict Resolution
Negotiation Skills
Integrity/Honesty
Passion and Engagement
Self-Development
Character
Stress Management
Diligence
Community Involvement and Service
Developing Relationships within the Legal Profession
Working with Others
Evaluation, Development, and Mentoring
Client & Business Relations - Entrepreneurship
Networking and Business Development
Providing Advice & Counsel & Building Relationships with Clients

FIGURE 5.3 Shultz and Zedeck Traits of a Good Lawyer Part 2, created by author, Nathalie Martin.

judges, and some clients,[8] asking questions such as, "If you were looking for a lawyer for an important matter for yourself, what qualities would you most look for? What kind of lawyer do you want to teach or be?" They gradually selected, added to, subtracted from, defined and redefined identified factors, seeking rough consensus through successive discussions with lawyers in many fields, settings, and career stages. They then distilled the interview results into a list of twenty-six "Effectiveness Factors." These are the qualities or traits they found most important to good lawyering in the eyes of the constituencies they interviewed. Though not in any particular order, the twenty-six factors are pictured in Figures 5.2 and 5.3.

The Shultz and Zedeck study confirmed that an effective lawyer is no doubt smart, but also that relationship skills, including interviewing, listening, persuasive

[8] Most of the interviews were done not with real clients but with attorneys and others playing the role of clients.

communication and conflict resolution, empathy, and compassion, are equally important. Study these two figures closely. You will be using the twenty-six Shultz and Zedek factors again in Chapter 6.

Particular Holloran Center Studies

Neil Hamilton and Jerry Organ of the Holloran Center have done extensive research into exactly what clients want and need. Through a recent study of large Minnesota firms, they created a hierarchy of values, virtues, capacities, and skills most valued by employers.[9] These traits, which dovetail with competencies emphasized in other studies, including a 2013 National Conference of Bar Examiner's New Lawyer Survey, show that preparing for a successful legal career requires both a high level of knowledge and skill in legal analysis and the ability to sustain relationships with colleagues but also to develop fiduciary relationships centered on understanding and serving the needs of clients.[10]

In other words, effective career development requires the cultivation of values and dispositions fully integrated with the mastery of technical skills and professional relationship competencies.[11] After years of research, Hamilton and Organ summarize these traits in order of importance, as follows:

- trustworthiness/integrity/honesty
- strong work and team relationship skills
- dedication to client/responsiveness to client
- good judgment/common sense
- habit of seeking feedback
- initiative/strong work ethic.

Technical legal skills such as researching and writing were found to be very important, of course, but the most critical skills were not the technical skills focused on in law school. Indeed, in subsequent studies, the Holloran Center confirmed that the number one cluster of traits lawyers identified as important for new lawyers hired in the office was integrity/honesty/trustworthiness.[12] Yet you won't find much training in integrity, honesty, or trustworthiness in the law school curriculum.

---

[9] Neil W. Hamilton, *Changing Markets Create Opportunities: Emphasizing the Competencies Legal Employers Use In Hiring New Lawyers (Including Professional Formation/Professionalism)*, 65 SOUTH CAROLINA L. REV. 571, 593 (2014).

[10] *Ibid.; see also* William M. Sullivan, *Professional Formation as Social Movement*, 23 ABA CENTER FOR PROFESSIONAL RESPONSIBILITY. THE PROFESSIONAL LAWYER 1, 1 (2017).

[11] Neil Hamilton, *The Qualities of the Professional Lawyer*, in PAUL HASKINS, ESSENTIAL QUALITIES OF THE PROFESSIONAL LAWYER (AMERICAN BAR ASSOCIATION 2013).

[12] Neil W. Hamilton, *Changing Markets Create Opportunities: Emphasizing the Competencies Legal Employers Use In Hiring New Lawyers (Including Professional Formation/Professionalism)*, 65 SOUTH CAROLINA L. REV. 571, 582 (2014).

The Foundations for Practice *Whole Lawyer Study*

While there have been others, we will share the results of one more study. In 2014, the Institute for Advancement of the American Legal System (the "Institute") launched a national multiyear project called the *Foundations for Practice* survey, designed to: identify the foundational skills entry-level lawyers need to launch successful careers; develop measurable models of legal education that support the development of these skills; and align market needs with hiring practices that incentivize positive improvements in legal education.[13]

Over 24,000 lawyers from all fifty states took the *Foundations* survey. The resulting study concluded that 76 percent of the characteristics lawyers needed most related to character, rather than technical legal skills.[14] These characteristics included traits such as integrity, work ethic, common sense, and resilience. The survey also split up the skills needed into two categories: those that could be developed over time in the practice of law, and those that young attorneys should have when they walk in the door. The study concluded that lawyers need many of the skills and characteristics right out of law school, in other words from day one of practice.

The survey discovered through its extensive dataset exactly what makes people – not just lawyers – successful. These traits include some expected traits such as a high IQ, as well as some less expected ones, such as emotional intelligence (EQ), as well as what the study authors call character quotient (CQ).

Perhaps not surprisingly, the *Foundations* study found that successful entry-level lawyers are not merely legal technicians or cognitive powerhouses. It noted that there is a dichotomous debate going in legal education, that pits "law school as trade school" against "law school as intellectual endeavor." The whole debate, however, misses the sweet spot and vision that recognizes the need for law school graduates to possess a broader blend of legal skills, professional competencies, and character competencies, which together comprise what the *Foundations* survey calls the *whole lawyer*.

To be a whole lawyer, the study found that lawyers require traits such as "character, industry, intellectual thoroughness, efficiency, honesty, loyalty, and judgment."[15] The study further found that being a "whole lawyer" requires a "beginner's mind" or "an attitude of openness, eagerness, and lack of preconceptions when studying a subject," and that "the universal overriding trait among exceptional lawyers is a dedication to systematic, continuous [self] improvement."[16]

Implicit in the *Foundations* report is what is likely obvious to you by now. Most law schools are only beginning to teach these critical professional skills, which

---

[13] Alli Gerkman and Logan Cornett, *Foundations for Practice: The Whole Lawyer and the Character Quotient, Institute for the Advancement of the American Legal System* (2016), available at http://iaals .du.edu/blog/foundations-practice-future-law-students-law-schools-and-profession.
[14] *Ibid.* at 1.   [15] *Ibid.* at 3 (quoting Paul D. Cravath, of Cravath, Swain & Moore).
[16] *Ibid.* (quoting small firm attorney Keith Lee).

include the ability to cultivate social and professional networks, manage stress, and get along well with others, all discussed elsewhere in this book. One of the study's most fascinating findings is that clients and lawyers recognize that developing legal skills in a particular field requires experience and can be developed over time, but that many of the character traits are needed from day one. More specifically, over 90 percent of participants expected starting attorneys to walk in the door with good listening skills and the ability and propensity to treat others with courtesy and respect.

While the *Foundations* study showed that one could develop the ability to read subtle interpersonal cues over time, skills such as tolerance, compassion, and sensitivity, as well as tact and diplomacy, had to be mastered pre-arrival, as did a strong work ethic, and an ability to take ownership (responsibly) for one's actions. On the other hand, development of many of the traditional skills that we fixate on in legal education, such as fact gathering, critically evaluating arguments, and substantive knowledge of the law, can develop over time while working as a lawyer.

More specifically, according to the *Foundations* study, the top foundational skills that new lawyers need at the beginning of their first law job, in this order, were the ability to:

- keep a confidence
- arrive on time
- honor commitments
- demonstrate integrity and trustworthiness
- treat others with respect
- listen attentively and respectfully
- promptly respond to requests
- be diligent
- work hard, and
- demonstrate attention to detail.

Note the absence of legal research and writing on this top ten list. Of course, you need to be able to research and write, but everyone who graduates will be able to research and write. The question becomes, how well will you achieve on these more subtle skills, which will separate the exceptional lawyers from the ones who are merely good technicians?

When comparing and combining the results of the Shultz-Zedeck study, The *Foundations for Practice Whole Lawyer Study*, and the various Holloran Center Studies, we see a convergence on the deep need for the following ethical-professional-identity competencies:

- trustworthiness
- respect for others and relationship skills including client relationship skills and teamwork

- strong work ethic/initiative/conscientiousness
- commitment to self-development including the habit of self-evaluation, and
- good judgment.[17]

THE MISSING LEGAL TRAINING

Despite the results of these studies, we have not traditionally taught empathy, compassion, listening, and so on, in law school. You may be thinking that most law students and lawyers already possess these people skills by the time they arrive in law school. Unfortunately this is not generally the case.

In one particular study of lawyers, Dr. Larry Richard and his colleagues at LawyerBrain interviewed over 1,000 law firm lawyers using the Caliper Profile, a personality test that has been in use for over thirty-five years. Through it, Richard and his collaborators found that lawyers exhibit the following traits, when compared to the general population:

- *High skepticism*: distrust; focus on motives instead of content, judgmental and cynical.
- *High abstract thinking*: preference for planning over action/paralysis by analysis.
- *High autonomy*: resistance to organizational rules and goals.
- *High urgency*: rushing for no reason; premature judgment; poor listening skills.
- *Low resilience*: defensiveness/resistance to feedback.
- *Low sociability*: a preference for minimal social interaction.[18]

Later, Richard and other colleagues used the Hogan Personality Inventory List of Success Traits to compile personality data on 1,800 large firm attorneys.[19] The study asked lawyers to rate one another. The researchers found that the lawyers, when compared to other high level professionals, lacked persistence, were distrustful of others, were detached, poor communicators, and had difficulty maintaining

---

[17]   Neil W. Hamilton, *Professional-Identity/Professional-Formation/Professionalism Learning Outcomes: What Can We Learn About Assessment from Medical Education?*, 13 St. Thomas L. Rev., App. C, p. 3 (2017, forthcoming, draft on file with author).

[18]   Dr. Larry Richard, *Herding Cats: The Lawyers Personality Revealed*, Managing Partner Forum, Advancing the Business of Law, available at www.managingpartnerforum.org/tasks/sites/mpf/ assets/image/MPF%20-%20WEBSITE%20-%20ARTICLE%20-%20Herding%20Cats%20-% 20Richards1.pdf. Richard also found that "there's a strong correlation between performance and motivation. People who are working in roles that are consistent with their personality, values and interpersonal characteristics generally outperform those who are less well matched—by a ratio of two-to-one." *Ibid.* at 3.

[19]   Jeff Foster, Larry Richard, Lisa Rohrer, and Mark Sirkin, *Understanding Lawyers: The Personality Traits of Successful Practitioners*, 2010, available at www.thresholdadvisors.com/wp-content/uploads/ 2011/04/Understanding-Lawyers-White-Paper-Oct-2010-revised.pdf.

relationships.[20] These same lawyers were found to lack focus and, while creative, as a group they lacked good judgment and were below average at supporting subordinates and coworkers. The study further found that the lawyers were generally low on altruism, unnecessarily direct in dealing with others, and often approached work with more of a sense of urgency than was necessary.[21] The study also found the lawyers to possess *below average* scores on these positive personality traits:

- *Adjustment*: steady in the face of pressure.
- *Ambition*: leader-like, status seeking, and achievement-oriented (this one surprises me).
- *Interpersonal sensitivity*: socially sensitive, tactful and perceptive.

It found that lawyers possessed *higher than average* scores on these potential problem areas:

- *Excitable*: initially enthusiastic but lack persistence; become tense and overly critical.
- *Cautious*: overly worried, resistant to change and risk averse; reluctant to take risks and make decisions.
- *Leisurely*: stubborn, procrastinating, and uncooperative; lax attention to rules.[22]

As Kiser, Richard, and Guthrie have all observed, lawyers often approach the world in an abstract, analytical way, which can make them "unskilled at dealing with emotional and interpersonal content."[23] Moreover, most studies show that lawyers are not particularly good listeners and that many have trouble recognizing verbal and non-verbal cues.[24] Worse yet, as Guthrie and other have noted, lawyers are frequently unaware of their deficiencies, meaning they also lack self-awareness.[25]

Stop and reflect on this for a moment. If lawyers often lack self-awareness, they may be less equipped than the general population to see their shortfalls. Add to this high degrees of skepticism and autonomy, and many lawyers may have little desire for self-awareness in any case.

> All lawyers need diligence, motivation, the ability to be self-reflective and take responsibility for one's actions, and the ability to communicate well and with respect.

---

[20] *Ibid.* at 3.   [21] *Ibid.* at 6.   [22] *Ibid.*
[23] Chris Guthrie, *The Lawyer's Philosophical Map: The Lawyer's Philosophical Map Impediments to Facilitative Mediation and Lawyering*, 6 Harvard Negotiation Law Review 145, 158 (2001).
[24] *Ibid.* at 164.
[25] *Ibid.* at n. 52, citing Beryl Blaustone, *To Be of Service: The Lawyer's Aware Use of the Human Skills Associated with the Perceptive Self*, 15 J. Legal Prof. 241, 243 (1990) ("few lawyers are intrapersonally developed; that is, few are self-aware of their own behavioral preferences, modes of communication, values, and sense of self").

IF A JOB CAN BE PERFORMED WITHOUT GOOD PEOPLE SKILLS, IT CAN BE DONE BY A MACHINE

Recall Karl Llewelyn's quote about the danger of the "legal machine." He meant that legal skills, without the good social skills, could be used for ill or nefarious means. I have another concern about legal "machines," namely that someday soon we will all be replaced by machines. Author, lawyer, and legal consultant Randy Kiser, who has written extensively on the role of emotional intelligence in lawyering, claims that "the quick test for determining whether a job will be automated within 5–10 years is whether it can be performed without [these critical professional] skills. If soft skills are not required, the job will be automated within 5–10 years."[26] I have no doubt that this is true.

Not long ago, consumer reports ran a story about the beauties of financial robo-advisors, such as Wealthfront, which use computer algorithms to choose diversified, low-cost, investment portfolios. The article claimed that these robo-advisors were found in most cases to be as effective as human advisors. As a result, robo-advisors are on the rise. Is there any reason to believe that law cannot be similarly robotized, or at the very least, outsourced overseas?

According to Thomas Morgan, author of *The Vanishing American Lawyer*, law jobs that can be automated are disappearing quickly.[27] Many new corporations that are incorporated today are incorporated not by lawyers but through internet services such as Legal Zoom. Additionally, a huge amount of litigation discovery and document review, which used to be done by attorneys, is now done by computers. One reason firms need to care a great deal about whether young lawyers possess good critical professional skills such as listening, empathy, and trustworthiness, is because in the past, lawyers who lacked these skills could be funneled to jobs reviewing documents and doing other discovery, in other words to non-people lawyering skills. Firms no longer need people to do these jobs. As a result, they need to ensure that the lawyers they do hire are skilled and adept at the critical professional skills.

One thing a computer will never be able to do is sit with a client's pain or really listen. Being able to do these things not only makes you an excellent attorney, but also provides job security. Much more critically, through the use of these interpersonal skills, you can know you did your best to serve your clients, and leave the world a better place than you found it.

CONCLUSIONS ABOUT LAWYER SKILL SETS

While the law schools of the past have largely ignored the non-technical, inter-personal skills lawyers need, today's legal market no longer permits this. There are too many pressures on the profession to ignore these aspects of lawyer preparation.

---

[26]   Randall Kiser, *From Strivers to Thrivers: Accelerating Professional Development with Soft Skills*, Presentation at University of Colorado Law School, Conference on "Mindfulness and Thriving Legal Practices," August 8, 2016, Boulder, Colorado.

[27]   THOMAS MORGAN, THE VANISHING AMERICAN LAWYER 91–98 (OXFORD UNIVERSITY PRESS 2010).

FIGURE 5.4 Word Cloud of What Clients Expect from Lawyers, created by author, Nathalie Martin.

In case you think skills such as trustworthiness, self-reflection, and an internalized moral code cannot be learned, the evidence suggests otherwise. As stated by Professor Neil Hamilton, "Each of us can grow toward being a virtuoso by practicing our art, seeking excellent mentoring and coaching, and reflecting on both our setbacks and the input our mentors and coaches give us. Try to use your three years of law school to start building your foundation of the attributes of a professional lawyer."[28]

The most effective strategy to foster self-development in professional formation is to actively seek feedback, reflect on it, and act on it, as discussed in Chapter 12. Affirmatively seek out excellent law professors, lawyers, and judges to act as coaches and mentors and give you honest and constructive feedback. You want coaches and mentors who will ask the right stage-appropriate questions, and challenge your current assumptions, beliefs, and performance.[29] As suggested by Hamilton and Organ, by identifying these coaches, you can create your own "personal board of directors" for this purpose.[30]

When all the words in these studies are placed in word cloud software, which pictures more common words in bigger font, the repetition of certain concepts becomes apparent. Figure 5.4 shows what clients of today expect from their attorneys.

---

[28] Neil Hamilton, *The Qualities of the Professional Lawyer*, in PAUL HASKINS, ESSENTIAL QUALITIES OF THE PROFESSIONAL LAWYER (AMERICAN BAR ASSOCIATION 2013).
[29] *Ibid.*   [30] *Ibid.*

In conclusion, strong interpersonal skills differentiate the good law school job candidate from the great law school job candidate. While base analytical competencies are always required in any job, the intangible qualities are what make a person stand out. The rest of this book is designed to help you deliver those skills.

6

Building Your Professional Identity

Kendall Kerew

Working hard for something we don't care about is called stress; working hard for something we love is called passion.

Simon Sinek

As you already know, law school can be an overwhelming experience. It challenges not only the way you think, but also the very essence of who you are and what you stand for. It takes the typical law student at least one semester, if not the whole first year, to adjust to the daily pressure of law school. Given that, you might be wondering why you need to focus on building your "professional identity," especially now when you are busy being a law student. The reality is that many law schools do not place an emphasis on building a professional identity, leaving law students to figure out who they want to be as a professional only after they graduate and enter law practice. The result: unfulfilled, unhappy, and, in some instances, unethical lawyers.

INTRODUCTION TO PROFESSIONAL IDENTITY FORMATION

The Third Apprenticeship

The Carnegie Report (referenced in Chapter 5) is one of a series of comparative studies examining how different professions educate students and prepare them to enter the profession. The report identified three apprenticeships necessary to legal education: the cognitive apprenticeship, the apprenticeship of practice, and the apprenticeship of identity and purpose. The concept of professional identity formation is rooted in this third apprenticeship, which is often overlooked in legal education.

The Carnegie Report suggested that:

[t]he apprenticeship of professional identity should encompass issues of both individual and social justice, and it includes the virtues of integrity, consideration,

civility, and other aspects of professionalism. The values that lie at the heart of the apprenticeship of professionalism and purpose also include conceptions of the personal meaning that legal work has for practicing attorneys and their sense of responsibility to the profession.[1]

Professor Neil Hamilton defines professional identity formation as involving "a change from thinking like a student (where he or she learns and applies routine techniques to solve well-structured problems) toward acceptance and internalization of responsibility to others (particularly the person served) and for the student's own pro-active development toward excellence as a practitioner at all of the competencies of the profession."[2] In other words, professional identity formation involves three distinct but interdependent components:

1. Self-awareness to identify what matters to you, your strengths and weaknesses, and who you want to be as a member of the legal profession.
2. Consciousness of the service-oriented nature of a profession in which lawyers are responsible to others, including those served, the judicial system and the larger community.
3. Self-motivation to capitalize on strengths while working to develop areas of needed growth, to set learning goals, and to seize learning opportunities for development of necessary lawyering competencies.

SELF-EXPLORATION AND BUILDING A PROFESSIONAL IDENTITY

As stated above, self-awareness and self-motivation[3] are two of the building blocks of professional identity formation.[4] Not surprisingly, "self" is the common theme.

---

[1] SULLIVAN ET AL., EDUCATING LAWYERS: PREPARATION FOR THE PROFESSION OF LAW 132 (JOSSEY-BASS 2007).
[2] This definition, which originally comes from William M. Sullivan, TEACHING MEDICAL PROFESSIONALISM (RICHARD CRUESS ET AL. EDS., CAMBRIDGE UNIVERSITY PRESS 2009), was applied to legal education in Neil W. Hamilton and Sarah Schaefer, *What Legal Education Can Learn from Medical Education about Competency-Based Learning Outcomes Including Those Related to Professional Formation (Professionalism)*, 29 GEO. J. LEGAL ETHICS 399 (2016).
[3] Unlike self-awareness and self-motivation, consciousness of the service-oriented nature of the profession is derived not from focusing inward but, rather, from focusing outward. In other words, a consciousness of the service-oriented nature of the profession often develops after one has had the opportunity to see and experience the realities of law practice through experiential learning (as described later) and other means. Although the main focus of this chapter is the self-exploration required of professional identity formation, developing a consciousness of the service-oriented nature of the profession is no less important.
[4] *See* Larry O. Natt Gantt and Benjamin V. Madison III, *Teaching the Newly Essential Knowledge Skills, and Values in a Changing World*, 256–60, BUILDING ON BEST PRACTICES: TRANSFORMING LEGAL EDUCATION IN A CHANGING WORLD (DEBORAH MARANVILLE, LISA RADTKE BLISS, CAROLYN WILKES KAAS, AND ANTOINETTE SEDILLO LOPEZ, EDS., CAROLINA ACADEMIC PRESS 2015)(identifying the following skills as fostering the core values of the profession: Self-awareness; empathy, ethical sensibility and other relational skills; reflective and decision-making skills; and the skill of self-motivation empowering the lawyer to act on his or her decisions).

What might be surprising, however, is the discomfort you feel with conducting a personal inquiry in the context of law school. After immersing yourself in the objective analysis employed to solve legal problems, engaging in a subjective analysis likely will feel foreign and uncomfortable. After all, "thinking like a lawyer" requires you to apply law to facts to predict an outcome. It does not require you to share your feelings about the facts, the parties to the case, or the inherent fairness of that outcome. As a result, it can be easy to dismiss your role, your ideals, and your feelings as tangential to your legal education. Professional identity formation, on the other hand, will necessitate a willingness to learn about yourself and to contemplate your professional future.

SELF-AWARENESS

At the center of professional identity formation is a concept introduced in Chapter 1 of this book: self-awareness – the ability to understand who you are, what you want for yourself, and who you want to be as a member of the profession. Developing self-awareness by identifying your personal core values, strengths and weaknesses, and career objectives is the first step to building your professional identity.

Core Values

As discussed in Chapter 1, personal core values define what is important to you and what gives you purpose. They are the values that will help guide both your personal and professional behavior and decisions. They should answer the questions: "What do I want in life? What are my must haves? Who is important to me?" They are not the values you think you should have or you want others to think you have. They are the core values that will guide who you want to be as a lawyer and what you view as meaningful professional employment.

Little Pause: Think back to the core values you identified in Chapter 1. Do you think the way you are living (approaching law school, your life, etc.) is currently aligned with those core values? If so, how so? If not, why not?

Professional identity formation requires not only integrity to one's personal core values, but also acceptance and internalization of the core values of the profession. Consider this list of professional core values set forth by Professors Natt Gantt and Benjamin Madison:

- Integrity: By displaying the same core values in their public and private lives.
- Honesty: Identified in ethical standards more than any other value, reaffirming its importance to the profession.
- Diligence: General obligation to be effective for clients. This includes enduring and completing strenuous work with craftsmanship and excellence.

- Fairness: Commitment to fairness, justice, and truth, for clients and the system.
- Courage/honor: The ability to remain consistently ethical under pressure.
- Wisdom/judgment: Ability to care for others and see the world through their eyes, while maintaining sufficient detachment to ensure that his/her reasoning is objective and not influenced by emotion.
- Compassion/service/respect for others: The role of lawyers is to serve both the clients and community.
- Balance: Although identified as a value, this is historically a struggle for lawyers.[5]

Little Pause: Do any of the core values listed above surprise you? How are your core values consistent with or in conflict with the core values of the legal profession? What do you think about the inclusion of "balance" in this list?

The intersection of personal and professional values may be difficult to envision in practice. Consider this observation from a student working as a judicial extern for the state Supreme Court:

> I noticed how attentive and precise [the staff attorney] was in his review of my work product. I relayed to him my observation and asked him how he cancels out the noise – facts and law from other cases – in his head to focus and afford to give quality attention to a new document. He said it was about not being lazy and spending time on it. He also added that the pace and the atmosphere of the Supreme Court allow him to give each case the focus it deserves.
>
> In the end, though, his answer did not point to a specific skill. His answer simply involved having a healthy respect for what he does. Understanding the implications his work has, he commits the necessary time to do it well. It was refreshing to see someone approach work with such a respect, especially in someone who has done it for many years and plausibly could have become too familiar with his work.
>
> Working with [the staff attorneys] overall has shown me the value of enjoying what I do and doing it excellently not because of a boss or a company but because I want to do it well. I feel challenged, because my initial work post-graduation will stretch me in this regard. Nonetheless, my goal and hope is to work excellently, not because of a boss or a company, but because of my values.

Little Pause: What professional core values did the staff attorneys illustrate?

Strengths and Weaknesses

The ability to evaluate your own strengths and weaknesses, not only regarding the technical, analytical skills you are learning in law school, but also the lawyering competencies not expressly taught or considered – empathy, ethical sensibility, and

---

5   *Ibid.*

other relational skills – is critical to building your professional identity. Without engaging in an honest assessment of your skills, you cannot effectively define the steps needed to achieve excellence in the competencies of the profession.

LAW PAUSE

Using the Shultz-Zedeck twenty-six Lawyering Effectiveness Factors identified in Chapter 5, identify the three lawyering competencies you believe are your strongest and the three lawyering competencies you would like to develop. Include the reason(s) for listing each competency. In thinking about your reason(s), consider past experiences in which you received recognition or constructive criticism.

If you are a first-year law student, you might find identifying your strengths and weaknesses difficult. After all, you haven't had much time to learn how to "think like a lawyer." But most of the Shultz-Zedeck's twenty-six Lawyering Effectiveness Factors do not involve cognitive skills but rather, relational skills – such as communication and working with others. As you progress through law school, you will want to revisit this list because, with attention and effort, what you identify as growth competencies now may be competencies you identify as strengths later.

Career Objectives

While it may be difficult to do, identifying a meaningful professional path that is both consistent with your core values and about which you are passionate is crucial. While it might feel premature, defining a career path early and revisiting it often will keep you on the route to becoming a fulfilled lawyer and will help highlight the steps needed to get there.

Ideally, we all want to find work that fulfills us. While it's possible you already know the kind of work you want to do when you graduate, it's more likely that you only have a vague idea of what lawyers do, let alone what you want to do with your law degree. Whatever you decide, you will have many opportunities to rebrand yourself and choose something else later, which is why both short-term and long-term career aspirations are important to consider. The path of least resistance may be to fall in line with what other students around you are doing or what others expect you to do. Focusing on your career now can keep you on the professional path *you* want to follow.

LAW PAUSE

Thinking about your remaining time in law school, describe your short-term career goals (up to three years after graduation). These goals should encompass something in addition to your assumed goals of performing well in class, graduating, and passing the bar exam. Be specific in stating your short-term career goals, explain why you selected them, and identify what skills you might need to achieve them.

Next, thinking about your long-term career goals (between five and ten years after graduation), describe your vision of your career as a lawyer and member of the greater community. Examine your career goals from a variety of perspectives (for example, the type of work environment and community in which you would like to live and work, the type of professional service you would provide, etc.), not just based narrowly on the type of law you think you might like to practice. Be specific in stating your long-term career goals, explain why you selected them, and identify what skills you might need to achieve them.

What may seem initially inconsistent about your values and your career goals may, in fact, help you to more concretely define your professional identity. Let's return to the thoughts of the judicial extern:

> I want privileges. I want to have a great platform which gives me influence in this world. But, I want to be humble. I want my humility to grow, not diminish, with privileges that come my way through lawyering. So as I lawyer, I plan to be a "down-to-earth" attorney whose lifestyle or character does not change because of privileges I experience over time.

Little Pause: Think back to Chapter 4 and the picture you produced of the lawyer *you* want to be. Are your personal core values and short-term and long-term career goals consistent with that picture? If so, how so? If not, why not, and how do you think that will impact your career satisfaction?

SELF-MOTIVATION

Perhaps the hardest part of building your professional identity is the need to be self-motivated – to be proactive toward excellence in all of the competencies of the profession – not only during law school but throughout your professional career. Professor John Lande's advice underscores this point: "Lawyers have always needed to keep learning. Each client brings new facts. The courts and legislatures continue to produce new law. Procedures and techniques evolve. Lawyers' ongoing need to learn is reflected in continuing legal education requirements you may need to comply with. So you need to be a learning machine."[6] Being a "learning machine" involves four separate but connected processes: assessing strengths and weaknesses (as described above), setting SMART learning goals, learning by doing, and learning from self-reflection.

---

[6]   John M. Lande, *My Last Lecture: More Unsolicited Advice for Future and Current Lawyers*, J. OF DISP. RESOL. 6 (2015).

Setting SMART Learning Goals

By determining and articulating SMART learning goals,[7] you create a standard against which you can evaluate your progress toward excellence in the competencies of the profession. A SMART goal is:

- Specific – sets forth a specific area for improvement.
- Measurable – sets forth ways to assess and evaluate your progress toward meeting the goal.
- Achievable – sets forth what you can accomplish, realistically considering resources and potential obstacles.
- Relevant – sets forth why achieving the goal matters to you.
- Time-related – sets forth a realistic timeframe in which you can accomplish the goal.

Following the SMART goal framework can help you to articulate meaningful learning goals. For example, let's assume you want to improve your legal writing. Instead of stating, "I want to improve my legal writing," consider how much more likely you are to accomplish that goal if you state it as a SMART goal. After all, you won't want to list a vague goal statement as a bullet point on your resume. Instead, you will want to demonstrate how you have worked to improve your legal writing (by writing, for example, different types of legal documents or several of the same type of legal document in multiple contexts). Of course, you are also going to have to consider what aspect of your legal writing needs improvement so that the writing you produce appropriately demonstrates improvement. In addition, you will want to keep in mind what is realistic given the nature of the work, the work environment, the amount of legal writing done, and the time you have to complete the work.

Little Pause: Think back to the areas for growth you identified above. How would you articulate ways to achieve this growth in SMART goal terms? What are the metrics you would use to determine whether you have advanced and/or achieved that goal?

Learning by Doing

Experiential courses in which students work in the role of a lawyer – simulations, externships, and clinics – provide some of the best opportunities to build your professional identity while in law school.[8] Why? Because experiential courses

---

[7] George T. Doran, *There's a S.M.A.R.T. Way to Write Management's Goals and Objectives*, 70 MANAGEMENT REV. 35–36 (1981). Although there is some debate about who came up with the concept, Doran has been credited as the first one to have written about it.

[8] *See* Timothy W. Floyd and Kendall L. Kerew, *Marking the Path from Law Student to Lawyer: Using Field Placement Courses to Facilitate the Deliberate Exploration of Professional Identity and Purpose*, 68 MERCER L. REV. 767 (forthcoming 2017). *See generally* David I. C. Thomson, *"Teaching" Formation of Professional Identity*, 27 REGENT L. REV. 303 (2015); Kelly S. Terry, *Externships: A Signature Pedagogy for the Apprenticeship of Professional Identity and Purpose*, 59 J. LEGAL EDUC. 240 (2009);

"integrate doctrine, theory, skills, and legal ethics; engage students in performance of professional skills; develop the concepts underlying the professional skills being taught; provide multiple opportunities for performance; and provide opportunities for self-evaluation."[9] Just as legal practice requires lawyers to integrate knowledge, skills, and values, experiential courses put you into practice situations that teach these critical aspects of lawyering in context.

Experiential courses also provide a realistic look at the service-oriented nature of the profession and illustrate the ways in which lawyers are responsible to others, including those served, the judicial system, and the larger community – a consciousness that, as described above, is essential to professional identity formation. Consider this observation from a student working as an extern in a criminal prosecutor's office:

> I think that as lawyers, we sometimes forget that it's not just the jury and judge who are watching us and listening to the things we say. We forget what it's like to be outside of the legal bubble and how different an environment it is once we're in it … As attorneys and future-attorneys, in our minds, it's easy to separate what happens in the courtroom from the rest of the world into distinct and independent spheres. But for others, it's one and the same. We forget that everyone we deal with doesn't have the ability to separate the courtroom from reality and in fact, for the people involved, now this *is* reality.

You will have a significant role to play in the quality of your experiential experiences. Not only will you want to consider your short-term and long-term career objectives when choosing the experiential course(s) you want to take, but you will also need to set SMART learning goals for yourself at the outset of the experience and ensure that you are taking affirmative steps to achieve those goals. You can do this by seeking work assignments that will help measure your progress toward meeting those goals and engaging your supervisor to ensure that you receive meaningful feedback.

Learning from Self-Reflection

When was the last time you really stopped to think? Hopefully, you have been able to learn and embrace some of the mindfulness and time management techniques discussed in Chapters 2 and 3 of this book. But to the extent you've had trouble doing so, consider the role technology is playing in your life. Go back and look at the *New Yorker* cartoon in Figure 1.4. Is this you? Let's check in and learn how much your cell phone is driving you.

---

and Timothy W. Floyd, *Moral Vision, Moral Courage, and the Formation of the Lawyer's Professional Identity*, 28 Miss. C. L. Rev. 339 (2009).
[9] *Ibid.*

Do you know how much time you actually spend each day on your phone? Do you look at it whenever you have a spare moment – while you are standing in line at the grocery store, waiting on food in a restaurant, riding on an elevator, stopped at a traffic light? If you don't know, you're not alone.

LAW PAUSE

To get a realistic sense of how much time you currently spend on your phone, download an app that tracks the amount of time you spend on your phone such as *Moment, RealizD, Time Tracker*, or *Cell Phone Addiction Timer*.

The 2014 *New York Times* article entitled, *No Time to Think*, puts into stark focus the discomfort we feel when we are left alone, without distraction, to consider our thoughts. Notably, the article reports that,

> in 11 experiments involving more than 700 people, the majority of participants reported that they found it unpleasant to be alone in a room with their thoughts for just 6 to 15 minutes. Moreover, in one experiment, 64 percent of men and 15 percent of women began self-administering electric shocks when left alone to think [rather than remaining in the room]. These same people, by the way, had previously said they would pay money to avoid receiving the painful jolt.[10]

What's more, the "studies suggest that not giving yourself time to reflect impairs your ability to empathize with others."[11]

Assuming you can find some time to be alone with your thoughts, you might wonder what's next. How do you engage in meaningful self-reflection? Consider this structured method to facilitate the process:

1 Ask and answer the question, *"What?"* This inquiry requires you to think about and describe the details of an experience related to your own work, observation of others, etc.

2 Ask and answer the question, *"So What?"* This inquiry requires you to describe why you picked that particular experience to discuss. The inquiry consists of two steps: a personal reaction in which you identify how the experience described made you feel, and a general reaction in which you identify the overall lesson learned about lawyering and any conclusions that can be drawn about the legal profession.

3 Ask and answer the question, *"Now What?"* This inquiry requires you to think about both the individual and lawyering lessons learned and how to apply those lessons to future practice.

---

[10] Kate Murphy, *No Time to Think*, New York Times, July 25, 2014, available at www.nytimes.com/2014/07/27/sunday-review/no-time-to-think.html?_r=0.

[11] *Ibid.*

Perhaps the following reflection, written by one of my externship students, will make the process of self-reflection and its relationship to self-motivation more concrete:

I have had three research projects since I started with my externship. The first one caused a significant amount of anxiety and strife in my emotional world, totally of my own doing. However, I told myself that certainly the more I researched, the less anxious I would become. Then I received my second research assignment. Once again, I tumbled down into my world of angst while perusing Lexis Nexis. The same thing happened with my most recent legal research assignment. Had I researched long enough? Did I shepardize effectively? Was the information as on point as I believed it to be? Was my analysis totally off base? My inner turmoil was enough to cause me to seek counsel in multiple ways.

I sent an email to the attorney that had assigned the research and requested to chat about the project. She eagerly agreed to do so. Leading up to the meeting, the anxiety returned but I told myself that without facing the firing squad of my inadequacies there was no way to the land of improvement. I sat down in her office fully expecting to get a lesson on researching thoroughly and applying the law more accurately. Instead, I received praise for my depth of research, to format, to application, and beyond. Don't get me wrong, praise is always lovely. I graciously thanked her for the feedback but trekked back to my cubicle more confused than I had left.

With time and rumination, I realized that perhaps the issue did not live within my abilities to research the law. Perhaps I needed to address my own self-development in an entirely different realm, the realm of stress management. As a lawyer, I am going to spend a significant amount of time not only researching, but placing myself in situations that are uncomfortable, unfamiliar and rife with the possibility of anxiety. If I was already falling into the rabbit hole of self-doubt on small externship projects, how could I possibly deal with the pressures of holding a client's future within my control? So I set out on a multi-faceted journey. First, I would address my concerns with legal research. As you know, I chatted with you about my doubts and learning when enough is enough. In hearing that my feelings were not strange and uncommon as well as reading the hints you provided regarding legal research, I am more confident than ever that with time, I will build confidence in my process. The real dragon to slay is much deeper within myself. It is in finding what is effective at easing the stress that I not only place on myself but that will be inherent in my chosen profession.

I began to think back on when I last felt fully relaxed. Believe it or not, it was while I have been in law school. It was a gift from the Mindfulness in Law Society called a Retreat. An entire day at the Indian Springs complex that was filled with yoga, meditation, and silence. An entire day of silence is never going to be a workable solution for an attorney under stress, unfortunately. However, I now understand that I must provide myself with quiet time each day within which I can address the little anxious voice in my head long enough to tell it to be quiet and let me meditate. Further, I have to make time for exercising. I know everyone faces this challenge, stressed attorney or not. But I now understand that I am going to have to make it a life or death priority when I am practicing in order to maintain my ability to cope with and ease my stress. The best laid plans of self-development, as Steinbeck would say . . .

To try and ensure that by the time my stressors outnumber my comforts I will be well equipped to cope, I am going to begin to implement my practices now, while still a pupil. I am going to implement the tools that I have been given to address my research concerns and continue to seek advice when new challenges arise in order to identify underlying triggers. I am going to turn off the "relaxing" television and give myself quiet time free from stimulation and sensory assault. I am going to spend at least 30 minutes each day using my body for more than sitting in a chair, even if it is walking circles around the law library in intervals. Most of all, I am going to take care of my own person and continue to identify how best to do so regardless of the discomfort and inconvenience that may be involved along the journey.

You don't need to wait for an unusual or especially remarkable event to practice the skill of reflection. Often, we unconsciously reflect when we think about a mistake we made or when something doesn't go as expected. Consider a car accident, for example.[12] First, we think about what happened. We recreate the details of the accident. What time of day was it? Was there heavy traffic? Was I distracted? Then, our mind shifts to how we feel about the accident – frustrated, lucky, etc. We might then think about the lessons we learned – texting while driving creates distraction and is illegal in most US states, speeding can make it harder to stop short if traffic unexpectedly slows, being tired delays reaction times, etc. Finally, we think about how we will apply the lessons learned the next time we get behind the wheel.

LAW PAUSE

Identify a time you made a mistake or something didn't go as expected in the last week, and work through the process of reflection outlined above.

CONCLUSIONS ABOUT PROFESSIONAL IDENTITY FORMATION

It's never too early to begin assembling the building blocks necessary to forming your professional identity. Law school is as much about learning to engage in an objective analysis of the law as it is about learning to engage in a subjective analysis of yourself. Developing the self-awareness and self-motivation necessary to a successful and fulfilling professional future takes time. Yet, in three short years, we will ask you to assume the responsibility of our profession to serve others: clients, communities, and society. Don't wait to figure out who you are and what you stand for until you are

---

[12] This example was developed by my colleague, Professor Kinda Abdus-Saboor.

walking across the stage at graduation. Put in the time now to ensure that passion, not stress, defines your professional future.

Professors Lawrence Krieger and Kenneth Sheldon's extensive empirical work on law student self-determination shows that three things most contribute to well-being: relatedness to others, autonomy, and competence, which we discuss in the next chapter on resilience.[13]

---

[13] Lawrence S. Krieger and Kennon M. Sheldon, *What Makes Lawyers Happy?: A Data-Driven Prescription to Redefine Professional Success*, 83 G. W. L. Rev. 554, 555–56 (2015).

7

Resilience

Joshua Alt and Nathalie Martin

The pessimist sees the difficulty in every opportunity.

The optimist sees the opportunity in every difficulty.

Winston Churchill

INTRODUCTION TO RESILIENCE THEORY

We start in this introduction with a short list of activities that can increase resilience, and return to this list at the end of this chapter:

- Don't run from things that scare you.
- Be quick to reach out for support when things go wrong.
- Learn new things as often as you can.
- Find an exercise regime you can stick to, usually something you love.
- Do not beat yourself up or dwell on the past.
- Rewrite your own story.
- Recognize what makes you unique and strong, and own it.[1]

As mentioned in the last chapter, the three things that most correlate with well-being are relatedness to others, autonomy, and competence.[2] Law school can undermine all three of these things. When it comes to competence in particular, it is critical to recognize that you will not be good at law school when you first arrive. The skills learned in law school are ones that improve only with practice, so that is why you are there.

As explained by George Washington University School of Law Professor Todd Petersen, virtually *all* legal training involves learning a skill, not a substantive knowledge base. It is not about learning torts or contracts, per se, but learning how to

---

[1] Mandy Oaklander, *Bounce Back*, TIME, June 1, 2015, at 36, 41.

[2] Lawrence S. Krieger and Kennon M. Sheldon, *What Makes Lawyers Happy?: A Data-Driven Prescription to Redefine Professional Success*, 83 G. W. L. REV. 554, 555–56 (2015).

develop the analytical skills needed to practice law. In other words, learning law is more like learning to play tennis than learning anatomy.[3] There is very little to memorize. You are learning to use and apply the law, and to analyze new situations, like those you will face when you see clients. For these skills, you need practice.

When we throw students into the Socratic method in law school classes, we do not explain that they are learning a skill, not substantive knowledge. If we did, they would understand that they are not supposed to be good at it when they start. Like tennis, only practice can improve the skill.

Fortunately, neuroscientists have long known that engaging in work and leisure that is outside your comfort zone can make you more resilient and help you traverse difficult life circumstances. You can think of these experiences, embracing new and difficult tasks, and enduring them involuntarily through life's twists and turns, as informal resilience training. If informal training is not enough, there is also formal resilience training.

Both formal and informal resilience training can help us deal with life's small annoyances as well as bigger traumas. Resilience training can also help us support others who are suffering from trauma, which is sometimes called vicarious trauma. Sheryl Sandberg's book, *Option B; Facing Adversity, Building Resilience, and Finding Joy*, is incredible in its ability to help us turn deep trauma into strength and even joy.[4]

Resilience training increases both the quality and the quantity of life, by creating a barrier to long-term health problems and the effects of constant low grade stress on the body and the mind. These techniques, a combination of mindfulness and positive psychology, can help ward off everything from heart disease to Alzheimer's disease, and other negative physical states.

Scientists have used brain scans to separate resilient people from others and then to measure how very resilient people are able to overcome even the largest of setbacks. Based upon this evidence, social scientists have designed step-by-step resilience plans that provide measurable increases in resilience.

In this chapter, we explore the theory of resilience, and then give you a chance to practice resilience using experiences in your own life. Unlike mindfulness in general, these techniques are especially useful in difficult circumstances.

Developing resilience involves:

- developing a core set of beliefs that nothing can shake
- recognizing what makes you strong and unique and owning it
- understanding that you have the choice and the ability to change
- finding meaning in stressful or traumatic events
- maintaining a positive outlook.

---

[3] Telephonic interview with Todd Petersen, June 21, 2017.
[4] Sheryl Sandberg, Option B: Facing Adversity, Building Resilience, and Finding Joy (Knopf 2017).

Little Pause: Think of someone who has overcome incredible obstacles and is still happy and healthy in outlook. Can you identify some of that person's traits?

Why Lawyers Need Resilience Training

We all have and use resilience in our lives, but if we are more conscious of this fact, we can use resilience more and with better results. Being a lawyer is rewarding but somewhat unique in what society and individuals ask us to do, namely to take on and use complex systems to solve problems for people who cannot resolve those problems on their own. Because of the combination of intellectual and emotional skills required of this job, lawyers may need resilience more than many other people in society.

Resilience helps us weather the storms of life. By developing resilience, lawyers can deal with the more difficult aspects of the job, more easily bouncing back from challenges. It starts with reframing our thinking. For example, a prosecutor such as Julie from Chapter 5 might experience anxiety and depression as a result of the horrors she sees every day, but she can develop resilience by realizing that she is a champion for the victim and the state, rallying behind that story, and moving past the trauma of the violence of the job.

Lawyers are storytellers. We often tell stories on behalf of clients. We can also design stories about ourselves to improve resilience. These stories can leave us open to change and even failure, as long as we know these stories will help in our lives. The job gives us many opportunities to design these reframed stories, for others or ourselves. Through resilience training, including mindfulness, we can rise from the trauma, disappointment, and burn out, stronger and better than before. We can use reframing and other resilience techniques when under stress from deadlines, workload, pressure from partners or clients to take a particular approach, client trauma, and other life events, to become stronger.

Law schools around the country teach resilience training. For example, Stanford Law Professors Barbara Fried and Joseph Bankman and Yale Law Professor Ian Ayres have designed and taught a two-hour course that teaches first-year law students cognitive behavioral therapy techniques to reduce anxiety.[5] Bankman provides notes to other professors around the country who would like to offer the course.[6]

---

[5] Peter Huang and Corie Rosen, *The Zombie Lawyer Apocalypse*, 42 Pepperdine Law Review 727, 769 (2015).
[6] To view Professor Bankman's entire wellness page, which includes teaching materials, see *Teaching materials, WellnessCast™, Articles, and Bloggers*, Stanford law School, available at https://law.stanford.edu/directory/joseph-bankman/wellness-project/#slsnav-the-wellnesscast.

What is Resilience?

According to the Mayo Clinic website,

> Resilience is your ability to adapt well and recover quickly after stress, adversity, trauma or tragedy. If you have a resilient disposition, you are better able to maintain poise and a healthy level of physical and psychological wellness in the face of life's challenges. If you're less resilient, you're more likely to dwell on problems, feel overwhelmed, use unhealthy coping tactics to handle stress, and develop anxiety and depression.[7]

Informal Resilience Tips for Beginners

Try New Things

We can develop resilience by trying new things and not being afraid to fail. You are already in great shape for this one as you are likely trying something new right now, law school! Michael Melcher describes four stages of knowing and learning things in life:

1. Unconscious competence, for those things we can do beautifully without thinking about it.
2. Conscious competence, for those things we can do well with effort.
3. Conscious incompetence, for those things we do not do well and we know it.
4. Unconscious incompetence, for those things we do not do well but for which we are unaware of our incompetence.[8]

While we want to avoid unconscious incompetence, it is good to be learning new things all the time and to regularly perform activities that fall into all of the other three categories. Being willing to try new things builds resilience by giving us permission to do things we are not good at, to observe improvement, and to learn to live with being just OK at some things. Being comfortable with not being an expert at everything improves our ability to grow from setbacks.

LAW PAUSE

Describe something you recently learned how to do. Can you recall how you felt when you were a total beginner versus how you feel now about this task? Which category of competence do you fall into right now in connection with this task?

Watch your perceptions, and know that you are not your thoughts.

---

[7] *Resilience training*, MAYO CLINIC, July 4, 2014, available at www.mayoclinic.org/tests-procedures/resilience-training/basics/definition/prc-20013967.

[8] MICHAEL MELCHER. THE CREATIVE LAWYER, 200–201(2ND EDN. AMERICAN BAR ASSOCIATION 2014).

FIGURE 7.1 Monkey Mind, created by illustrator, Pamela "Zen" Miller.

We often think negative thoughts about ourselves that are not true. Father of modern mindfulness Jon Kabat-Zinn reminds us that we are not our thoughts. We know this logically because those thoughts do not exist outside our heads. One way to internalize the reality that we are not our thoughts is to watch our thoughts for a set period of time.

If you actually try watching your thoughts as they come and go, you will see that you could *never* be all the things you think about yourself. Meditators call this constant barrage of thoughts "monkey mind," a state of mind in which we just spin from thought to thought.

Once you see that you are not your thoughts, you can become more intentional about your actions and perceptions. You can use purposeful, trained attention to decrease the negative thoughts and to bring greater focus to the more meaningful aspects of an experience, which increases happiness and decreases stress and anxiety.

This is informal resilience training, which allows us to withstand moderate stressors and bounce back from larger stresses. Our thoughts seem real because of the attention we give to them, especially the redundant, negative thoughts that keep replaying in our heads. Instead of replaying those negative thoughts and allowing them to become our "reality," we can focus on more positive ideas, or practice one of the breathing exercises outlined in this book.

The more attention we pay to our present moment awareness, the more we realize that we don't have time or psychic energy to waste on redundant, negative thoughts. These thoughts are not reality and not us. Allowing them to take over our minds wastes our precious mindspace, meaning that special space inside the brain that we need to use to our best advantage.

Move Your Body and Reorient Your Mind, aka Get Off Your Butt and Do Something

If you get any form of exercise, you will feel accomplished. It will blow off steam, relieve depression and hopelessness, and you will feel like less of a failure. If exercise and physical movement is not your thing, spend some time on a hobby, go shopping, send a note of gratitude to a friend, or call someone. You can at least say, today I did something; I got off my butt and exercised, or called a good friend, or went to the mall and bought a friend a gift.

FORMAL RESILIENCE PLANS

Resilience can also be called grit.[9] Martin Seligman, one of the fathers of positive psychology,[10] is a former president of the American Psychological Association. He attributes that position and his overall professional success to the popularity of his book, *Learned Optimism*,[11] in which he sets out his views on optimism and pessimism,[12] thoughts attributable to pessimism,[13] and practical methods we can use to shift from pessimism to optimism.[14] When you read Dr. Seligman's books, you begin to realize that despite his success, he has had a rather rough life. A pessimist by nature, he admits that being resilient and optimistic do not come easily for him. Seligman appears to have written this book to address problems he saw in his own life, which makes the work even more credible. You may already be using some of these techniques without knowing it.

Resilience Training from Martin Seligman's Learned Optimism

Seligman uses four factors to measure our level of optimism/pessimism. The three primary factors are permanence, pervasiveness, and personalization. There is also hopefulness, found at the crossroads of permanence and pervasiveness. All of these factors overlap somewhat, but the framework is still helpful. In her book, *Option B: Facing Adversity, Building Resilience, and Finding Joy*, Sheryl Sandberg describes how she used Seligman's framework to build resilience after

---

9   Angela Lee Duckworth, *Grit: The power of passion and perseverance*, TED, May 9, 2013, available at www.youtube.com/watch?v=H14bBuluwB8.

10 *Authentic Happiness*, University of Pennsylvania, available at www.authentichappiness.sas.upenn .edu/.

11 Martin Seligman, Learned Optimism: How to Change Your Mind and Your Life iii (Vintage Books 2006).

12 *Ibid.* at 3–16.

13 *Ibid.* at 17–53. This includes Chapters 2 and 3, which discuss how pessimism is learned helplessness and provides a test to determine if you are more optimistic or pessimistic.

14 *Ibid.* at 208–80. This three-chapter series gives different applications to the same techniques. The first chapter deals with optimizing (my word, not Seligman's) the self. *Ibid.* at 208–34. The second chapter deals with applying the optimization techniques to your children. *Ibid.* at 235–53. The final chapter of the three deals with applying the techniques in your work life. *Ibid.* at 254–80.

the sudden death of her husband David.[15] As she explains in reference to perso-nalization, pervasiveness, and permanence, hundreds of studies show that adults and children recover more quickly when they realize that most bad things that happens to them are not their fault, don't apply to every aspect of their lives, and will not follow them everywhere forever.[16] The elements of this framework are descried in more detail below.

Permanence

Permanence is tested by looking at "how permanent you tend to think the causes of bad events are."[17] For example, assume a scenario in which you make an obvious mistake at work or in school. How you think about the mistake will determine whether or not you address it pessimistically. If you are optimistic regarding permanence, you might think, "I didn't impress today." If you are more pessimistic, you might think, "I can never impress my peers."

Either way, you acknowledge the mistake, which is healthy. The difference between the optimist and pessimist is that the optimist considers the mistake a one-time event, while the pessimist considers the event part of a permanent personality flaw. The ability to view problems as temporary is the hallmark of one who is more optimistic.

Pervasiveness

The next attribute, pervasiveness, is about space[18] and how far and long we stretch a particular thought or event. More particularly, is the event universal or specific? Returning to the previous example, if you think, "I can never impress my peers," then you are thinking about the problem universally – and pessimistically. Conversely, if you think, "I didn't impress Professor Moore today," then you are thinking about the problem more specifically and in a more limited way, that is, more optimistically.

In other words, if you make a mistake, try not to assume that is how you are and who you are. Try instead to assume you made one mistake. Don't blow things out of proportion. Avoid all or nothing thinking and avoid the words always and never. Make problems smaller rather than bigger through your thinking. To overcome the drag of negative events on us, we need to be willing to shrink the problem and move on.[19]

---

[15] SHERYL SANDBERG, OPTION B: FACING ADVERSITY, BUILDING RESILIENCE, AND FINDING JOY (KNOPF 2017).
[16] *Ibid.* at 16.
[17] MARTIN SELIGMAN, LEARNED OPTIMISM: HOW TO CHANGE YOUR MIND AND YOUR LIFE 45 (VINTAGE BOOKS 2006).
[18] *Ibid.* at 46.
[19] This deals with proportions. When our problems are small (in time, spatially, and conceptually), then we can crush those problems. I am not sure of the clinical efficacy of such a concept, but it is certainly helpful. For example, when someone is a coward or weak, they are described as "small." Courage and bravery are BIG. Heroes are BIG, muscular, and "larger than life." Cowards and weaklings shrink. While the strong may have an empathetic response to the weak, the strong do not become weak because of those feelings.

FIGURE 7.2 Hopeless and Forlorn Attorney, created by illustrator, Pamela "Zen" Miller.

Hopefulness

In the context of Seligman's pessimism test, hopefulness is at the crossroad of permanence and pervasiveness.[20] The pessimist views his or her problems as both universal and permanent, which can lead to future failure. Try to adjust your thinking from "I am always a failure, not just today, but always. I suppose I always will be too" to "I made a mess of things today, but I won't make the same mistake again."

Seligman characterizes hopefulness as the most important attribute for resilience.[21] Why is hope so important? If hope is a combination of permanence and pervasiveness, then hope is a sum of the parts. Permanence deals with our view of how long a problem will last. Pervasiveness deals with our view of how "big" the problem is. If the problem is big and long-lasting, can we see an end to it? Probably not, at least, not easily. Hope is the ability to see a problem as small, specific, finite, and a one-time event, the capacity to hold out for a positive change in the future. If you view problems as small and brief, then you are more likely to work toward and find a solution.

[20] *Ibid.* at 49.   [21] *Ibid.*

Personalization

Personalization involves how we take responsibility for good and bad situations. This is a tricky trait to describe because it involves a dichotomy. Personalization requires us to balance reality with emotional well-being. For example, if you bump into someone in the hallway, is it your fault or theirs? We may say things like, "That's my fault, I'm so sorry" but is that what you really feel? If you attribute the bad to external events and consider yourself to be the cause of the good, then you are more optimistic in life. Just don't be in denial either. If you are the cause of the trouble, see it, change it, and make it better.

In summary, the optimist views problems as short, specific to a situation, and external, while viewing success as internal.

Can Optimism Actually Be Learned?

This discussion and these techniques are all well and good, but can we actually become more optimistic?

LAW PAUSE

Recall a personal disappointment or setback, perhaps something you had no control over. How did you respond? Would others say you overreacted or responded appropriately?

Resilience is not fixed but can grow, particularly through enduring difficulties.[22] You can unquestionably train yourself to be more resilient in the face of adversity, and perhaps even come out ahead as a result of the personal growth resulting from the experience. This does not mean we ever choose to endure horrible circumstances, but if we must, we might as well see if there is a way to gain from the experience in some way.

We need to become good at spotting pessimism and nipping it in the bud. We can do this by watching our thoughts and seeing if they are optimistic or pessimistic. If you can't do this yourself, ask a friend to help you. Since all thoughts and expressions are personal, and not ourselves, we can then see the separation between us and our thoughts. We can also examine the ways in which we think and feel about our problems, and intentionally change some of that thinking.

Seligman's ABCDDE Method of Building Resilience

Seligman uses the acronym "ABC" to build resilience, which stands for "Adversity," "Belief," and "Consequences."[23] Create a chart or log on a piece of paper and write out information for each factor.

[22] SHERYL SANDBERG, OPTION B: FACING ADVERSITY, BUILDING RESILIENCE, AND FINDING JOY 10 (KNOPF 2017).
[23] MARTIN SELIGMAN, LEARNED OPTIMISM: HOW TO CHANGE YOUR MIND AND YOUR LIFE 210–17 (VINTAGE BOOKS 2006).

1. **Adversity:** Under adversity, write down a problem that triggered a negative reaction. For example, pretend a woman on her cell phone crashes her car into your car in the law school parking lot. Enter this fact in the adversity column. Adversity refers to an objective factual scenario that gives rise to negative thought processes and emotional responses. But here, just write the fact or facts.[24]

2. **Belief:** Beliefs are thoughts. Here write down the thoughts that came to mind as a result of the adversity. These thoughts may reflect some of the characteristics we describe above, such as permanence, pervasiveness, hope, and personalization. Thinking about the woman who ran into you in the parking lot, depending on your explanatory style, you will react either optimistically or pessimistically. If you think, "That idiot! Didn't she see my *parked* car in the *parking* lot?" then you "believe" that she, not you, is at fault. This belief column is filled with subjective thoughts, but not emotions.

3. **Consequences:** Under consequences, write down the pure emotional response to your belief about the adversity. In the same example, you might write down, "I was so angry at the little ingrate. I am so upset about having to pay for repairs. And I hate how slow insurance is to compensate me" or whatever. Writing down your consequences completes the ABC record.

LAW PAUSE

Complete five or six entries in the chart or log referred to above, over the next few days.

So how does this help? Essentially, by helping us understand how we perceive, think about, and feel about a given situation. When we are able to understand our explanatory style in action, we can take action to correct them.[25]

A Few More Tools from Learned Optimism

In *Learned Optimism*, Seligman provides a few more tools to combat our negative beliefs. The first of these items is distraction,[26] then disputation, and finally, energizations. In essence, he has added D, D, and E, to A, B, and C.

4. **Distraction:** With distraction, you simply distract yourself from the beliefs running through your mind. How do you do this? Perhaps you could start thinking about a beautiful bird in your favorite tree, which is Professor Martin's choice, or for Joshua, a little red corvette.

---

[24] *Ibid.* at 213.   [25] *Ibid.* at 215.   [26] *Ibid.* at 217–18.

Alternatively, you could yell "stop" and slam your hand on the table, hopefully when you are alone. Either approach should make the thought go away, but it might be back soon, which is why we also need a long-term strategy.

5. **Disputation**: Seligman calls his long-term strategy disputation,[27] which involves challenging our beliefs about our limitations and failures. Like Jon Kabat-Zinn, Seligman asks us to acknowledge that our beliefs are not facts, just like our thoughts are not facts.[28] He suggests we find ways to create distance between belief and reality and use that distance to build up some toughness. Disputation is a reasoned, measured approach to our problems, used to combat negative beliefs. Since lawyers love logic, you might find this one particularly useful. For example, if you wrote down the belief "I am not smart enough for law school," then your "D" disputation would be "I wouldn't be here if I wasn't smart enough. I am smart enough."

6. **Energization**: Energization is mostly just reaffirming the D. You write down something like, "I feel better about my intelligence. Now, I can get that memo done."[29]

LAW PAUSE

Take a moment and think about your own level of resilience and optimism. Write a few sentences about this. Next, take the *Learned Optimism* test found at https://web.stanford.edu/class/msande271/onlinetools/LearnedOpt.html and reflect on it in a journal entry. See if there are things you can learn through this comparison. Also, keep in mind that these are mutable characteristics, so you can change them.

RESILIENCE IN THE PRACTICE OF LAW

Obviously, resilience is not needed in happy times, but rather when we are weak. Resilience is our ability to power through adversity because of positively adapting to our stressors. Recovery is healing from damage.

If a parent becomes ill and seems close to death, and we have developed consistent resilience, then we can cope in such a way that we will be resistant to the negative effects of the stressor. We will be more likely to find positive coping mechanisms. If we are not sufficiently resilient, then we may experience a trauma at the news of the parent's declining health, and use negative coping mechanisms such as overspending and substance abuse. If we suffer trauma that we are unable to

---

[27] *Ibid.* at 218–25.   [28] *Ibid.* at 219.

[29] Seligman also tells the reader to look toward evidence, alternatives, implications, and usefulness when we dispute with ourselves. *Ibid.* at 220–23. Does the evidence disprove our beliefs? Are there alternative explanations for something? Even if you are right about yourself, what are the implications of those beliefs? Even if the situation is true ("I'm so bad at eating healthily!"), is it helpful for you to actually think it? These are some examples of his section on arguing with yourself.

power through, we suffer a psychological injury, and recover from that injury over time. If we are not resilient, this could take a very long time. If we are resilient, the recovery time will be much less, perhaps years less.

While all lawyers need resilience, family law attorneys witness a unique form of personal tragedy. As Gabriel Cohen explains in his family law article, *A Better Way to Break Up*: "Shaken by an unexpected separation, blindsided by a custody dispute, betrayed – the path of divorce can bring us to our knees. What if there's a way not to just regain our footing but to step onto a new emotional path?"[30] Cohen tells the story of Joe, an IT specialist from Central Pennsylvania, who found out that his wife was having an affair with another man. Joe's wife wanted a divorce and prime custody of their daughter. The custody news in particular threw Joe into a total panic attack. He blamed the other man and fantasized about what it would be like to tell him off. Joe also had recently picked up Cohen's book, *Storms Can't Hurt the Sky: A Buddhist's Path through Divorce*,[31] in which he described his own divorce.

Remarkably, when Joe serendipitously ran into the other man in a parking lot, rather than tell him off, Joe apologized, saying, "I want to apologize for making you the focal point of anger that should have been directed at myself. I realize that I contributed to my damaged marriage before you ever showed up."

Joe did not explicitly forgive the man, because "I forgive you" can signal blame or assert dominance. Joe said he felt very free after the exchange, recognizing for the first time that his vow was with his wife, not this man. The lover was also grateful for the exchange and in the coming days, the wife softened on the custody issue.

The good result did not necessarily occur because Joe was nice rather than nasty to his wife's lover, but that niceness didn't hurt. Family law attorney Wendy Samuelson helps people develop resilience by focusing on their own needs and tamping down stress and anxiety though mindfulness. Unlike some lawyers, Samuelson works hard to discourage anger and confrontation in clients. She asks them to focus not on getting back at an ex, but on getting what they need. Samuelson uses breathing exercises to help clients calm anger, anxiety, and fear.

In general, lawyers can help clients *not to judge* themselves as a big mess or a failure, and to see anger and sadness not as something being imposed upon us by society but as natural feelings intensified by the way in we think about our circumstances.

As Cohen explains in the context of his own divorce, instead of struggling to make ourselves feel better by changing other people, we can find peace only by working on ourselves. We can ask ourselves, what can I learn from this situation? We can teach

---

[30]   Gabriel Cohen, *A Better Way to Break-Up*, Spirituality and Health, available at www.spiritualityhealth .com/articles/better-way-break.

[31]   Gabriel Cohen, Storms Can't Hurt the Sky: A Buddhist's Path through Divorce (Da Capo Press 2008).

this skill to our clients, but we need to learn to use it on ourselves first. Again, put your own mask on first before assisting others.

SPECIAL RESILIENCE TIPS FOR WOMEN AND PEOPLE OF COLOR

The need for resilience is not equally distributed among the general population, nor among lawyers. Most lawyers in the western world are white men, and while things are slowly changing, the profession can be more difficult for women and people of color.

White men still occupy the vast majority of top law jobs. For example, when looking at large law firms, just 5.3 percent of the partners are men of color, and just 2.7 percent are women of color.[32]

Some law students may hold the distinction of being the "first" in their family (or perhaps their entire community) to graduate from college or law school, or to become a lawyer. Dean and Professor Zuni Cruz describes being the first Pueblo Indian woman in the country to become a tenured law professor. She claims that the experience is surreal and in some ways wrong, particularly given the incredible loss of intellect and intelligence of all the people who came before her and never had the chance to make that kind of contribution. As she explains:

> [A]ll those Indian people before me . . . with their great intellect and intelligence, for whom the legal profession was never an option, and I think, "What a loss." In the specific context of Pueblo people, I think, "What a loss," because Pueblo people have been involved with outsider legal systems since the 1500s. It was over 450 years ago that the Spaniards first encountered the Pueblos, not far from [Albuquerque], and there are accounts of Pueblo delegations appearing before *audencias* in Mexico, and *protectores* being appointed for Indians. Under the Spanish and the Mexican legal systems there were no [Pueblo] Indian attorneys, and it is always necessary to point out, lest we forget, it wasn't until very recently, under the American system, that we even had Indian attorneys [in any number]. In the last forty years, in the late sixties and early seventies, we saw our first Indian attorneys and in July of 2002 the University of New Mexico (UNM) officially tenured its first Pueblo law professor.[33]

Dean Zuni Cruz goes on to describe a conversation she had with colleague Margaret Montoya on being first:

> Professor Montoya . . . said being first is hard on the soul of that first person, because it is like we are put through a sieve not made for us. And going through that tiny hole that wasn't designed for us, hurts, bruises, and tears us; but as we go through that

32 Renwei Chung, *Diversity in the Legal Profession Has Flatlined since the Great Recession; Who Is to Blame?*, ABOVE THE LAW BLOG, Jan. 6, 2017, available at http://abovethelaw.com/2017/01/diversity-in-the-legal-profession-has-flatlined-since-the-great-recession-who-is-to-blame/.
33 Christine Zuni Cruz, *Toward a Pedagogy and Ethic of Law/Lawyering for Indigenous Peoples*, 82 N. D. L. REV. 863, 865 (2006).

hole, we also misshape that hole, making it larger for those who follow us, so that it doesn't hurt and tear and bruise the next person coming after us quite so much; and that pretty soon, the hole is appropriately shaped for those like us, who follow, so that they pass through easily, so much so, that there is not even the knowledge of the assault on the soul of that first person. I understand that line, "[m]y heart doesn't hurt anymore, but my soul does" and I suspect, most of you will, if you don't already.[34]

Some lawyers will need more resilience than others, perhaps due to race, gender, or gender identity. We can all find strength in the challenges, and solace from and gratitude for those who came before us.

Women law graduates now outnumber male ones,[35] which some call the feminization of the profession. This could lead to better access to justice, the subject of Chapter 17, because women lawyers might represent unrepresented groups at higher rates than male attorneys. Nevertheless, some people will not welcome these changes in the profession. Older male lawyers may be less familiar with practicing with women. They may even wonder why these women are not home with their children or their husbands. They might think the female attorneys do not need as much money as the men, because the men need to support families. Thankfully these types of thinking are mostly part of our past, but they do still exist.

Some attorneys and judges even today are hostile to women attorneys. Randy McGinn reports on a particularly drastic case of sex discrimination in one New Mexico judge's courtroom. At first the judge just ignored the women attorneys, calling the men up to a bench conference while leaving the women sitting at counsel table, essentially engaging in ex parte communications with one side of a case.[36] When he was told by colleagues that this behavior had to stop, he acknowledged the women but called them Mister.[37] As McGinn explains, "[n]eedless to say it was quite confusing for the jurors when he called 'Mister' McGinn to the bench. You could see them looking at each other, wondering if there was something they didn't know about me. Was I a cross-dresser? Was the judge senile?"[38] All lawyers should assume they will be well-received but also be ready for outliers who live in the past and are unfamiliar with the diversification of the profession.

---

[34]　*Ibid.* at 867.

[35]　Elizabeth Olson, *Women Make Up Majority of U.S. Law Students for First Time*, New York Times Deal Book Blog, Dec. 16, 2016, available at www.nytimes.com/2016/12/16/business/dealbook/women-majority-of-us-law-students-first-time.html?_r=0.

[36]　Randi McGinn, Changing Laws, Changing Lives 156 (LLC 2014).　　[37]　*Ibid.*　　[38]　*Ibid.*

PRACTICE BUILDING RESILIENCE

Read this Story of Resilience to Prepare to Write your Own Resilience Story

A young teenage girl, who we'll call Terry, suddenly finds her grandmother living with her family. Her grandfather had passed away almost a year before, and the grandmother's descent through Alzheimer's left her living in filth, diabetic from eating loaves of bread and jars of peanut butter as her only food, and bankrupt, facing foreclosure. Terry's mother, Christine, works as an insurance agent. Her father, Jack, works as an exterminator. Terry's oldest brother has moved out of the house, but her other brother, Paul, lives with the family. Because Christine and Jack are so busy with work, the responsibility of watching grandmother passes to Terry and Paul. Paul, a stalwart and selfish jerk, does everything he can to not be home. Terry, alone, cares for her grandmother on top of tending to her homework. Terry helps bathe and feed her ailing grandmother, and most of her time is consumed with tending to her. The rest of the family only helps when convenient.

Terry's grades begin to steadily decline. Instead of taking on adult responsibility, Christine blames Terry for not keeping her grades up. Terry manages. Despite the crushing responsibilities thrust upon her, Terry passes her classes, gets a job after high school, and moves on to be a functional adult. She does not experience any depression. She is effective at working, and even has a knack for business. Terry eventually meets a young man who appreciates her strength and resilience, her humor and emotional intelligence. Terry marries that young man, whose name is James.

James comes from a complex background. When he was a boy, both of his uncles – his father's only two brothers – died violent deaths. One was murdered by a motorcycle gang, and the other committed suicide. James never had the opportunity to learn about death gradually. He was baptized in the cruelty of the world at age seven. Still, he grew up. He did well in school until sophomore year of high school when a deep depression triggered a perceptive teacher's inquiry.

This teacher helped James get help, and explain to his family what he was going through. The teenager reformed and became deeply interested in eastern religious traditions. He attended university to study poetry and Japanese. Throughout this time, he experienced many more losses, both of friends and family. "Somehow," he would tell himself in his loneliest of loneliness, "I am able to move on." In his final year of university, he met a young woman named Terry who accepted his wounded psyche but appreciated his ability to persevere in the face of some of the most potent loss. They were married and remain so after many years.

James and Terry probably do not understand that they are real-life warriors. They have overcome powerful trauma to meet each other, love each other, and build a life together. Each of them has been knocked down in different ways. Both of them got back up. Both of them kept fighting. It wasn't always easy for them. James had times when he was sure that he was down and out. Then, with help, he got back up. And, somehow, he was able to move on through the tragedy in his life. Terry was able to overcome the guilt and shame her family put her through. Because of her resilience, she found her way into a steady job as a phlebotomist. James got a corporate job. They earned their own money, bought a house by the time they were twenty-five years old, and never missed a payment.

Terry and James are happy and secure despite the past. Or are they happy and secure because of the past? Recall the dichotomies. You can't know happiness without sadness. Some of the most unhappy and purposeless lives we have seen have been those of people who had it all but didn't realize it.

LAW PAUSE

Write your own story of resilience, drawing on the times when you overcame challenges. Tell the story in the third person and change the names. After you write the story, read it aloud to a friend or loved one. Ask them what they think of the hero of the story. This works even better when the person doesn't know the story already. You will come to know how much of a champion you are in your own right.

As it turns out, a relatively difficult childhood helps people be more resilient and more creative. These early adversities also help us weather less-than-perfect life circumstances when they arise. These skills help us thrive in most any job, including law jobs. Thus, there is a silver lining to experiencing some diversity early in life.

CONCLUSIONS ABOUT RESILIENCE

> Resilience is the ability to persevere through adversity and come out better than before.
> Resilience is the ability to power through trauma, difficulties, and stress because you can believe in yourself, which keeps adversity at bay.
> Resilience is the ability to resist stressors, which allows you to persevere through adversity.
> Resilience is the ability to persevere again and again.

Rocky, in the movie *Rocky Balboa*, understood resilience when he said:

Let me tell you something you already know. The world ain't all sunshine and rainbows. It is a very mean and nasty place and it will beat you to your knees and keep you there permanently if you let it. You, me, or nobody is gonna hit as hard as life. But it ain't how hard you're hit; it's about how hard you can get hit, and keep moving forward. How much you can take, and keep moving forward. That's how winning is done. Now, if you know what you're worth, then go out and get what you're worth. But you gotta be willing to take the hit, and not pointing fingers saying you ain't where you are because of him, or her, or anybody. Cowards do that and that ain't you.[39]

Someone who is resilient is able to take blows from life and get back up.[40] It takes awareness and practice but pays off.

Once again, try these resilience tips:

- Don't' run from things that scare you.
- Be quick to reach out for support when things go wrong.
- Learn new things as often as you can.
- Find an exercise regime you can stick to, usually something you love.
- Do not beat yourself up or dwell on the past.
- Rewrite your own story.
- Recognize what makes you unique and strong and own it.[41]

---

[39] *Rocky Balboa*, QUOTES, available at www.imdb.com/title/tt0479143/quotes.

[40] This is different from grit because grit requires long-term goals which aid in one pushing through the difficult, but also reflect one's dogmatic adherence to a goal (i.e., becoming the best player in the state of the game, *Magic: The Gathering*). Resilience is your ability to push through a trauma or bad event. Resilience does not necessarily require a long-term goal to satisfy it. In fact, such a goal might be enough to turn resilience into grit.

[41] Mandy Oaklander, *Bounce Back*, TIME, June 1, 2015, at 36, 41.

8

Mindfulness: Theory and Practice

Nathalie Martin

A Wild Bull

The effort to make the mind quiet,
Is like holding a wild bull on a leash.
The leash is held on to, and he drags you around,
And you are determined not to release.
One day maybe the bull will stop moving,
And finally you can rest.

Or you can stop expecting the bull to be still,
And let go of the leash, instead.
Once you don't care what the bull does,
When you no longer seek to control him,
Wherever he goes and whatever he does,
Does not affect the one watching.

A bull moves around, that's what it does,
If you fight him, he fights you back.
Don't ask the mind to be silent,
Then silence is all that you have.[1]

Adam Oakley

I love the image of the mind as this raging bull in Adam Oakley's poem above. The mind is often like that, off on its own, pulling us all over the place and causing us to go way off track from where we want and need to be. Most of this severe agitation is unnecessary. We all know that our thoughts are not us and that our thoughts are not reality, but we still have moments when those raging bull thoughts, particularly our negative, repetitive thoughts, control the majority of our mindspace.

---

[1] ADAM OAKLEY, INNER PEACE POETRY: POEMS ON INNER PEACE, THE SELF, LIFE AND HUMAN NATURE, available at www.goodreads.com/videos/112361-a-wild-bull.

As a result, we get less done and are less happy in life than we could otherwise be. In a sense, by allowing the bull to rage, we are wasting our precious time on this earth. This chapter provides an introduction to some modern mindfulness practices that can be used to slow the raging bull down.

This chapter starts by describing the world's first mindfulness practices, developed over 3,000 years ago. It then describes what drew people to these practices back then, and why there is an upsurge in these practices now. Meditation, for example, has been scientifically shown to improve concentration, allowing one to get more done in less time and with less effort, to help one establish "flow," and to find enhanced meaning and purpose in life. This chapter builds upon the science of the mind described in Chapter 2 and summarizes some of the scientific evidence that practices such as meditation, journaling, visualization, and mindful yoga can do to enhance mental and physical well-being, overall happiness, and cognitive abilities.

HISTORY OF MINDFULNESS PRACTICES

Mindfulness traces back to Patanjali, the father of yoga, but societies around the globe have been using similar techniques in one form or another since the beginning of time. These practices range from the secular to the deeply spiritual. Patanjali

"Nothing happens next. This is it."

FIGURE 8.1 *New Yorker* Cartoon "Nothing happens next. This is it," Image I.D. no. TCB-45164, licensed from *The Cartoon Bank, a feature of Condé Nast Collection.*

wrote the first yoga text, the yoga sutras, around 1500 BCE in the context of the yoga affiliated with the Hindu religion. Mindfulness can be traced to Daoism beginning in around 600 BCE through the mind-body practice of qì gong, and to Buddhism around 535 BCE.[2] All the major western regions then incorporated mindfulness in one form or another into their faith.

> Historically, meditation was used not for stress relief but to strengthen the capacities of the mind. In other words, meditation has been used for ages to make us smarter and to make our brains stronger.

Positive psychology is a branch of psychology that emphasizes successful development rather than the treatment of mental illness. It uses science to prove that positive affirmations and attitudes can lead to greater mental and physical health. According to one positive psychology source, in order to remember and recall the long texts, high priests or Indian Brahmans had to concentrate and free their thoughts, which led to a practice very close to what we now call meditation. Once Buddhism was founded, Buddhists adopted meditation and redefined it as a tool to enhance both memory and presence of mind.

Later, these practices were incorporated into Judaism, Islam, and Christianity, where they remain an important part of religion today. You can call them meditation, mantra, prayer, speaking in tongues, focusing on the creator, clearing the mind, or many other things, but at their core, the practices are more similar than they are different. All religions share an emphasis on mindfulness and mindful living. These practices have persisted for over 3,000 years.

HOW DID MINDFULNESS BECOME SO POPULAR IN THE WEST?

While the band The Beatles likely began the westernization of mindfulness in 1967,[3] modern mindfulness really came to be when Kabat-Zinn founded the Stress Reduction Clinic at the University of Massachusetts Medical School in the late 1970s. Since that time Kabat-Zinn has trained over 18,000 people in his Mindfulness

---

[2] *History of Mindfulness: From East to West and from Religion to Science*, POSITIVE PSYCHOLOGY PROGRAM, March 13, 2017, available at https://positivepsychologyprogram.com/history-of-mindfulness/.
[3] *The Beatles meet Maharishi Mahesh Yogi*, THE BEATLES BIBLE, NOT QUITE AS POPULAR AS JESUS ..., Aug. 24, 1967, available at www.beatlesbible.com/. In 1968, The Beatles visited the Maharishi's spiritual training camp in Rishikesh, India. Songs such as *Let the Sun Rise, Let it Be*, and many others reflect the spirit of mindfulness and of meditation in particular. Not long after The Beatles' entry into meditation, the mindfulness movement got another big PR boost, this time from well-respected physician at Massachusetts General Hospital, Jon Kabat-Zinn. If you decide to read just one book on mindfulness, other than this one, you might consider Kabat-Zinn's *Full Catastrophe Living*. We have this book in hard copy and on CDs. We have listened to the e-book over and over again. While listening to a CD is not the same as meditating, John Kabat-Zinn will give you a full secular view of how and why meditation, and mindfulness in general, works.

Based Stress Reduction (MBSR) program, which is designed to help with very practical everyday problems such as chronic pain, heart disease, anxiety, psoriasis, sleep problems and depression. It definitely works for these purposes, though mindfulness meditation can help with much more. It can be a way to find not just stress and pain reduction, and targeted focus in life and work, but also one's purpose in life.

Another influential person for mindful practices in the West is Vietnamese Buddhist monk Thich Nhất Hạnh, who lives in France but travels internationally to give retreats and talks. He is best known for coining the term "Engaged Buddhism" in his book, *Vietnam: Lotus in a Sea of Fire*. Nhất Hạnh has published more than 100 books, including more than forty in English. He is active in the peace movement, promoting nonviolent solutions to conflict and promoting nonviolence toward nonhuman animals.

Though Nhất Hạnh's writing does not arise from a secular setting, it can be applied to a person of any (or no) faith. For example, he has said: "We will be more successful in all our endeavors if we can let go of the habit of running all the time, and take little pauses to relax and re-center ourselves. And we'll also have a lot more joy in living."[4]

WHY HAS MODERN MINDFULNESS TAKEN ON SUCH SIGNIFICANCE?

I have a few ideas about why mindfulness is now so popular. First, the world has changed more in the past twenty years, 1997–2017, than it had in the past two centuries, at least in terms of how, how often, and in what medium people communicate. Globalization and the digital age make it possible to be in minute to minute contact with individuals and groups around the globe at any moment in time. There is just no comparing the technology, virtual connections, and complexities of today to our past.

On the other side of the coin, finding time to let the brain lie fallow is a bit like finding a two dollar bill – not completely impossible but unlikely to happen by chance. We are frenetically busy, often juggling several things at once, which may explain why mindfulness is surging in popularity.

WHAT EXACTLY IS MINDFULNESS AND HOW DO I PRACTICE IT?

Since mindfulness is now discussed regularly in popular media sources such as the *New York Times*, *Time*, *National Geographic*, and even the *Wall Street Journal*, you have likely heard that a more mindful approach to life can help with everything from

---

[4] Marianne Schnall, *Exclusive Interview with Zen Master Thich Nhat Hanh*, HUFFINGTON POST THE BLOG, MAY 21, 2010, available at www.huffingtonpost.com/marianne-schnall/beliefs-buddhism-exclusiv_b_577541.html.

job performance, personal relationships, to overall stress in life. But what does it actually mean to become more mindful, and how does one do "it"?

Jon Kabat-Zinn describes mindfulness as "paying attention in a particular way, on purpose, in the present moment, and nonjudgmentally." British meditation teacher and author Paul Wilson describes meditation, the main portal to mindfulness, as "just being." He goes on to say:

> When you learn how to live only in the moment, when there is nothing to distract you, when you are not tied to the past or anxious about the future, when your mind and your emotions are your servants rather than your master, your consciousness (your awareness) is in the most perfect state possible. This state is simply "being." Meditation is about *being* not *doing*.[5]

Wilson claims that we need cultivate just *one* skill in order to be mindful, the skill of thinking about just one thing at a time. This one skill is a gold mine for lawyers because the ability to focus on one thing at a time fosters intense brainpower and creativity. Also, if the one thing you are focusing on is a person, for example a client, learning mindfulness can give you a market edge. As Chapter 5 pointed out, the listening lawyer is a rare breed indeed.

The concept of mindfulness is much broader than meditation. Meditation is one form of formal mindfulness practice, but mindfulness is more of a philosophy or way of looking at the world than a "practice" per se. The idea is to look at the world, and yourself, with increased awareness and focused attention, to observe and to see but not to judge. Put simply, see, note, and of course, breathe. Just don't judge.

Deep belly breathing improves every function in the body, calms the mind, and makes life easier. To try it, lie down or sit up tall, and put your hands on that sweet beautiful belly of yours. Breathe as deeply as you can into your belly and then exhale. You can even imagine that you are breathing in love and beauty, and breathing out anything that you no longer need. If that is too New Age for you, just practice deep breathing in and out. Next up, see if you can pause and practice this breathing throughout your day. Then, do it when you are nervous. Finally, try it when you are angry, before you do or say anything.

To attain knowledge, add things every day,
To attain wisdom, remove things every day.
Tao Te Ching

The question of how to "practice mindfulness" reminds me of a silly joke my husband's Uncle Mickey used to tell me all the time. He was not a fan of lawyers, and would often say, "Practicing, practicing, when are you lawyers going to get it right?"

---

[5] PAUL WILSON, THE CALM TECHNIQUE 13 (THORNSONS PUBLISHING 1987).

Here we discuss what it means to "practice" mindfulness, but first, what is mindfulness?

Mindfulness Defined

Mindfulness is present awareness of one's thoughts as they arise and minute to minute awareness of one's existence. Mindfulness can also include non-thinking or simply clearing the mind. In either case, mindfulness allows you to pay clear and particular attention to the things around you, so you can do what is best for yourself, those you care about, and the world at large if you take it that far. Jon Kabat-Zinn talks about being alive in the moment. As he explains, life is full of moments, not just years and decades.[6] He asks if we can stop and be present, even for one moment, and goes on to say: "A good way to stop all the doing is to shift into the 'being mode' for a moment. Think of yourself as an eternal witness, as timeless. Just watch this moment, without trying to change it at all. What is happening? What do you feel? What do you see? What do you hear?"[7] Stopping just for a moment and simply observing is often harder than it sounds.

Little Pause: If the idea of stopping and observing is somewhat new to you, try it right now and see how you feel compared to how you felt before the exercise.

Really, try it. As Jon Kabat-Zinn explains, most of us have never even tried to live in the moment, as we toggle between regretting the past and worrying about the future. If you experience the present moment for just a minute, you may find that you like the sensation enough to try it again. And again.

While mindfulness can reduce stress, at its essence it is so much more than that. Mindfulness is about being more aware. As Law Professor Scott Rogers explains:

> While mindfulness is often discussed in the context of feeling less stressed and being better able to focus, the mindfulness practice (and living a mindful life) is not really aimed at these changes—or any change, for that matter. Mindfulness is about much more—it's about relating more effectively to challenging situations without needing people and circumstances *to change* in order to be okay—and the practice of mindfulness can help bring about these useful, even transformative shifts.[8]

THE SCIENCE BEHIND MINDFULNESS

Using mindfulness techniques to calm down and to think clearly about your life, your work, and your impact on others, is not new by any means. Variations of these techniques have been used over thousands of years to bring about a sense of peace,

---

[6] JON KABAT-ZINN, FULL CATASTROPHE LIVING 26 (DELTA TRADE PAPERBACKS 1990).

[7] JON KABAT-ZINN, WHEREVER YOU GO, THERE YOU ARE 11 (HYPERION 2005).

[8] Scott Rogers, *Mindfulness, Law and Reciprocal Practice*, 19 RICHMOND PUB. INT. L. R. 330, 331 (2016).

calm, and equanimity. We refer to all of these techniques as "mindfulness," though the variety of techniques is endless in the modern world. The sense of peace and calm that can result from any of these techniques can also lead to periods of intense and deep concentration, enhanced productivity, a heightened ability to think through complex problems, and of course, a calm, peaceful state of mind.

While the two concepts just mentioned above – deep intense thought on the one hand and a calm state of mind on the other – may seem at odds, they are not. Rather, when we are stressed, stress hormones interfere with concentration by flooding the brain with cortisol and making it impossible to "think straight."[9] For this reason, mindfulness techniques can enhance one's ability to "think like a lawyer" – a mindful, clear-thinking lawyer, that is.

Scientists have been studying the effects of meditation and other mindfulness techniques for over fifty years. Beginning in the 1960s and 1970s, researchers began to study the scientific effects of meditation and other mindfulness practices on the brain. In all studies, people who engaged in these practices reported feeling better, but researchers wanted to know if the practices resulted in any physiological changes in the body. As it turns out, they do. First, meditation produces a deep state of relaxation, which Paul Wilson calls the Calm State.[10] Unlike sleep or hypnosis, the mind is very alert and awake, which shows in your brain waves. In fact, there is an increase in slow Alpha waves, which are typically present only when you are wide awake. Beta waves are also found in the brain. These Beta waves are typically only found in the brain during a very deep sleep. This combination of brain waves reflects a unique state in which the meditator is highly alert and in a deep relaxed state, both at the same time. You cannot achieve this state of being by walking along singing, listening to music, or dozing off in bed, though you might get different benefits from those "practices." The key is and always will be training the mind to do one thing at a time.

Some of the other physiological changes that take place during mediation include a lower production of carbon monoxide, drastic decrease in heartbeat and respiration rates, and a dip in lactate levels in the bloodstream. Lactic acids contribute to feelings of anxiety, tension, and fatigue. Blood pressure also drops and the skin gets a more elastic look and feel. Meditation also improves mental health and creates a sense of well-being.[11] These physiological changes are all good for the body.[12]

---

[9]   Clemens Kirschbaum, Oliver T. Wolf, Mark May, Werner Wippich, and Dirk H. Hellhammer, *Stress and Treatment Induced Elevations and Cortisol Levels Associated with Declarative Memory in Healthy Adults*, 58 LIFE SCIENCES 1475 (1996).

[10] PAUL WILSON, THE CALM TECHNIQUE 22 (THORNSONS PUBLISHING 1987).

[11] Charles N. Alexander, Howard M. Chandler, Ellen J. Langer, Ronnie I. Newman, and John L. Davies, *Transcendental Meditation, Mindfulness, and Longevity: An Experimental Study with the Elderly.*, 57 J. PERSONALITY & SOC. PSYCHOL. 950–64 (1989).

[12] PAUL WILSON, THE CALM TECHNIQUE 22–23 (THORNSONS PUBLISHING 1987).

More specifically, Eileen Luders at UCLA's Lab of Neuro Imaging has found that meditation increases gray matter in the brain, creates stronger connections between brain regions, and reduces age-related brain thinning.[13] In 2012, she reported finding mindfulness meditation to be associated with larger amounts of gyrification, the process of creating folds in the brain cortex. Gyrification is thought to allow the brain to process information faster, which is particularly relevant to the work we do as lawyers.[14] This means that an intentional shift of awareness can even rewire neurological pathways to create long-term benefits in health and wellness.[15] This rewiring can improve physical as well as emotional health.[16] It can also foster emotional intelligence, allowing one to react to difficult situations in ways that enhance one's well-being as well as the well-being of others.

Many other studies have found similar results, leading some people to conclude that taking time to be mindful and clear the mind of debris can make people better at virtually anything.[17] Meditation helps us concentrate and also sleep better.[18] Internet company Google, major US banks, and even law firms are offering programs for their employees to get them meditating, and they are not doing this to be nice. Meditating employees improve the bottom line.

Going even deeper, mindfulness is now regularly used to treat personality disorders, depression, and mild to serious anxiety. It has been used to treat post-traumatic stress disorders (PTSD) in returning soldiers through the Mindful Warrior Project, as well as to help police departments think before they shoot. Meditation and yoga programs in prisons have transformed the most horrible situations into tolerable ones, and yoga teacher James Fox has trained more than 1,000 teachers to teach over 75,000 people nationwide. Finally, using yoga in schools has been transformative in reducing disciplinary problems, even in elementary school and pre-kindergarten. At least one school has replaced detention with meditation,[19] and the non-profit Breath for Change offers a 200-hour yoga teacher training program for educators. Clearly, mindfulness is not just for gurus any more, if it ever was.

---

[13] Scott Rogers and Jan Jacobowitz, Mindfulness and Professional Responsibility 27 (Mindful Living Press 2012).

[14] *Ibid.*; see also *Meditation Strengthens the Brain, Raises Consciousness*, Natural News, Mar. 15, 2012, available at www.nyrnaturalnews.com/mind-body/2012/03/meditation-strengthens-the-brain-raises-consciousness/.

[15] *Ibid.*

[16] *Ibid.*; see also Scott Rogers and Jan Jacobowitz, Mindfulness and Professional Responsibility 27 (Mindful Living Press 2012).

[17] Leonard L. Riskin, *The Contemplative Lawyer: On the Potential Contributions of Mindfulness Meditation to Law Students, Lawyers, and their Clients*, 7 Harv. Negot. L. Rev. 1, 46 (2002).

[18] Julie Corliss, *Mindfulness Meditation Helps Fight Insomnia, Improves Sleep*, Health Blog, Harvard Health Publications, Harvard Medical School, Feb. 18, 2015, available at www.health.harvard.edu/blog/mindfulness-meditation-helps-fight-insomnia-improves-sleep-201502187726.

[19] James Gaines, *This School Replaced Detention with Meditation. The Results are Stunning*, Upworthy, Sept. 22, 2016, available at www.upworthy.com/this-school-replaced-detention-with-meditation-the-results-are-stunning.

Probably above all else, mindfulness techniques improve thinking and focus. A recent study proves that engaging in mindfulness techniques improved graduate record exam ("GRE") scores.[20] Studies show that regular meditation increases gray matter in the brain.[21] Besides these physiological changes, these techniques also help control emotions and reduce stress, scientifically proven over and over again. They literally help restructure the brain in ways that lead to better concentration, improved immunity, greater compassion, and thus better interpersonal relationships.

Another Harvard University study found that spending twenty-seven minutes meditating a day can change the structure of the brain by developing and growing the hippocampus region of the brain, while at the same time shrinking the amygdala, which is the part of the brain associated with anger, jealousy, aggression, and even depression.[22] This has many applications to today's society and might explain why some elementary schools are replacing detention with meditation training.

These findings confirm that the brain can be changed and improved through our actions. For example, several studies by neuroscientist Eleanor Maguire of University College London show that London taxi drivers had larger-than-average hippocampi because to get licensed they needed to memorize a labyrinth of 25,000 streets within a ten kilometer radius.[23] Maguire's studies showed that drivers who earned their licenses had larger hippocampi than those who failed, and also that the drivers' hippocampi grew over time in the cab.[24]

MINDFULNESS AND PRACTICE OF THE LAW

So how do we know that mindfulness can help attorneys in particular? Scientific research, of course. Private sector lawyers often bill time in six minute increments,

---

[20] Michael D. Mrazek, Michael S. Franklin, Dawa Tarchin Phillips, Benjamin Baird, and Jonathan W. Schooler, *Mindfulness Training Improves Working Memory Capacity and GRE Performance While Reducing Mind Wandering*, 24 PSYCHOLOGICAL SCIENCE 5, 776–81 (May 2013), available at http://pss.sagepub.com/content/24/5/776. This study found that mindfulness training improved both GRE reading-comprehension scores and working memory capacity while simultaneously reducing the occurrence of distracting thoughts during completion of the GRE and the measure of working memory. These results suggest that cultivating mindfulness is an effective and efficient technique for improving cognitive function, with wide-reaching consequences.

[21] Britta K. Hölzel, James Carmody, Mark Vangel, Christina Congleton, Sita M. Yerramsetti, Tim Gard, and Sara W. Lazar, *Mindfulness Practice Leads to Increases in Regional Brain Gray Matter Density*, 191 J. PSYCHIATRY RESEARCH NEUROIMAGING 1, 36–43 (2011).

[22] Sue McGreevey, *Eight Weeks to a Better Brain: Meditation Study shows Changes Associated with Awareness, Stress*, HARVARD GAZETTE, Jan. 21, 2011, available at http://news.harvard.edu/gazette/story/2011/01/eight-weeks-to-a-better-brain/.

[23] Ferris Jabr, *Cache Cab: Taxi Drivers' Brains Grow to Navigate London's Streets: Memorizing 25,000 city streets balloons the hippocampus, but cabbies may pay a hidden fare in cognitive skills*, SCIENTIFIC AMERICAN, Dec. 8, 2011, available at www.scientificamerican.com/article/london-taxi-memory/.

[24] *Ibid.*

meaning a tenth of an hour. In one study, clever researchers decided to see how lawyers would respond to sitting for just six minutes a day for twenty-one days, figuring the billing lawyer's mind was already trained to do tasks in tenth increments.[25]

The study results were surprising. The lawyers in the study reported greater well-being after practicing mindfulness for six minutes over twenty-one days. The most interesting finding is that productivity skyrocketed. These lawyers who agreed to meditate could do more work in less time. This is a big benefit given that we can never produce more time.

Generally speaking, lawyers have a tendency to live from the neck up, using their mind constantly, and never ever letting it rest. Our work involves primarily logic and intellect, and with practice, some empathy and people skills to go with them. Other jobs do not require brainwork alone. Think about construction workers, potters, mechanics, and bus drivers. Even doctors use their hands for something other than typing or holding a phone. In many ways, lawyers live as if the body is not even there.

> To combat the occupational hazard of living from the head up, work the body more and rest the mind more! Indeed, scientific studies confirm the physical and mental benefits of regular mind-clearing activities.

Many scholars have reported the effects of meditation on the lawyer's mind. In his book, *Making Waves and Riding Currents*,[26] Professor Charles Halpern, former CUNY Law School Dean and Arnold & Porter attorney, talks about the first time he ever experienced meditative moments, which occurred on a canoe in the lakes of northern Ontario. These experiences later led to a more formal meditation practice, which he claims altered his life and law practice in measurable positive ways. As he explains:

> I found that in the midst of turmoil I was able to respond to strong pressure with less anger and reactivity. I was able to see things more clearly. I was able to empathize with a broad range of people and identify the things we shared . . .
>
> Each of us can return to times in our lives when we had an awakening—an insight that suggested that the world was larger than what we had thought it was. Often these are not the sort of incidents that show up on résumés, and we sometimes don't talk about them with the people we work with. By sharing such incidents in my life, I want to encourage each of us to lift up to such events, to reflect on how they enrich our lives and how they can be more fully integrated into our work for a more peaceful and just world.[27]

---

[25] Jeena Cho, *Mindful Pause Meditation: Mindfulness for Lawyers in 0.1 Hour*, SOUNDCLOUD, available at https://soundcloud.com/jeena-cho/sets/mindfulness-for-lawyers-in-01-hour.

[26] CHARLES HALPERN, MAKING WAVES AND RIDING CURRENTS (BERRETT-KOEHLER PUBLISHERS 2008).

[27] *Ibid.* at 5.

Another law professor, Leonard Riskin, teaches dispute resolution and mindfulness in law at the University of Florida as well as Northwestern School of Law. Riskin recounts the many benefits of meditation for lawyers in a 2002 *Harvard Law Review* article,[28] where he quotes one Wilmer Hale attorney, stating that meditation helps her to:

- think through things and respond more effectively
- manage stress better and not be so affected by it
- be more tolerant and less judgmental
- listen better
- pay more attention to other people
- get to know people better
- develop harmony between work-self and other-time-self.[29]

Another of Riskin's students reported that meditation causes him to feel better, be more efficient, be less likely to jump to conclusions and better able to see issues from more perspectives, all keys to solving legal problems.[30]

Still finding it hard to believe meditation is worth trying? After a quote from Kabat-Zinn stating that mindfulness is not about sitting like a statue but about living your life as if it really mattered, one popular columnist continued: "And [mindfulness] is not just for type-A CEOs, traders, and venture capitalists looking for fast-tracked success. It is a rich practice that can be as simple or as complex as you want it to be – a tactic for being productive at work, acting more present in your relationships, or moving closer toward [meaningful] relationships."[31] Who knew that mindfulness was *primarily* known as a tool for type-A CEOs? Quite a few people, as it turns out. A recent Case Western Reserve study found mindfulness in the workplace to be a valuable management tool that improves employees' focus (through enhanced stability, control, and efficiency), helps them manage stress, and helps people work better on teams. Improved capacity for teamwork or collaboration was also one of the motivators for Google's well-known mindfulness program, *Search Inside Yourself.* Not to be outdone by Google, tech company Intel now has its own mindfulness program, Awake@Intel, and insurance giant Aetna has a program designed to increase productivity, happiness, creativity, and relationships with coworkers. By the time this book goes to print, this list will look quaint and out of date. There is even a CEO conference called Wisdom 2.0 that attracts thousands of business people to learn these "new" "secrets to success," which are neither new nor secrets. Now you can learn them too.

As people become more open to these practices, more lawyers open up about using them. Coral Gables litigator Harley Tropin is known for his unflappable,

[28] Leonard L. Riskin, *The Contemplative Lawyer: On the Potential Contributions of Mindfulness Meditation to Law Students, Lawyers, and their Clients*, 7 HARV. NEGOT. L. REV. 1, 41 (2002).
[29] *Ibid.*   [30] *Ibid.* at 44.
[31] Amanda Mascarelli, *The Mindfulness Meditation Guide: Our mindfulness meditation guide can help you get around roadblocks and on the path to contentment*, YOGA JOURNAL, Feb. 6, 2015, available at www.yogajournal.com/meditation/mindfulness-meditation-guide.

quick-response courtroom style in high-impact cases, and also now for his fifteen minute daily office meditation. As he explains in a news article, meditation helps him and other lawyers lower stress levels, curbs anger and negative thinking, and ultimately enhances their performance. As Tropin, a partner at Kozyak Tropin & Throckmorton explains, "It helps you not take everything so personally and intensely." The article continues, stating that "no one knows why lawyers — considered by many to be among the most aggressive and least zen-like professionals — in particular have embraced mindfulness, but they have." Scott Rogers, head of the Mindfulness in Law Program at the University of Miami School of Law and an early proponent of mindfulness in law, explains the development:

> [Mindfulness] is conducive to the high-stress, high-stakes environment in which lawyers, judges and others in the legal profession work … It helps them with concentration and focus and the ability to regulate emotions as well as providing medical benefits … While mindfulness began making inroads [in the legal community] 25 years ago, I believe it's now reaching a tipping point across society.[32]

Paul Singerman, a top bankruptcy lawyer at Berger Singerman in Miami, brought Rogers to his law firm to teach a five session course to the entire staff in 2013. Explaining this decision, Singerman reports that:

> [the] study and practice of mindfulness has changed my life profoundly in positive ways …. It's a discipline that enlightens me on the difference between reacting and thoughtfully responding, and it facilitates more effective communication and keener powers of observation. The study of mindfulness in law school is very important in shaping the thinking of young lawyers and helping them manage the stress of legal education and prepare for a legal career.[33]

Mindfulness is taught in many law school classes, and also in state and local bar associations around the country. Many judges and others in high-stress jobs receive training in mindfulness. Tony Recio, a partner with Weiss Serota Helfman Cole & Bierman in Coral Gables, started practicing mindfulness six years ago. At the time, the land-use attorney was unhappy, stressed, and overindulging in food and alcohol. Recio practices mindfulness at the beginning and end of his day. He said mindfulness has improved his memory, health, critical thinking, and even led to his losing twenty pounds and cutting down on drinking. He explains: "This has definitely put space between a stimulus and my reaction to a stimulus. When something doesn't go your way, there's a tendency for it to snowball and dominate your thinking. This helps me not tear my hair out."[34]

---

[32] Julie Kay, *Mindfulness Programs Help Produce Less-Stressed Lawyers*, DAILY BUSINESS REVIEW, July 30, 2015, available at www.law.com/dailybusinessreview/almID/1202733529895.
[33] *Ibid.*   [34] *Ibid.*

The mind works best when we clear it of debris. Ironically, a great way to clear the mind, improve creativity, and increase productivity is to stop thinking for a while. You already have experienced this when searching for an answer to a perplexing and enduring problem. Answers remain elusive despite your hardest and deepest concentration, and then boom. The answer comes to you on a dog walk, or in the shower, or while you are floundering on the elliptical machine at the gym.

MINDFULNESS TECHNIQUES

Early Buddhists meditated in one of two basic ways – one focused on the breath to calm the mind, and the other focused on the breath to discover and uncover the meaning of life. Note the commonality there. Like they did, it is best for the rest of us to also keep our mindfulness practices simple. After all, it would be ironic if the best mindfulness techniques were complex. The whole idea is to return to a simpler, more natural, state of mind. To start, channel Faith Hill, Pearl Jam, or Christian rocker Johnny Diaz, and "just breathe."

Breathe deeply and note how you feel. Focus on the breath, and as thoughts arise (and they will), acknowledge them and let them go, bringing your attention back to your breath. Remember that the brain can only focus on one thing at a time, so rather than trying to eliminate a thought, worry, or trouble, focus instead on your breath, thus giving your mind something simple to do.

Do this focused breathing practice throughout your day from time to time, and also do this for a set period of time. I try to do six minutes a day as a minimum, and the minute I wake up, based upon the lawyer study. I also pause throughout my day, and focus on my breath for a moment or two. This is no big complex "practice," just a few minutes in the morning and a pause here and there. If you don't meditate already, this is really all you need to know.

Although more is sometimes less, here is a bit more if you like. I like to mix it up myself and have fun and yes, purchase an app or two from time to time. But don't go crazy. Mindfulness is simple and free.

LAW PAUSE

Find a regular place to practice or "sit." Choose a certain time of day for a certain amount of time. If you miss it, try to do it later, as something to look forward to. Again, first thing in the morning works best for me and a little time goes a long way. While a longer "sit" goes much further, see how it feels. In the beginning, few can sit for more than a few minutes at a time. You can work up to more if you like it. Set a timer on your phone and see how it feels. While there, either:

- focus on your breath, counting your breath if you like,
- focus on a piece of nature out a window, or
- repeat a mantra, something that speaks to you.

The idea is to slow down thoughts and have fewer of them, so you can calm the mind and clear it, making way for peace, productivity, and growth. This is why we say that we shouldn't judge ourselves for having a thought. Rather, acknowledge that thought and then show it the door, like clouds passing in the sky. I sometimes say "OK thought, this is not my time to think, you'll have to go now, as this is my time to focus on my breath." Ultimately you are learning to focus on one thing at a time. Train your mind to focus on what *you* want it to focus on – your breath and the moment.

Another technique that some people love is to just accept the thoughts and watch them. See what comes up and how many thoughts there are! I am always surprised at the sheer number and variety of thoughts that occur, and frankly, I find this practice pretty exhausting. Nevertheless, it serves one great purpose. It demonstrates what Buddhists call "monkey mind," which is easy to remember through the visual in Figure 8.2. Monkey mind is the mind that is unsettled, restless, confused, indecisive, and out of control.

After seeing how out of control the mind typically is, you can learn not to take those thoughts so seriously. You will learn firsthand that you are not your thoughts. Realizing that you are not your thoughts can help you with self-compassion and self-forgiveness, and perhaps deeper compassion for others, a topic taken up elsewhere in this book.

FIGURE 8.2 Monkey Mind, created by illustrator, Pamela "Zen" Miller.

Watching the thoughts come and go, as opposed to focusing on the breath, can be easier for beginners. One woman in a trial lawyers' association mindfulness training said that in a ten minute silent meditation, in which I instructed people to focus on the breath, the breath, and nothing but the breath, she finally just gave up on the breath and got more done than she had in weeks, more shopping lists, more oral arguments formulated, etc. I can appreciate that she found the peaceful time to be a good time to get things done, but wow! That surely was not what I was aiming for. Some of the others nodded; they also worked during the meditation.

LAW PAUSE

In addition to your "sit," try to stop and pause throughout your day, every time:

- the phone rings
- you touch a doorknob
- you ride an elevator
- you take the stairs
- you use the restroom
- you wait in line.

Each time you do this, note your breath and how it helps you stay present in the moment, in a nonjudgmental way.

You can meditate in grocery store lines (my favorite because otherwise you might get frustrated waiting, and you can instead turn a potentially bad thing into a good thing), on elevators, while touching any doorknob, or while firing up a computer.

You can even learn to use technology mindfully, by sending mindful emails, using phone calls to practice mindfulness and full attention, and meditating on an office focal point or object in order to bring focus and creativity to a particular task. To try this focusing on an object technique, place a red thumbtack on the wall and focus on it whenever you find a good breaking point in your work.[35]

I am a bit jealous of those who have not yet tried any of these mindfulness techniques because the beginning of learning mindfulness is so interesting and exciting. There is a lot to learn about yourself at that stage, and little things make you feel a lot better.

---

[35] This idea traces back to my first mindfulness practice as a lawyer, at Fine and Ambrogne in Boston. Thank you to my former colleague and mentor, George Kelakos.

We have between 12,000 and 60,000 thoughts a day, and 80 percent of those are negative.[36] Every time we beat ourselves up or worry about the future catastrophes that may not even happen, we sell ourselves and our clients short.

LAW PAUSE

Do a little self-exploration. After a short sit or mindful walk, answer this question: Would you rather think or feel? Why? We will use your response to this Law Pause in the next chapter, on emotional intelligence.

[36] WILLIAM URY, GETTING TO YES WITH YOURSELF 27 (HARPER ONE 2015).

PART II

You and Others Around You

9

Introduction to Emotional Intelligence: Theory and Practice

Nathalie Martin

INTRODUCTION TO EMOTIONAL INTELLIGENCE

We ended Chapter 8 with a Law Pause, in which you answered this question:

Would you rather think or feel?

There is a place for each of us in the world of law, and in fact, there is more need for lawyers in the world than there are lawyers to fill that need. In Chapter 17 on professional identity, professional responsibility, and access to justice, we will talk more about this. For now, just know that there is a place for you, and not just any place, but a meaningful and important place.

We each bring something unique to the table, which is why we are all needed in our own way. I like to ask people whether they would rather think or feel because it helps me understand them better as individuals. It also helps me see what parts of lawyering each new lawyer will likely struggle with the most. We all must do both – think and feel. There will be struggle. It is just a question of what kind of struggle.

I would rather think than feel. It is a fact, and not a close call. Thinking is just easier for me, and I suspect for many lawyers and lawyers to be. When I feel, I often feel too much. I sometimes start to cry and sometimes get blue. When I think on the other hand, I wonder, I write, I read, I research, I teach, I model, I succeed. Not only do I succeed, but I feel strong. Yet all of the people closest to me are "feelers." My husband would rather feel than think. My two closest friends at work, Fred and Jenny, would both rather feel than think. My closest non-work friends, Connie, Kim, and Pat, also all would rather feel than think. I assume these feelers are emotionally healthier than I am, but again it is not a competition. I need to be able to feel in order to do this job, and so do you.

Of course, you can't be a lawyer without being able to think, but let's face it, most of school is about teaching us to think. Nowhere is this truer than in law school. So for you feelers, again, you are fortunate to be a bit ahead of the learning curve. You may not need many of the lessons in this chapter and the next, but read them anyway. You also might pick up a thing or two, which might help you better understand the others around you in law school. I personally struggle with every lesson in this and the following chapter. None of this comes easy for me, so believe me, I am not judging you or preaching to you. Still, it might feel like I am. This is not easy material to read about to practice.

GOING TO THE BALCONY

Emotional intelligence, or EQ (coined after the IQ abbreviation), is the capacity to be aware of, control, and express one's emotions, and to handle interpersonal relationships with empathy. EQ is thought to be the key to both personal and professional success. Knowing how to form deep, lasting personal relationships is another sign of EQ, and one of the keys to a happy, successful life in any field or walk of life. Other people are our primary source of learning. This chapter discusses how to develop relationships and good "people skills" in general. While no doubt this topic has always been relevant, the modern trend is to call these people skills "emotional intelligence" or EQ.

Emotional intelligence builds upon mindfulness. You usually need to become somewhat mindful and self-aware before you can improve your emotional intelligence quotient. William Ury, author of the bestseller, *Getting to Yes*, and the sequel *Getting to Yes with Yourself*, calls the ability to watch your own reactions to situations without becoming outwardly reactive "going to the balcony."[1] Ury explains that we give up a lot of control and advantage over situations when we react to other people's words, tone, voice, or actions. If we feel attacked, we attack back. Or we retreat. Or we accommodate. Ury says we tend to rely on one of the three A's:

- Attack
- Accommodate
- Avoid.

We may start by avoiding or accommodating, and then get so sick of the situation, we eventually attack back. None of these three reactions serve our true interests. Once we are in flight or fight mode, our ability to think clearly diminishes, we forget our purpose, we act contrary to our purpose, and we give up our power to influence other people or change a situation for the better. When reacting, says Ury, we say no to ourselves and to our own best interests.[2] We also say no to our client's interests.

Ury explains that rather than reacting, we can instead choose to observe ourselves. We can retreat to our private balcony, a metaphor for a "mental and emotional perspective, calm, and self-control."[3] He suggests we learn to go to the balcony

---

[1]　WILLIAM URY, GETTING TO YES WITH YOURSELF 20–21 (HARPER ONE 2015).　　[2]　*Ibid.*　　[3]　*Ibid.*

throughout our days but especially before, during, and after difficult negotiations or conversations.

Ury also explains that our anxiety can rub off on others. When he and his wife were suffering from fear about their daughter's debilitating illness, their daughter could pick up that anxiety.[4] Conversely, when they were able to calm themselves down, their daughter also became more calm.[5] Ury uses the analogy of inviting all of his emotions to the kitchen table and welcoming them all, one by one. OK, here comes fear. Oh, there is disappointment. Here comes a little hope. Through this approach we can observe, go to the balcony, and keep the emotions from overtaking us. We can choose to control our emotions rather than allowing them to control us.[6]

EQ THEORY: WHAT IS EMOTIONAL INTELLIGENCE?

Emotional intelligence is the external side of mindfulness. Mindfulness is an internal journey, an "inside job," and if it takes hold, you will live your life with a greater understanding and appreciation of yourself. This can lead to enhanced emotional intelligence, an "outside job." If you can cultivate mindfulness, emotional intelligence will be easier. You will have a better understanding of others and also better insight into them. You will cultivate empathy, good listening skills, and many other skills that will make others want to be in your company.

Because of the connection between mindfulness and emotional intelligence, I refer to them as "siblings." While mindfulness is centuries old, its sibling emotional intelligence is quite modern. The phrase, developed by Daniel Goleman in his internationally acclaimed book, *Emotional Intelligence*,[7] refers to the ability of people to become talented in any field through self-awareness, self-regulation, awareness of the feelings and reactions of others, and highly effective communication skills, all critical to the modern practice of law. Empirical data show that people with high EQ scores excel in leading others as compared with people with lower EQs.[8]

Data also show that with training, EQ skills can be improved. Like most of the other topics in this book, EQ is not a fixed trait, particularly if you maintain a growth mindset. In her book, *Mindset: The New Psychology of Success*, Carol Dweck explains the critical

---

[4] *Ibid.* at 59–62.   [5] *Ibid.* at 62.   [6] *Ibid.* at 29.

[7] DANIEL GOLEMAN, EMOTIONAL INTELLIGENCE (BANTAM BOOKS 1995). This book spent more than a year and a half on *The New York Times* bestseller list. Goleman also developed the argument that noncognitive skills can matter as much as IQ for workplace success.

[8] Incidentally, economists such as Nobel Prize winner Jim Heckman have consistently found that traits such as perseverance, dependability, and consistency predict wealth and success better than IQ as well. William Harms, *Heckman's Research Shows Non-Cognitive Skills Promote Achievement*, UNIVERSITY OF CHICAGO CHRONICLE, http://chronicle.uchicago.edu/040108/heckman.shtml (discussing the work of Nobel economist Jim Heckman).

difference between fixed mindsets and growth mindsets.[9] If you believe that you can create change through your own efforts and through past mistakes, you have a growth mindset. Conversely, if you believe that abilities are inherent and can't be changed, you have a fixed mindset. Because people with fixed mindsets believe their intellect and other traits are set in stone, they have constant self-doubt and no real strategy for improvement.[10] People with growth mindsets, on the other hand, learn from past mistakes because they believe their past will help them improve in the future. Maintain a growth mindset and you can improve your EQ.

We start our discussion of EQ with more thoughts on mindfulness because mindfulness is the most common way to develop EQ. For example, engineer Chade-Meng Tan runs the mindfulness program at internet giant, Google.[11] As Meng Tan explains throughout his book, *Search Inside Yourself*, one can build emotional intelligence skills. While Meng Tan leaves the door open to other possibilities, he claims that meditation and reflective journaling are the only methods he knows for learning emotional intelligence.[12] To this I would add seeking out and attempting to implement meaningful feedback.

In his program at Google, Chade-Meng Tan was able to prove empirically that mindfulness practices increase professional success, by improving emotional intelligence and interpersonal interactions.[13] Similarly, by improving emotional intelligence, investment advisors at financial services corporation American Express with mindfulness training also made more money on average than those without the training.[14] Tan explains that the main difference between good and great leaders is that great leaders have observable compassion for others and are deeply ambitious for the greater good, whether that is the good of the organization or some other societal good.[15] In other words, those trained in mindfulness had the rare capacity to show both ambition and humility, as well as a concern for something greater than their own advancement.

Recognizing and controlling emotions is discussed in the next chapter at length, but for now, just know that controlling emotions is a big part of emotional intelligence. While it is impossible to stop an emotion from occurring (it'll just bubble up somewhere else), we do have the power to welcome the emotion and then let it go, and perhaps with practice, to let it go immediately. Meng Tan describes this through the Buddhist metaphor of "writing on water."[16] We can train ourselves to let the emotion come, but then to let it go in the same way that writing on water disappears.

Emotional Intelligence 2.0, one of many popular books on the subject,[17] describes the steps involved in improving emotional intelligence. First a person becomes able

9   CAROL DWECK, MINDSET: THE PSYCHOLOGY OF SUCCESS 7, 48–49 (BALLANTINE BOOKS 2006).
10   *Ibid.* at 38.   11   CHADE-MENG TAN, SEARCH INSIDE YOURSELF xi (HARPER ONE 2012).
12   *Ibid.* at 19–27.   13   *Ibid.* at 83.   14   *Ibid.*   15   *Ibid.* at 201.   16   *Ibid.* at 106.
17   TRAVIS BRADBERRY, JEAN GREAVES, AND PATRICK M. LENCIONI, EMOTIONAL INTELLIGENCE 2.0 (TALENT SMART 2009); *see also* DANIEL GOLEMAN, EMOTIONAL INTELLIGENCE (BANTAM BOOKS 1995); JESSICA CAMBRIDGE, EMOTIONAL INTELLIGENCE: HOW TO QUICKLY DEVELOP YOUR EMOTIONAL INTELLIGENCE, COMPLETE GUIDE TO IMPROVING YOUR EMOTIONAL INTELLIGENCE (AMAZON DIGITAL SERVICES, INC. 2014); TRAVIS BRADBERRY AND JEAN GRAVES, THE EMOTIONAL INTELLIGENCE QUICK BOOK (FIRESIDE 2003).

to recognize one's own emotions and how they affect one's thoughts and behaviors. Then one learns to identify strengths and weaknesses.[18] This is the self-awareness stage. Next, in step two, one becomes more able to self-regulate,[19] meaning better able to control impulsive feelings and behaviors, manage emotions in healthy ways, take initiative, follow through on commitments, and adapt to changing circumstances. The third step in improving emotional intelligence is awareness of others or "social awareness," which allows one to understand the emotions, needs, and concerns of other people, pick up on emotional cues, feel comfortable in any social setting, and recognize the power dynamics in a group or organization. People trained in these skills demonstrate more empathy than usual, a concept we will look at in more detail in Chapter 13. Finally, emotional intelligence training includes a fourth step, which helps us manage relationships by teaching us how to communicate clearly, inspire and influence others, work well in a team, and manage conflict. There is no question that these skills are highly useful to attorneys. Nor is there any doubt that some lawyers lack many of these skills.[20]

The authors of *Emotional Intelligence 2.0* researched various businesses and identified people with high EQs. They then asked people who worked with these high EQ persons to describe their management styles. Some of the most common traits of the high EQers were:

- takes time to assess a situation before offering suggestions for change
- is calm, cool, collected, sensitive to the feelings of others, yet direct and to the point
- is open and authentic, aware of tone and impact of communications on others
- is able to help others separate feelings from logic
- handles confrontation well
- can spot and address an elephant in the room
- can read a room and the emotions of others.

LAW PAUSE

Take a second and reread those traits. Can you find a common theme in each? It seems that concern and/or awareness of the feelings and perspectives of others is high on the list of EQ traits. Now think of a mentor, teacher, guide, or role model in

---

[18] Of course, confidence in law students isn't always lacking. As teachers, sometimes we need to strengthen the weak and weaken the strong. Some students think they already know it all, and for them the lesson is in learning that in reality they do not.

[19] The authors of *Emotional Intelligence 2.0* call this "self-management." TRAVIS BRADBERRY, JEAN GREAVES AND PATRICK M. LENCIONI, EMOTIONAL INTELLIGENCE 2.0 97–114 (TALENT SMART 2009).

[20] Lawyers are known to talk all the time and to be pessimistic, argumentative, and poor listeners. *See* Chapter 5 of this book.

your life. Can you identify times when you saw that mentor think of others and put others above him- or herself?

While, admittedly, EQ is not just for lawyers, lawyers who exhibit EQ have a huge edge. By becoming more in touch with ourselves internally through mindfulness, we can "look under the hood" and see how we are doing. We can make sure our own emotions are not like Adam Oakley's raging bull (see his poem in Chapter 8), stirring things up to no good end. We can allow our calmer selves to be in control, to the extent we need to be in control at all. We can also better gauge, guide, and appreciate our lives and our work.

After we have developed a practice of working internally on ourselves, we can become more attuned to others externally, through emotional intelligence. We can better encourage, engage, and empathize with others. This will enrich not just their lives, but also our own.

Through mindfulness practices and greater emotional intelligence, we are also able to control our stress and our emotions and build self-awareness, all of which lead to a more successful career and a more satisfying personal life. This is because people who accurately assess their own strengths and weaknesses are more successful both at work and at home.[21] Again, everyone appreciates self-awareness in others.

MINDFULNESS IDEAS FOR ENHANCED EMOTIONAL INTELLIGENCE

Here we open the mindfulness umbrella a little further and add a few more mindful practices to try. As you can see in Figure 9.1, there is more than one path to a more insightful day. There are many ways, besides meditation, to create space for the life you want, and remain calm, effective, focused, happy, and fulfilled at the same time.

By incorporating a few of these practices, or others you have learned earlier in this book or elsewhere, you can live more happily with others as well as yourself. You just need to create the time and space to practice, whatever that practice may be.

Developing a Daily Practice

To work best, these need to be daily practices. Recall that in Chapter 1, we offered up these practices to get you started, for just ten minutes a day:

- Exercise vigorously. Run, jog, or otherwise tire your physical body out. If you already exercise, pick something new to add.
- Meditate using one of the techniques found in Chapters 2, 8, and this chapter, or on the internet, for six to twenty minutes a day.

---

[21] TRAVIS BRADBERRY, JEAN GREAVES AND PATRICK M. LENCIONI, EMOTIONAL INTELLIGENCE 2.0 19–22 (TALENT SMART 2009).

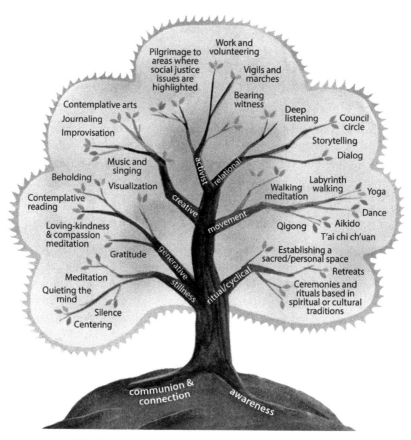

FIGURE 9.1 The Tree of Contemplative Practices, used with permission from *The Center for Contemplative Mind in Society*, as copyright holder, image found at www.contemplativemind.org/practices/tree.

- Do yoga.
- Journal out three notebook pages of gobbledy-gook writing (nothing you or anyone else ever needs to read) as suggested by Julia Cameron in her book, *The Artist's Way*.

Now we add to those and suggest you add another ten minutes a day. Try two or more of these and see how they work for you, spending at least ten to twenty minutes a day on some combination:

- Do a loving-kindness meditation each day, until you get to the point where you mentally wish that each person you pass be happy, healthy, and loved.
- Keep a gratitude journal, where you write down three things you are grateful for each day.

- Write a list of three positive words each day, using the dictionary, thesaurus, or computer when you start to run out of ideas.
- Do a daily mantra in English, Spanish, or Sanskrit – or whatever language you speak.
- Do a calming twenty-minute yoga practice each night before bed or before dinner.

Since these are daily practices, you'll want to pick just one or two to try at a time, and eventually stick with the one or ones that speak to you, based upon what is keeping you happy, healthy, and sane. These will help you think better, sleep better, and play better with others, the topic to which we now turn.

DEVELOPING PARTICULAR EQ LAWYER TRAITS: EQ 101

In the next few pages, we discuss a few of the emotional intelligence skills critical to good lawyering, and describe ways to help develop them. These skills are developed through general awareness of your own actions and the actions and feelings of those around you, and through self-awareness activities.

The EQ 101 traits discussed in this chapter are humility, giving up control through non-attachment, listening, showing an interest in others by avoiding talking just about yourself (including the most boring topic of all, how busy you are and how important your work is), honoring and learning from your mistakes, and finally, a brief introduction to receiving and giving feedback, the subject of Chapter 12. These skills build on one another, more or less in the order in which they are presented here.

In the next chapter, we will learn about some advanced EQ topics, such as nonjudgment, controlling emotions, dealing with difficult people and situations, and forgiveness. Neither I nor anyone else has mastered *any* of these skills. We are all works in progress, which is itself inspiring. After all, "youth is a gift, age is a work of art." There is still so much to learn, so much to look forward to, and so many opportunities!

Honing Humility

The humble lawyer. Is this an oxymoron? I think not, but some of us could use a hand in this department. It is hard to reach our potential without humility, and most of us struggle with this.

For example, a former student of mine, whom I helped find a job at a very good law firm, recently threatened two of our law school clinic students with sanctions for a very well-substantiated complaint the students had filed. My former student was representing the defendant in a case brought by our students for wage theft. Wage theft cases involve situations in which an employer pays less than minimum wage, or otherwise knowingly violates wage and hour laws. The result of this former student's threat, if successful, would be that our clients would need to pay the other side's legal fees. The claim in the complaint was a good one, we knew, so the threat was an empty one. There was no way we would be sanctioned for bringing this cause of action.

The fact that our former student opposed our complaint was not a problem at all. Indeed, that was his job. That was totally normal. What was not normal was that in his threat, this former student referred to these clinic students, who by definition were just learning to practice law, as "inexperienced counsel bringing unfounded claims." This was so disheartening for me. Seriously, he was just there in law school himself, and now only a few years later, he was saying this to our students? This experience taught me the importance of humility in lawyers, and reminded me to recommend humble students for the best jobs.

Great lawyers are always humble, rarely egomaniacal. As reported by Michael Melcher in *The Creative Lawyer*, a lawyer named Chris found better lawyers as she moved up the ladder of success, and they were less egotistical:

> When I started out litigating cases with the ACLU, we were litigating against local U.S. attorneys in various districts. They were generally abrasive, aggressive, sort of swaggering, testosterone-laden, even when they were women. They seemed to be people who relied on having the power of the government behind them.
>
> But as we went to the circuit courts and eventually the Supreme Court, the quality of the lawyering got much better, and a lot of this was because the lawyers were better people. The opposing counsel had a lot more empathy and were a lot more reasonable in a lot of ways.
>
> I've also noticed this working in commercial litigation. The top law firm partners I work with are really fun to be around as people. They may be adversaries, but they are respected adversaries. They engage you. They express an interest in different people in the room. Even when they show their aggressive side, they're showing it in a way that is not offensive.[22]

Maintaining humility throughout a law practice is hard work. It costs a lot to gain a law degree, both in terms of money and wages lost while you are doing it. You also learn a lot about life and the law, and this can cause us to forget how scary the law is to the average person. If you don't believe me, talk to someone who has been sued and see how they felt. You might even have gone through it, which will give you an advantage in the empathy and emotional intelligence category because you've been there.

I recently asked a former student what job experience he had before law school that would help him most as an attorney. He answered that his most useful experience was being a restaurant server. As he explained, lawyers serve, just as waiters and waitresses serve.

---

[22] MICHAEL MELCHER, THE CREATIVE LAWYER 130 (2ND EDN. AMERICAN BAR ASSOCIATION 2014).

This same student told me that his parents had a really bad bankruptcy lawyer, not because the lawyer did not understand the law but because the lawyer did nothing to allay his parents' fears. The lawyer was literally considered "unqualified" by his clients because he did not attend to his client's feelings. The lawyer did not serve.

Clients are frequently intimidated by lawyers, and even feel that their own lawyers sometimes put them down. Most of this stems from failing to develop humility "muscles." Why is it so difficult to be humble? Why do we lawyers always need to prove that we are the smartest person in the room? Ironically, that need to prove often comes off not as knowledge but as deep-seated insecurity, and a lack of humility.

In his book, *After the Ecstasy, The Laundry: How the Heart Grows Wise on the Spiritual Path*, which deals with the overall topic of mindfulness and humility in a very general way, Jack Kornfield explains the experience of learning humility in the Forest Monastery where he trained to become a Buddhist Monk.[23] As a westerner, bowing was deeply awkward for Kornfield, but he gradually got used to doing it each time he entered the monastery. After some time, a monk pulled him aside and explained that Kornfield also needed to bow to each "elder" as he met him or her in passing. But Kornfield wondered, "Who are these elders?" As it turned out, everyone who arrived at the monastery before Kornfield was his elder. "Everyone" included the usual elders whom Kornfield (like most of us) would deeply respect, but also a twenty-one-year-old monk full of hubris, there only to please his parents. The elders also included an elderly rice farmer there on a retirement plan, who chewed beetle juice and never meditated a day in his life.

Kornfield was conflicted about this bowing, but found a way to make it work. He found one worthy thing about each person he bowed to. He bowed to the wrinkles around the old farmer's eyes as he imagined the hard work that went into this life, he bowed to the vitality and playfulness of the young monk, he bowed to something in each person, like one does in a loving-kindness meditation in which you silently wish each person you pass to be happy and healthy.

Bowing eventually became part of Kornfield's practice. As he explained:

> I began to enjoy bowing. I bowed to my elders, I bowed before I entered the dining hall and as I left. I bowed as I entered my forest hut, and bowed at the well before taking a bath. After a while, bowing just became my way – it was just what I did. If it moved, I bowed to it.[24]

Humility, Kornfield learned, teaches us that there is always something to learn from others. I like to have this philosophy about every student. Each student has

---

[23] JACK KORNFIELD, AFTER THE ECSTASY, THE LAUNDRY: HOW THE HEART GROWS WISE ON THE SPIRITUAL PATH ix–x (BANTAM 2001).

[24] *Ibid.*

something to teach me. Kornfield asks us in our lives to bow both to beauty and suffering, enlightenment and confusion, and his message in *After the Ecstasy* is to accept life's lessons and grow from them. There is a great deal in any life or profession that is unpleasant and hard to accept or even endure. Kornfield suggests that we accept things as they are, at least initially, so we can see and really understand those truths.

One cannot do any of this without humility. Without humility, one already knows everything. There is nothing left to learn, nowhere left to grow. Without learning and growth, no one can improve. In many ways, all people must find an emotionally intelligent way to strengthen the weak and weaken the strong. This may sound harsh, needing to weaken anyone or anything, but an overdeveloped ego makes it harder to succeed in the practice of law.

Little Pause: Honestly answer this question: Do you typically think you are better than most people in the room, or not as good?

Either way, try this mantra: *No one is better than me. I am no better than anyone else.*

Giving Up Control by Exercising Non-Attachment

Whoever forces it spoils it. Whoever grasps it loses it.

Lao Tzu

Much of our work as lawyers involves changing or controlling situations. We clearly need to work as hard as we can to get the results we need and want for our clients. There is no question about that. We need to put in the necessary effort to know that we have done all that we could have done for our clients.

There is a challenging balance, however, in figuring out when we have done all that we can and when, on the other hand, our work is done. We often use great physical and mental energy to change a situation that is really outside our control. Finding that sweet spot is enlightening. Many of us (myself included) have a hard time letting go, even in matters that are none of our business, or that are or should be outside our control. One way to look into this is to ask: "Is this within my jurisdiction? Or is dealing with this someone else's job?"

Little Pause: Have you ever been called "controlling?" If so, read on.

Trying to control everyone and everything around you could be driving everyone around you crazy. It could also be making you less happy. The need to control everything can hurt your career, assuming you try to control things that are not yours to control, or that are already outside your control. Here are some of the ways that controlling situations that are already outside your control or expertise, or that are none of your business, might hurt you:

1. Controlling others can annoy them. It can place them in a position of servitude to your needs, leading you to minimize their needs and desires, disrespect them, ignore them and the fact that they are equal to us. It presumes superiority on our part toward others.
2. If something is really outside your control, trying to control it can waste your time and emotional energy and that of other people. In reality, despite your largely wasted efforts, you cannot control a great deal of what you encounter.
3. Constantly trying to control everything may demonstrate that you are not living in the present. While trying to control others, you are thinking only about the future, never about the here and now, and you are not accepting things as they are. You are in constant non-acceptance.
4. It might demonstrate that you are worried and not happy.
5. It might make you less productive than you could be, due to your preoccupation with what is not. Again, many of these things may not be your business, or may be outside your control, expertise, or jurisdiction.

Again, giving up control doesn't mean you don't work hard on a brief or a client matter. It simply means that you work hard, do your best and accept what will be. It means being non-attached to any particular outcome or result, but doing your best and letting go, trusting that your best will be enough.

LAW PAUSE

Recall a situation in which you exerted a great deal of control over a situation and that turned out to be a good thing. What conditions made the decision to get so involved such a good decision? Be very specific. Finally, consider whether you could have achieved the same good goal in this scenario without exerting so much control, by doing your best and assuming that it would work out.

Now recall a situation in which you exerted a great deal of control over a situation and that turned out to be a bad thing. What conditions made the decision to get so involved such a poor decision? Be very specific. What do you think would have happened had you *not* exerted this pressure in the same degree or to the same extent?

The irony is that if you push too hard, your efforts can backfire. You can push people away and they may resist even the best advice from you. There are still many situations in which you will need to influence others. The key is learning to differentiate between situations in which we should try to influence others and those in which we should not do so – those where we should do nothing, stay out of it, keep our own counsel, or just let others make the decisions. Talking and properly discussing difficult or controversial issues is one thing; strong-arming is quite another. So how can you tell? Try answering these questions with a situation in your own life in mind, where you pushed hard to get someone to do something and expressed strong opinions to another:

1. How would you feel if someone you disagreed with was saying these things (or the opposite) to you?
2. Was this already out of your hands?
3. Had you already expressed your views?

Have the courage to get real feedback on whether you come off as controlling in a few different settings in your life. See if you can implement this feedback in order to improve. Studies show that people who can accept and embrace feedback can become better listeners and communicators. I have also seen from experience that the healthier you are emotionally, the more willing you will be to seek out real feedback.

Remember that when working with and living with others, the only thing you can ever change is yourself, never anyone else.

Finally, slow down, use intention in your interactions with others, and try not to control the outcome. As the mantra above articulates, you and your peers, professors, clients, colleagues, family, and friends are all equally valuable. Forget what people think of you when interacting with others, as you cannot control other people's thoughts. Instead think about what *you* think of you while interacting with others, while listening and attending with real attention.

Developing the Patience to Listen

The greatest compliment ever paid me was when one asked what I thought, and attended to my answer.

Henry David Thoreau[25]

According the International Listening Association,[26] we spend 45 percent of our time on earth listening but catch less than half of what we hear.[27] While most lawyers and law students are actually introverts,[28] we tend to stereotype lawyers as people

---

[25] Thoreau: Political Writings, Cambridge Texts in the History of Political Thought 103 (Cambridge University Press 1986).

[26] International Listening Association, www.listen.org/. Thanks to meditation teacher Mirabai Bush for informing me of the existence of this organization. According to the association's website:

The International Listening Association (ILA) was formed in 1979. Since then, we have grown into an international community working in more than 19 countries. We are involved in listening in education, business, healthcare, hospitality, spirituality, music and many other fields. We promote the study of listening, exchange information, and pursue research into the ways in which listening can develop understanding in our personal, political, social and working lives. The International Listening Association serves as a dialogue space, a resource network, a news source and a worldwide community.

[27] Mirabai Bush, Working with Mindfulness Audio CD (2012).

[28] Michael Melcher, The Creative Lawyer 106–107 (2nd Edn. American Bar Association 2014).

with gregarious type-A personalities. Although extroverts in law are in the minority, you will notice quite a few opinionated, gregarious people around the law school and law firms. These people tend to take up extra space, commanding and demanding attention. These same people can also sometimes be controlling and self-centered. They have some excellent attributes too, but an "I know best" attitude is common and not always appreciated by others. Can you tell if any of the descriptions in the paragraph above apply to you? Are you self-aware enough to be honest with yourself?

If any of these descriptions fit, you may want to put extra effort into learning to be a good listener. Listening well will help you become a good lawyer and a good leader. Because lawyers are often community leaders, gaining control of these traits (which we'll call the "G" traits for gregariousness) can help you use your newfound power and education to serve society and yourself.

Little Pause: How often have you found yourself in meetings, planning carefully what you plan to say but giving little thought to how you will think about and be influenced by the comments of others? Do you attend a meeting with an open mind hoping to learn something, or with the sole intention of getting your way? Are conversations with you a give and take, or more of a speech by you, followed by the need for you to leave and get more important things done?

The most successful people in nearly *all* professions are good listeners who value others and are perceived as fair. They have well-developed people skills, which can be learned. Virtually all jobs require good people skills, and these can bring success in all fields.

Listening binds people together. True listening is powerful and rare. In fact, some of the best advice in looking for a job is to ask your interviewers what they are working on that excites them and really listen to what they say. You can also ask about something difficult they deal with at work. They will deem you the most interesting person they have met in a long time, though all they have done is talk about themselves and been truly heard.

To get ready to do the Law Pause exercise below, think about a time when someone did not listen to you. Perhaps you were waiting in a doctor's office for thirty minutes only to have the doctor rush in, ask a question but not hear the answer, then waltz out just as quickly.[29] How did this make you feel?

Studies show that most people find lawyers to be aloof, arrogant, users of jargon, expensive, conceited, and so on.[30] Listening well is one way to counter these beliefs, at least as they apply to you. Good listening skills have always been critical to good lawyering. There is even a blog about listening by Professor Jennifer Murphy Romig at Emory University School of Law, called *Listen Like a Lawyer*, where she collects and discusses research, articles, checklists, and other resources to help lawyers, law professors, and law students to improve their listening skills.

---

[29] GERALD A. RISKIN, THE SUCCESSFUL LAWYER 52 (ABA 2005).   [30] *Ibid.*

To show you are both listening and hearing, engage in active listening. To actively listen, take notes, make lots of eye contact, and verbally restate back in your own words what you think the other person said so you can make sure you fully understand. Many who experience this approach to active listening say it is the first time they have ever felt truly heard.

We also need to cultivate the ability to listen not just for facts, but also for emotions. Remember the student whose parents had a bad lawyer, who was deemed bad solely because he did not allay the fears of his clients? He was not really listening, even if he could parrot back what the clients were saying. That is because he was not listening for his clients' emotions, perspectives, or points of view. Sure, the lawyer heard the facts, but the student's parents were not *heard*.

While you are listening for facts, also listen for emotions. When dealing with a client, for example, see if you can relay back to the client what the client said, but also what you think he or she is feeling as well, not just what happened. If you get it wrong, ask for clarification until you get those feelings right. Then, as recommended in *The Successful Lawyer*, show that you understand how the other person feels and, importantly, let that person know you do understand. Finally, don't be afraid of silence. Try as hard as you can (and this is so difficult) not to talk over people and fill in the silence gaps. Let it be about them, not you. Let the other person have space to communicate and actually be *heard*.

Focus on People Not Electronic Devices

Be particularly aware of device distraction. Others know when you are not fully present, so watch this very carefully. For extra motivation, go back and read the story about Malcolm Smith and Thomas Golisano in Chapter 2, and the *New Yorker* cartoon in Chapter 1.

When it comes to clients in particular, you will want to let them know that you understand how badly they want a particular result. Tell them that you are on their side and will do your very best to help in any way you can. If you do these things, you will be far more successful than the lawyers who don't. Here is an opportunity to practice these skills.

LAW PAUSE LISTENING EXERCISE

For the next couple of weeks, set aside five or ten minutes once a week to just sit and listen to another person – your friend at work, your parent or grandparent, your child. Take the posture of listening. Drop whatever you are doing, make eye contact, and face the person. Make it obvious that you are really listening. Repeat back some of what you think the person is saying, thinking, and feeling. Ask if you are right. Write a brief journal entry about the experience.

When we practiced this exercise in our first semester, first-year law class, the students relished being heard. If you follow through and do this exercise on your own, and you are very accomplished so if you put your mind to it you can, this might be the only time in weeks, months, or years that the other person has really been listened to.

One of my favorite stories about the power of listening comes from William Ury's book, *Getting to Yes with Yourself.* Ury, founder of the Harvard Project on Negotiation and a world-renowned negotiator, was once hired by the United Nations and former president Jimmy Carter to help resolve a political crisis in Venezuela. Millions of Venezuelans had taken to the streets to demand the removal of then president Hugo Chavez. Ury was asked to meet with Chavez to try to de-escalate the problem and avoid imminent civil war.[31]

To prepare, Ury went for a walk in the park to seek clarity. He began outlining the various recommendations he would offer to Chavez. Eventually, though, Ury's thinking became more clear and it occurred to him that it might be best to offer Chavez no advice at all. Ury's voice in his head told him: "Don't offer advice unless of course requested to do so. Just listen, stay focused on the present moment, and look for openings."[32]

When the meeting came, tensions were high. Ury thanked Chavez for meeting with him and broke the ice by asking about Chavez's daughter, who was about the same age as Ury's. Ury let the conversation unfold naturally from there, and Chavez began telling his personal story in great detail. He described his life, his passions, and the many political events in his life. Ury just listened. Finally, Chavez turned to Ury and said, "OK Professor Ury, what do you think of the conflict here in Venezuela?"[33]

Ury explained that he had worked as a third-party negotiator in many civil wars and that once bloodshed began, it was hard to stop. Ury said that he thought there was a great opportunity here to avoid civil war. When Chavez asked how, Ury said, "By talking to the opposition." This outraged Chavez, who considered these opponents traitors. Ury then went to the balcony, right there in the meeting, and focused on the present moment. Then this question occurred to Ury and he asked it: "What action if any could they possibly take tomorrow morning that would send you a credible signal that they were ready to change?" Eventually Chavez said, "Well they could stop calling me a mono (or monkey) on their TV stations. And they could stop putting uniformed generals on television calling for the overthrow of the government. That's treason!"[34]

Within minutes of this conversation, Chavez had designated a public official to develop a list of practical actions each party could take to build trust and de-escalate the crisis. Chavez even asked Ury to come back and meet with him regarding their

[31] William Ury, Getting to Yes with Yourself 89–90 (Harper One 2015).   [32] *Ibid.* at 90.
[33] *Ibid.* at 91.   [34] *Ibid.* at 91–92.

progress the very next day. A constructive process developed, which defused a grave political crisis affecting many millions of people. Ury reported that because he deliberately gave up the idea of giving advice and decided to just listen and stay in the present moment, he was able to help avert the crisis. Ury also claims that Chavez would likely have ejected Ury from the meeting within minutes if he had shown up with his list of recommendations instead. Ury used mindfulness to build a solution to a national and international crisis.[35]

Like Ury, you can choose to use mindfulness to further develop patience and listening skills. In mindful meditation, when a thought takes your attention away from the breath, you can acknowledge the thought and let it go, bringing your awareness back to the breath. You can do the same thing when practicing the listening exercise. Listen as long as you can and when an unrelated thought arises (and it will), bring your attention back to what the person is saying, repeating back some of those thoughts to see if you are getting them right. While listening, try to discipline yourself to *not* prepare your reply or response. Try to just sit and listen. Developing the capacity to really listen will help you well beyond the workplace. Imagine what this could do for your personal life.

While you are learning to listen better to other people, also listen to yourself, to what you are saying. Do people seem to care about what you are saying? Are you engaging them? Are they bored? Are *you* bored by what you are saying? What reactions are you creating in others and yourself?

Showing an Interest in Others by Avoiding Constant Talk About Yourself

Show an interest in others. This sounds easy and obvious, but is it? For most of us, it is often all about us, about how busy, stressed, or crazy we are. How many times have you heard "I am so busy" or "I am so stressed out?" This conversation starter rates right up there with "I am so tired." Incredibly boring.[36] When people start talking like that, most people just tune out. No one listens. No one cares.

Consciously try to put others before yourself. Start small, by choosing not to talk about how stressed, busy, and exhausted you are.

Little Pause: Try not to say "I am so busy," and try to limit these two phrases too: "I am so stressed" and "I am so tired." Every time you think about saying that, instead change that thought (or statement if you can't help yourself) to "I am so boring."

Instead, try replacing those phrases with something positive or engaging, such as: "I am happy to see you," "What have you been up to?" or "I worked on something cool the other day."

---

[35] *Ibid.* at 92–94.
[36] Michael Melcher, The Creative Lawyer 177 (2nd edn. American Bar Association 2014).

Experiencing Your Emotions

The next chapter covers this very broad topic in more depth, but know this: like writing on water, as Chade-Meng Tan says, you can't just *not have* the emotion. The emotion will come out some other way, and usually not in a good way or at a good time. Deep breathing, exercise, yoga, and meditation can help you to process your emotions, as can guided visualizations. Anger, in particular, causes all sorts of problems, including physical ones such as heart disease and heart attacks.

Little Pause: Think of a time when you got angry and the consequences were dire.

As *Star Wars* Jedi master Yoda famously said: "Anger leads to hate. Hate leads to suffering." Fortunately, anger can be neutralized with a little effort. Notice your own patterns for getting angry, and what triggers this. Keep a journal. Watch your words and avoid saying words such as "always" or "never," "must" or "can't," and other absolutes.[37] These absolutes will rarely be accurate, are often exaggerations, and can make your comments less credible.

PARTING WORDS ON EQ: GENERAL ACTS OF KINDNESS
AND CONSIDERATION THAT KEEP YOU SANE

We finish here with a few tips that show emotional intelligence and also will keep you happier.

1. Try to show up five or ten minutes early for every lunch, meeting, or commitment, and bring something to do while you wait. Don't expect to get in early. The point is to be prepared to wait. Being on time is one of the most powerful forms of respect you can show another person. I recall my mother-in-law saying, "I don't like to make other people wait for me." Wow, put in that light, "Sorry I will be ten minutes late" takes on a whole new meaning.

2. When nervous about a meeting, presentation, or an argument, remember that it is NEVER about you. Do what you can to allay your own fears, so you can focus on the point and on others. Some tips:
   • Go to sleep having written out and practiced your notes.
   • Set out your clothes the night before.
   • Practice with a friend.
   • Do some deep breathing.
   • Always keep in mind who and what this is all about and remember, it is not about you but the person you are serving.

3. Try not to overschedule. In the language of management science, you want to have valuable slack available. Recently, I was in the parking lot and saw a student I enjoy speaking with. I looked away to avoid being late for an appointment.

---

[37]   MICHAEL F. ROIZEN AND MEHMET C. OZ, YOU STRESS LESS 49 (SIMON AND SCHUSTER 2011).

Being that busy is being too busy! Try to leave enough space in your day to stop and talk to the people you run into. In the language of modern finance theory, try to make room to be able to exercise valuable real options. Leave time and space for serendipity. Many of the good things I have experienced in life have come in moments of unscheduled time.

10

Advanced Emotional Intelligence Skills

Nathalie Martin

This being human is a guest house
Every morning a new arrival.
A joy, a depression, a meanness,
some momentary awareness comes
as an unexpected visitor.

Welcome and entertain them all!
Even if they are a crowd of sorrows,
who violently sweep your house
empty of its furniture,
still treat each guest honorably.

He may be clearing you out for some new delight.
The dark thought, the shame, the malice,
meet them at the door laughing,
and invite them in.

Be grateful for whoever comes,
because each has been sent
as a guide from beyond.

                                                        Rumi

The Sufi poet Rumi states the truth when he says that "this being human is a guest house." We need to experience and welcome the full range of emotions if we are to truly live. In this chapter, we discuss some of the most complex emotional intelligence skills, including processing emotions, practicing nonjudgment, dealing with difficult people, and forgiving others. Everyone who is fully alive struggles with these issues. Indeed, many of the authors who share advice on these subjects admit that they write about these topics because the issues challenge them. Many of the world's greatest leaders exhibit these advanced emotional intelligence skills, while at the same time struggling with them. I guess that means, just like the rest of us, they are human.

As in the last chapter, it is helpful to see difficult situations as opportunities. We now turn to the topics of practicing nonjudgment, processing our emotions, dealing with difficult people, and forgiveness. Like the subjects of Chapter 9, these skills build on one another, in roughly the order in which they are presented here.

LEARNING TO RECOGNIZE AND PRACTICE NONJUDGMENT

What is love?
Love is the absence of judgment.

Dalai Lama

LAW PAUSE

Think of a time when someone judged you and the person was incorrect about that judgment. What made the person judge, and did he or she find out that the judgment was incorrect? How?

Now think of a time you incorrectly judged someone. How did you find out the judgment was incorrect?

Reserving judgment whenever possible makes us more astute because we assume less, we are open to the truth, and we miss fewer facts. Nonjudgment, however, is hard work. Watch your thoughts throughout the day and you see the extent to which we judge.

Telling a lawyer not to judge is like telling a bird not to fly. Nevertheless, if we can withhold judgment, even some of the time, we can achieve better results as attorneys. Consider this parable:

> There once was a man whose ax was stolen and he suspected that his neighbor's son stole it. The boy walked like a thief, looked like thief, and spoke like a thief. But one day, the man found his ax while digging in his valley, and the next time he saw his neighbor's son, the boy walked, looked, and spoke like any other child.[1]

By reserving judgment when possible, we can increase our capacity to practice law successfully, and also improve relationships with others. We can also become happier. To this end, you might have at least two questions:

1 How can *just* practicing mindful nonjudgment improve so many facets of life and make me more successful as a lawyer?
2 Wait just a minute here. I am at the beginning of my career, preparing to become a lawyer, and I am *not* supposed to judge? I am studying to become a lawyer but I

---

[1] WAYNE MULLER, HOW THEN SHALL WE LIVE? 15–16 (BANTAM BOOKS 1994).

shouldn't judge? In fact, many of us will even become judges, yet we are now going to train ourselves not to judge? Isn't this our job as lawyers, to differentiate, to discern, to judge?

To the first question, there is nothing minimal about *just* learning to practice mindful nonjudgment. It is not *just* learning one little thing, it is learning one small thing that can, in turn, create seismic shifts in thinking and being.

To the second question, no, it is not your job to judge. It is your job to do your best, by serving people and getting to know those people as best you can, in order to achieve the best results for them. Judging impedes this process.

Some Practical Lessons in Nonjudgment

It is helpful, where possible, to assume that people who think and feel differently from you are just different, not flawed human beings. Yet many of us attribute differences to flaws, rather than just being different. If someone is unique in certain ways, we often look at that as a negative, rather than something out of the ordinary. It can be hard not to assume negative things about people with whom we disagree, so we turn the tables and judge them, focusing on their differences as flaws or, at the very least, flawed behaviors.

Practicing nonjudgment means not being judgmental. This involves observing a situation and describing it in our minds or on paper, but not attaching an adjective to it, or giving it a "yes" or "no," or a good or bad ranking. Nonjudgment means describing something but not always noting if we like it or not, just noting and observing. Rather than judging, we are better served in our profession by looking at each situation with fresh eyes, with a beginner's mind, and with the open-hearted acceptance to see, as if for the first time, what is now before us.

This is a tall order for most of us. Most of us feel that *it is our job* to straighten out the world, and in many ways, this is our job, but not until we have observed, listened, and taken stock of each new situation, without jumping to conclusions and without judging.

Jack Kornfield, in *After the Ecstasy, the Laundry*, tells the story of a military officer who was studying meditation for stress reduction.[2] On his way home from class, he stopped at a supermarket and stood in line behind a woman with a baby, buying just one item. She could have just as easily used the express lane and gotten out of his way. It really annoyed the officer that he had to wait for her before he could check out. Worse yet, she and the clerk were delaying things further by chatting, and the customer even handed the clerk the baby to

[2] JACK KORNFIELD, AFTER THE ECSTASY, THE LAUNDRY: HOW THE HEART GROWS WISE ON THE SPIRITUAL PATH 244–45 (BANTAM 2001).

hold at one point! The officer tried to use the class lessons to allay his anger, breathe deeply, and calm down, noticing for the first time that the baby was cute. When he reached the clerk, he commented, "Cute boy," at which point the clerk told him that the woman was her mother and that the baby was hers. Her mom was bringing the baby by to say hi. Kornfield's example shows that we don't know what is actually going on in another person's life. As a result, judging others creates incorrect information and inappropriate emotions.

Judging Dog Owners: An Example

Judgment is everywhere. I seem to have a long history of judging people for the way in which they treat their pets. For a long time, I judged people for leaving their dogs outside, until I found myself with a dog that preferred to stay outside when no one was home. Then I judged people who kept their dogs in cages or crates, until I had a dog that enjoyed her crate. A close relative judged people who left dogs inside and walked them on leashes. After all, a dog should be free to walk around, right? Once again, judging creates misinformation and inappropriate emotions.

People judge certain breeds of dogs. In some cases this is justified and in others, it is not justified. Recently I found a puppy, a five-week-old Pitbull, who was shivering in the dark at 10 p.m. in November, standing in my neighbor's driveway. This was not the neighbor's puppy, but rather an abandoned puppy. She was absolutely beautiful but my older dog did not appreciate her. As a result I set out to find a home for the new puppy. Many people were interested and she ultimately found a wonderful home.

Not long afterwards, I ran into the neighbors in whose driveway I found the puppy. They had heard that I found her a home and told me that she had been hanging around their yard and home but bothered their older dog. I asked them if, once they discovered that she could not get along with their dog, they just put her back outside at 10.30 at night? They said yes dismissively, as if to say, "Of course, she was a Pitbull. Who cares?"

Having spent money on vaccination shots and two days finding the puppy a new home, I was angry and surprised. These neighbors are dog-friendly and their dog is part of their family. I know that not everyone feels this way about dogs but these people do. Judgment literally took me over. I could not believe what I was hearing, and then realized I was witnessing discrimination between dog breeds. They did not feel that a Pitbull puppy was worth saving.

Still, why is it my right to judge that? Was this my jurisdiction? I do not save every stray dog I see and I certainly do not try to catch every dog I see running in the street. What gave me the right to judge them?

More critically, how, why, and when should I stop?

Practicing Nonjudgment

In our society, and perhaps in all societies throughout the millennia, the brain automatically judges things as good or bad, right or wrong, fair or unfair, important or unimportant, urgent or non-urgent, and so on.[3] This happens so fast that if we don't work at it, we never get to experience life without judgment. Indeed, we lose the present moment, the only thing we ever really have, the only time we really live. Our experiences become a series of comparisons, automatically colored by judgment, which changes and distorts our present-moment perceptions.

This reality is bad for good lawyering. When we judge, we do not experience reality, but rather the judgment, good or bad, right or wrong. We will talk about what to do when we know something is truly wrong later in this section, and also how to differentiate, but the only way to truly live your life to the fullest is to cultivate nonjudgmental awareness.

If you watch your mind at work, you will notice yourself judging virtually everything you encounter. We judge experiences, other people, ourselves, foods, interactions, drivers, music, everything and anything. We label each of them good or bad as we move on to the next thing. Even while attempting to read the first few pages of this chapter, some of you liked what you read while others did not. We "like" or "don't like" online products or services, and even the comments made by others.[4] That is a lot of judgment.

How different would our lives be if we dropped this automatic judging and experienced life as it rolled out? What would it be like to just live, listen, and see, if we were able to see judgmental thoughts, and then replace them with nonjudgmental observations? We could then bring awareness to the present moment so we could live in that moment. We could bring intentionality to our lives, and live and experience each new moment rather than sleepwalking through comparisons to the past and anticipations of the future.

We can become aware of our judgments first just by watching them come and go. Then we can slow the judgments and even stop them in cases where they do not serve us. As Dr. Elisha Goldstein explains in a Huffington Post blog:

> Be aware when the brain is automatically judging a situation or a person, and we can pause and get some perspective. Was this judgment just something that popped in my mind? Is there another way I can see this? Is the checkout person in the checkout line just a checkout person or someone with their own history or triumphs, perceived failures, moments of adventure, and wanting the same things I do, to be understood and cared about?

---

[3] Elisha Goldstein, Ph.D., *What Is Non-Judgmental Awareness, Anyway?*, Huffington Post the Blog, May 3, 2013, available at www.huffingtonpost.com/elisha-goldstein-phd/non-judgmental-aware ness_b_3204748.html.

[4] Leo Babauta, *Practicing Non-Judgment*, Zen Habits, May 15, 2015, available at https://zenhabits.net/ dislike/.

Bringing mindfulness to life means being alive. It allows us to bring back the choice and wonder that is inherent in everyday life.[5]

Try for a brief time, say five minutes, to just note things around you. Be aware of your thoughts and try not to judge things and people around you; instead just experience them for what they are. Try not to think about whether something you see or hear is good or bad. Instead, just observe the sensations of the moment. Don't label them good or bad, pleasant or unpleasant – just experience them. Now write down a few observations about this exercise.

In the exercise above, we asked you to dedicate just five minutes to nonjudgmental awareness. Some teachers may ask you not to judge for one day, but a whole day without judging may be a bit much as a place to start. Try the five minutes and work your way up. Nonjudgment is challenging. Start small. It is freeing and can quickly become habit-forming, but not overnight.

The Ego and Judgment

You may have more difficulty not judging given your chosen profession. Even if you are just beginning your studies, the law often attracts people with high goals and strong egos. Big goals are critical and you can achieve them (see Chapters 16–17), but your ego might need to be taken down a notch if you are going to do so. If the ego is too strong, you can get in your own way, end up serving only yourself, and have difficulty finding larger purpose or meaning.

Judgment and Separation

Judgment separates us from ourselves and what we are judging. If a situation arises and we judge it as bad, we separate ourselves from that situation. Through nonjudgment, we realize that we are not separate from the situation at all. In fact, we are a part of that situation. Whatever needs to be done to make the situation right will flow naturally from us and others. Right action will just happen. Forgive the passive voice, but I really am asking you to let go here. Let it happen, as in the song, "Let it go" from the movie, *Frozen*. Become one with the whole messy situation and watch what happens without judgment.

The ego loves to judge things because, as said above, the judging is what keeps that separate little voice going, what keeps it alive. This is just the mind again, not you,

---

5   Elisha Goldstein, Ph.D., *What Is Non-Judgmental Awareness, Anyway?*, HUFFINGTON POST THE BLOG, May 3, 2013, available at www.huffingtonpost.com/elisha-goldstein-phd/non-judgmental-aware ness_b_3204748.html.

conjuring up those judgments. You can actually stop the judging if you practice enough, and there is a nice silver lining to all that work. When you find a relaxed state of nonjudgment,[6] you enjoy life more.

Judgment separates us from the present, and from other people. It causes us to see people and events in the light in which we have categorized them, and not as they really are. We are blinded to actual reality. We separate ourselves from a particular person or event, and from this moment in time.

Little Pause: Think about this: if you judge a person, that person becomes a non-person They become a concept or an archetype.

There is that separation again. That person is no longer who he or she actually is, but something you have conjured up instead. If you do not judge the people you run across in your life, but instead just let them be who they are, you will receive a better outcome with less suffering, stress, and pain. And *a lot* less work! You will gain a better understanding of the other person and of what needs to be done and does not need to be done. You may be trying to change things you don't need to take on, things outside your jurisdiction.

Nonjudgment applies to clients and adversaries, not to mention children and partners. You will achieve more and be much happier if you train yourself not to judge others. You will see the real people before you, understand them better, listen more and better, and achieve a better outcome for everyone involved.

Little Pause: Practice looking at an object and just noting its attributes. Forget what you like or dislike, or whether the object is good or bad, pretty or ugly, worthless or valuable. Just look at it without judgment or mental labeling. As Adam Oakley explains, you might be able to actually see stillness emanating from that object.[7] Chances are, if you get to this point, you will notice stillness in yourself at the same time. That is because you and the object are not separate after all.

What if you don't like a situation or a person and have labeled that situation or person negatively? Labeling will not do anything to improve the situation, though taking action might. If you need to do something to make things better, go ahead by all means. If you are going to act, do not bother to label, as labeling will get in the way of what needs to be done. Labeling is baggage. As explained by Leo Babauta, these sensations and even your thoughts are just:

> phenomena in the world, happening without any good or bad intention, just happening. They aren't happening "to" us, nor are they there "for" us. They just happen, without thinking about us as the center of the universe.
>
> What I've noticed, when I experience anger, frustration, disappointment . . . is that I am judging my experiences (and others, and myself) based on whether they are what I want, whether they are good for me or not. But why am I at the center of

6   Leo Babauta, *Practicing non-judgment*, ZEN HABITS, May 15, 2015, available at https://zenhabits.net/
     dislike/.
7   Adam Oakley, *Inner Peace Poetry, on Inner Peace, the Self, Life and Human Nature*, available at
     www.goodreads.com.

the universe? What about the other person? What about the rest of the universe? If I drop away my self-centeredness, I no longer have reason for frustration. The experiences are just happening, and have nothing to do with me. They are neither good nor bad, they're just happening.[8]

Just by reading this section, judgment is likely loosening its grip on you. Let it. When others judge, note it and let it go, moving on to the next moment. Don't judge others for judging and don't jump in and participate – just observe it, and let it go.

LEARNING TO BOTH WELCOME AND PROCESS OUR EMOTIONS

All emotions serve a purpose, which is why we need to welcome them in the way that the mystic poet Rumi suggests. Go back to the beginning of this chapter and read that poem again. We welcome some emotions more than others, but we need to feel them all in order to process them. We need to experience all emotions, even the difficult ones such as sadness, anger, loneliness, even depression. These emotions tell us about our current lives, something we can learn from. It is important, as Chade-Meng Tan says in *Search Inside Yourself*, to have and really feel all emotions.[9]

> Screenwriter and creativity teacher Barnet Bain explains that creativity is unleashed when we allow ourselves to deeply and intensely feel a negative emotion, consciously let it go, and then replace it with a positive emotion.[10] How do you know you have fully experienced an emotion? You force yourself to sit with it long enough to get very, very sick of it. Usually ninety seconds works well.
>
> Ignored emotion = negative emotion = repetitious negative emotion
> Any acknowledged and felt emotion = a positive emotion
>
> As Bain further explains, there is no such thing as a bad emotion except for the emotion we refuse to actually feel. The unfelt and unacknowledged emotion is bad because it causes us ongoing pain and suffering. It never works its way through our system. It just keeps cycling through our heads, time after time after time.[11]

We can't ignore emotions, otherwise they will pop out at an inopportune time, taking control of us in ways few of us enjoy. That creates an irony. Some of the most emotional people may actually be less in touch with their emotions than the quiet ones among us. Highly emotional people can be so unfamiliar with the boundaries

---

[8] *Ibid.*   [9] CHADE-MENG TAN, SEARCH INSIDE YOURSELF 105–107 (HARPER ONE 2012).
[10] BARNET BAIN, THE BOOK OF DOING AND BEING: REDISCOVERING CREATIVITY IN LIFE, LOVE, AND WORK 93–96 (ATRIA 2015).
[11] *Ibid.* at 93–95.

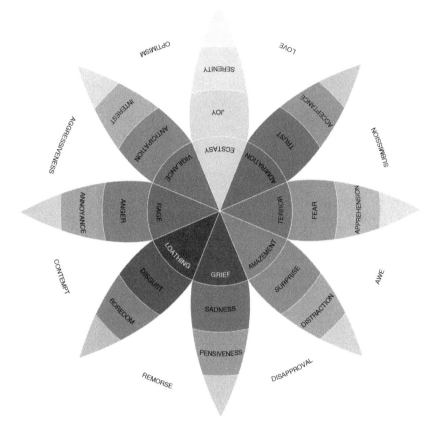

FIGURE 10.1 *Robert Plutchik's Wheel of Emotions, Plutchik-wheel de.svg*, WIKIMEDIA COMMONS.[12]

of their emotions that when those emotions come out, the person has no idea what to do. The person can be as surprised about what transpires as are observers.

We won't talk about the entire spectrum of emotion here, but please take a few minutes to look at Plutchik's wheel, pictured in Figure 10.1. Human beings have the capacity to experience a wide range of emotions, as this emotional intelligence visual aid shows.[13]

---

[12] Robert Plutchik, *Robert Plutchik's Wheel of Emotions, Plutchik-wheel de.svg*, WIKIMEDIA COMMONS, available at https://commons.wikimedia.org/wiki/File:Plutchik-wheel_de.svg. This file is ineligible for copyright and therefore in the public domain because it consists entirely of information that is common property and contains no original authorship.

[13] www.theatlantic.com/health/archive/2014/02/new-research-says-there-are-only-four-emotions/283560/. Psychologists and scientists originally recognized six essential emotions – joy, surprise, fear, anger, sadness, and disgust. Now scientists think there may be just four primary emotions – joy, sadness, fear, and surprise. Either way, these primary emotions give context to the emotion wheel.

LAW PAUSE

Bring to mind a recent unpleasant situation you endured, and identify the emotions you feel or felt on Plutchik's wheel. Now try that with a pleasant situation.

I love this wheel. I love to ask students how they feel when certain situations come up, to ask them not to respond but just notice what is coming up. You can also take a look at the atlas of emotions found at this website: www.huffingtonpost.com/paul-ekman/introducing-the-atlas-of-_b_9939728.html.

Experiencing an emotion will change your present moment for better or for worse. Through your own mental resolve, once you have experienced and identified an emotion you can often move a negative emotion such as rage, grief, or loathing, from the center circle of emotions into the emotions found in the middle area of the chart, meaning anger, disgust, or sadness. You may even be able to neutralize that emotion out into the outer circle of emotions, such as annoyance, boredom, and pensiveness. After enough observation and experience with these emotions, they may eventually be felt only briefly and then just go away, almost on their own.

You can also neutralize an emotion by bringing its opposite emotion to mind. This is harder to do but give it a try if you like a challenge. You can only successfully replace the negative emotion with a positive one *after* you have allowed yourself to truly feel the original emotion, even if just for a few seconds.

Sometimes it is important to neutralize an emotion on the spot, to protect your client and yourself. After all, it is always best *not* to be the one who blows up or breaks down in public.[14] The Law Pause below suggests another effective way to neutralize anger, from Mirabai Bush, in her CD, *Mindfulness at Work*.[15]

LAW PAUSE

The ninety-second feel: Bring a recent situation to mind that made you really angry. Set a timer for ninety seconds. Tighten your fists as much as you can. Force yourself to feel that anger as hard and as much as you possibly can, for the full ninety seconds. Do not let go and keep squeezing. At ninety seconds, release the fist and release the thought. Pretty cool, right?

You can try this with sadness too if you, like me, are more prone to sadness than anger. You can also try it with any circular, repetitive, negative thought. It is amazing how sick of that emotion or thought you can become after ninety seconds.

From here we will briefly discuss dealing with two emotions that, if left unchecked, will likely interfere with your lawyering capacities – anger on the one

[14] Randi McGinn, Changing Laws, Changing Lives 137, 139 (Trial Guides LLC 2014) (discussing her "no crying in court" rule).
[15] Mirabai Bush, Working with Mindfulness Audio CD (2012).

hand, and sadness or depression on the other. As attorneys, we want to be the strong ones upon whom others can rely. We need to be able *not* to jump into the emotional tornado with our clients.

Dealing with Anger

Like all other emotions, anger is sending a message. In his book, *Overcoming Destructive Anger: Strategies That Work*, Bernard Golden explains that anger lets us know that we are suffering from distress, and can motivate us to address our underlying needs, desires, or perceived threats.[16] Because *unprocessed* anger often leads to "conflict, social isolation, problems at work, substance abuse, depression, shame, and even incarceration," Golden describes what triggers anger, how it affects our bodies and our minds, and what we can do to manage it. According to Golden, we all feel anger. Some people are biologically or socially predisposed to feel more anger than others, but we all feel anger and deal with it somehow, often through one of three unconstructive ways: to get outright aggressive, to get passive aggressive, or to turn that anger on ourselves.[17]

Golden offers the following tips, but if anger is an issue for you, his entire book is worth reading:

1. Manage your expectations. Try to figure out what expectations you have of others and study those. For example, Golden says, you may feel that your friends should always be available to help when you need them, or that you should never have to feel the effects of aging. Obviously expectations like these will lead to disappointment because they are unrealistic.

2. Assess how you appraise or view a triggering event. We often attribute much deeper meaning to events than these events actually have. This occurs most when we are focused exclusively on ourselves and our own needs and insecurities, rather than also considering the needs and insecurities of others. Golden uses the example of a spouse who comes home late from work. This lateness feels disrespectful to the spouse waiting at home, unless you consider it from the late, stuck-in-traffic spouse's point of view. Getting caught in traffic is a real pain!

3. Consider whether the anger is connected to some other emotion or event, or perhaps even hiding a more subtle emotion such as sadness, hurt, disappointment, anxiety, embarrassment, shame, loneliness, or even depression. Golden suggests we use mindfulness to identify the emotions underlying the anger, more specifically, mindfulness meditation, self-compassion, and self-awareness, to get to the root or real cause of the anger.[18]

---

[16] Bernard Golden, Overcoming Destructive Anger: Strategies That Work (John Hopkins University Press 2016).
[17] *Ibid.*   [18] *Ibid.*

> You can choose how you respond to a particular event or emotion.

There is a physiological reaction to every emotion we experience. Every emotion carries with it a physiological response, and scientists have had a heyday studying those responses. Studies show that mindfulness helps us differentiate between different emotions and as a result, better regulate negative emotions. In one study, Daphne Davis and Jeffrey Hayes found that high levels of mindfulness predict "relationship satisfaction, ability to respond constructively to relationship stress, skill in identifying and communicating emotions to one's partner, amount of relationship conflict, negativity, and empathy."[19] In addition, "people with higher trait mindfulness reported less emotional stress in response to relationship conflict and entered conflict discussion with less anger and anxiety."[20]

The Importance of Self-Compassion

While we have talked at length about mindfulness and meditation, and indirectly about self-awareness, we have not (until now) broached the subject of self-compassion – kindness toward one's self. Like many other topics in this book, I find self-compassion to be difficult. Self-compassion, however, may be the most useful skill you can develop.

Kristen Neff's book, *Self-Compassion: The Proven Power of Being Kind to Yourself*, is packed with useful self-compassion lessons.[21] Neff's extensive research on self-compassion shows that it increases emotional resilience and stability, and decreases negative self-evaluations, defensiveness, and the need to see oneself as better than others.[22] Neff's work compares self-esteem with self-compassion and finds that self-compassion creates more benefits and fewer detriments (such as judgment) than mere self-esteem.[23] Self-compassion was found to provide a stronger buffer than self-esteem on other dimensions as well. In contrast to people with high self-esteem, for instance, self-compassionate people were less likely to compare themselves to others. They were also less likely to get angry at others for perceived offenses.

Self-compassion reduces negative association with self-focused emotions such as public self-consciousness or self-rumination.[24] People high in self-compassion also thought about negative events in ways that reduce the effects of these negative

---

[19] Daphne M. Davis and Jeffrey A. Hayes, *What Are the Benefits of Mindfulness? A Practice Review of Psychotherapy-Related Research*, 48 AMERICAN PSYCHOLOGICAL ASSOCIATION 198, 201 (2011).

[20] *Ibid.*

[21] KRISTEN NEFF, SELF-COMPASSION: THE PROVEN POWER OF BEING KIND TO YOURSELF 85–88 (MORROW 2011).

[22] Kristin D. Neff, *Self-Compassion, Self-Esteem, and Well-Being*, 5/1 SOCIAL AND PERSONALITY PSYCHOLOGY COMPASS 1, 1 (2011).

[23] *Ibid.* at 6–7.   [24] *Ibid.*

events,[25] and self-compassionate participants had more thoughts reflecting self-kindness, common humanity, and mindful acceptance.[26] All of this helps process and neutralize our anger and leads to greater professional success, not to mention happiness.

You will make mistakes in your life. That means you will need both humility and self-compassion. How will you choose to respond to your mistakes? With self-compassion? With humility? With defensiveness? With worthwhile knowledge from which you can learn? With hubris? While mistakes are our quickest path to self-improvement, few of us learn from them. Most of us are too stubborn. Making mistakes is human. Put simply, mistakes happen, but the pain does not have to be wasted. We can live and learn. Often the seemingly biggest mistakes come with huge rewards.

LAW PAUSE

Write a few sentences about a big mistake that ended up creating huge personal rewards for you.

My friend and collaborator, Bonnie Bassan, says that every time she makes a mistake, she tells herself, "I'm sexy," a tip she learned from a life coach. The idea is to accept that you will make mistakes and not beat yourself up over it. You can also just tell yourself, "Thank goodness I made that mistake. Now I can learn something that will really help me in my life."

Dealing with Really Hard Times: Sadness and Depression

There is a big difference between sadness and depression. Sadness is a normal human emotion.[27] We all experience sadness in response to difficult, hurtful, challenging, or disappointing events, experiences, or situations. In other words, we tend to feel sad *about something*. These feelings of sadness come and go. We adjust to the cause or come to terms with the cause, and the sadness eventually disappears.

Depression, on the other hand, is an *abnormal* emotional state, a mental illness that affects our thinking, emotions, perceptions, and behaviors in pervasive and chronic ways. When we're depressed we feel sad about *everything*. Depression is not necessary triggered by an event. It is a general malaise that permeates our very beings. Experts say that experiencing five of these at a time indicate that one is likely to be depressed and could use professional help:

---

[25] *Ibid.* at 8.   [26] *Ibid.*
[27] Guy Winch, Ph.D., *The Important Difference Between Sadness and Depression*, Psychology Today Blog, Oct. 2, 2015, available at www.psychologytoday.com/blog/the-squeaky-wheel/201510/the-impor tant-difference-between-sadness-and-depression.

1. A depressed or irritable mood most of the time.
2. A loss or decrease of pleasure or interest in most activities, including ones that had been interesting or pleasurable previously.
3. Significant changes in weight or appetite.
4. Disturbances in falling asleep or sleeping too much.
5. Feeling slowed down in your movements or restless most days.
6. Feeling tired, sluggish, and having low energy most days.
7. Having feelings of worthlessness or excessive guilt most days.
8. Experiencing problems with thinking, focus, concentration, creativity, and the ability to make decisions most days.
9. Having thoughts of dying or suicide. [28]

While everyone feels sad from time to time, depression is also common in our culture. Between 6 and 7 percent of the US population suffers from it. Among lawyers, 24 percent are clinically depressed, and among women lawyers, 41 percent report being clinically depressed. Chronic depression must be treated by a health-care professional. This is obviously a serious occupational hazard.

Thinking about this distinction between sadness and depression, read this poem by Adam Oakley. Do you think he is describing depression or sadness?

> What if you were born into a world that told you this:
> "There will be a time when depression comes for you.
> It doesn't always come for everyone, but if it comes for you, we want you
>   to be aware of it.
> When it does come, if it does come, then tell us.
> We will arrange a party.
> We hope, dearly, that one day the depression will come.
> The heaviness, the lethargy, the sadness, the sense of being tired of life.
> If that comes for you, my dear, then you will have made it.
> That depression is the pinnacle of the human existence.
> If it comes for you, you are the blessed chosen one, and together we can
>   celebrate as a family, that you are finally depressed.
> You've made it.
> Congratulations."
>
> Adam Oakley[29]

I read this poem to remind myself that sadness will pass. The poem also makes me wonder if the studies about lawyer depression are really about lawyer sadness. Sadness is natural but depression is not. Sadness comes and goes, but depression does not.

---

[28] *Ibid.*

[29] Adam Oakley, *Yes! I'm Finally Depressed*, INNER PEACE NOW, Nov. 15, 2016, available at https://medium.com/@InnerPeaceNow/yes-im-finally-depressed-735c3cc12fd5.

We all get sad for short spurts now and then. I am generally optimistic and cheerful, but found grief, sadness, despair, and even depression after losing two parents within one year. The best thing I have found to feel better is to let the feelings come and to welcome them in, just as Rumi said. There are times when I do not want to do this, when I literally assume that letting these feelings in will simply overtake me, so that I can never come back. In those cases, I push the feelings away. But they come back even stronger, so it seems best to just sit with them. Letting them in prevents a public sneak attack.

Depression or at least sadness will come for you, as it does for all of us. How will you react? If you allow yourself to truly experience the sadness rather than pushing it away, you can process the sadness and keep it from materializing into that more constant state of being called depression. You may even decide to create a ritual around letting sadness come to you. For example, George Washington School of Law Professor Todd Petersen suggests creating a "sad" playlist to listen to, when you need to work through and truly experience sadness. He also suggests that you ask yourself, "Why am I sad? What is the triggering effect?"[30] This practice reminds us that sadness will come and go, along with its trigger.

Three weeks after my dad's death, I suffered the loss of a pet, and I am a huge animal lover. With no children to distract, a dead father, and a dead cat, I was in a bad way.

Believe it or not, even these sad events have a silver lining. It is difficult to have true empathy, as opposed to sympathy, for someone who is going through something you yourself have not experienced. My empathy has increased, a silver lining indeed. As German philosopher, Friedrich Nietzsche and others have said, "That which does not kill us, makes us stronger."[31] It will work in the same way for you as well, when those hard times hit. It is good to be prepared and to know in advance that "the only way out is through."

THE LAWYER'S DICHOTOMOUS RELATIONSHIP
WITH THE EMOTIONS OF CLIENTS AND CASES

Up to now, we have been talking about self-awareness and processing emotions. Now we turn briefly to our obligation to respond to the emotions of clients. When dealing with the emotions arising in relationships with clients and others in our cases, which we'll call "case emotions," we need to delicately balance expressing empathy with clients with not getting sucked into the drama. Attorney analyst and

---

[30]   Telephonic Interview with Todd Petersen, June 21, 2017.
[31]   *What Doesn't Kill You Makes You Stronger*, THE BEST BRAIN POSSIBLE, Sept. 12, 2014, available at www .thebestbrainpossible.com/what-doesnt-kill-you-makes-you-stronger/; *see also* Kelly Clarkson, *Stronger (What Doesn't Kill You)*, available at www.youtube.com/watch?v=Xn676-fLq7I.

emotional intelligence expert Randy Kiser refers to lawyers who skillfully strike this balance as "emotionally attentive" lawyers.[32]

To balance these emotional dichotomies, we need to first recognize that clients often *need* our emotional involvement, particularly in litigation. Clients in litigation need to know that we can feel emotions and that we empathize with their plight. One lawyer describes this as follows:

> People do not realize the emotional effect litigation has on clients. Young attorneys do not realize the damage that is done by having to relive the trauma of an emotionally devastating event like wrongful death. Humans have a capacity to mend, to recover over time, and litigation reopens memories that people are trying to recover from. They do not realize the damage they will do to their own clients even if they win. [Clients] have to relive all the painful events they are trying to put behind them. Most attorneys do not realize that winning is resolving a case earlier rather than winning at trial.[33]

Despite that much of law school is dedicated to teaching students how to repress emotions and focus only on logic, we need to be capable of expressing empathy.[34] You will still hear many lawyers in law offices questioning whether lawyers have any business expressing emotions, and insisting that lawyers must remain detached at all times. People who espouse this view often have difficulty developing relationships with clients, however, which is why some lawyers state the obvious in saying that "if you are not emotionally involved, your client is not getting your best effort."[35]

Once again, balance is key. It is important to be emotionally involved with clients, to listen and to welcome their feelings, while at the same time remaining detached enough to do your job. If you allow yourself to express more emotion than is desirable in the situation, you might get sidetracked and lose your concentration.[36] You need to be mindful and self-aware, be able to watch where your emotions are taking you, and be able to stop that emotional train.[37] As one attorney explains, in the context of medical malpractice cases:

> Maintaining a professional distance is important to accurate evaluation ... but a lawyer really serves two roles: that of an advocate, putting the client's best case forward to the outside world, and, on the other hand, serving as a neutral (this is the real point for evaluation) advisor about the likely outcome of the case. I am not sure

[32] Randall Kiser, *The Emotionally Attentive Lawyer: Balancing the Rule of Law with the Realities of Human Behavior*, 15 Nev. L. J. 442 (2015).

[33] *Ibid.* at 450.

[34] Melissa L. Nelken, *Negotiation and Psychoanalysis: If I'd Wanted to Learn About Feelings, I Wouldn't Have Gone to Law School*, 46 J. Legal Educ. 420, 421 (1996).

[35] Mark Curriden, *Lions of the Trial Bar: Joe Jamail*, A. B. A. J., Mar. 2009, at 32, 34.

[36] Randall Kiser, *The Emotionally Attentive Lawyer: Balancing the Rule of Law with the Realities of Human Behavior*, 15 Nev. L. J. 449 (2015).

[37] *Ibid.*

many lawyers appreciate this distinction or realize that they have these two roles that must be separated.

In the advocate's role, feeling the emotion of the case, even for a defendant who will not pay a dime [because of insurance coverage] if the case is lost, is important to the best advocacy. Letting oneself feel the emotion, without being overcome by it, helps trial advocacy. During almost every trial, I end up crying sometime, away from court, not because of unhappiness or fear of loss, but just from the over-whelming emotion I feel during trial. I don't know if I am unique in this respect. I do think some lawyers lose this as they age—a sort of cynicism can creep in. I consider myself lucky that I can genuinely feel the emotion in every case.[38]

While author and master trial attorney Randi McGinn has a very strict rule of "no crying in court" even for clients,[39] she acknowledges that everyone in the office cries outside the courtroom for the very same reason, to process overwhelming emotions that come up in trial. To ensure that she keeps her rule of not crying in court, she does the following:

How do you keep from crying in front of a jury when you are dealing with the saddest facts imaginable in a case? You cry the first day your client tells you about her lost child. You cry when you visit their home to see that, months or sometimes years after that child's death, her bedroom remains untouched, the same as it did the day she died. You cry at night when you are preparing your witnesses to testify at trial. And if you are still not cried out by the time you walk into the courtroom, you pinch yourself or bite the inside of your cheek until it bleeds to keep from crying in front of a jury before the verdict comes in.[40]

Overwhelming emotions will come up in many cases. After all, we are only human. At least I hope we are still human, despite being lawyers.

DEALING WITH DIFFICULT SITUATIONS AND DIFFICULT PEOPLE

Dealing with Difficult Situations

As Michael Melcher explains in *The Creative Lawyer*, every career has its trade-offs, as careers are *prix fixe*, not *à la carte*.[41] Every career has its benefits and rewards, but also its petty annoyances. There are no exceptions. Even a self-employed attorney who chooses her own cases must deal with some people she does *not* choose.

In any job, you will need to do things you don't want to do, be with people you don't particularly care for, and endure situations you'd rather avoid. Whether you are a doctor, an electrician, a television star, a cowboy, or a Supreme Court Justice, there will still be annoyances and annoying people at work. Melcher suggests you

---

[38]   *Ibid.* at 463.
[39]   Randi McGinn, Changing Laws, Changing Lives 137, 139 (Trial Guides LLC 2014).
[40]   *Ibid.* at 143.
[41]   Michael Melcher, The Creative Lawyer 61 (2nd Edn. American Bar Association 2014).

actually make a list of small job annoyances you can handle, even though you don't love them, to find the limits of your capacity to put up with these things and determine which annoyances are indeed minor and which are deal-breakers.[42] You may be leaving jobs that are not that bad, or putting up with things that anyone would find intolerable. Find out by thinking about your personal limits, making the list and creating the two categories.

LAW PAUSE

Make a list of annoyances in your life in general. Next to each one, write down how you might eliminate some of those. Now make a list of things that would be intolerable in life. Instead of listing annoyances in life in general, list annoyances in a job if you have one.

Lawyers have a great deal of autonomy and the power to help people in meaningful ways. Lawyers help when society is at its most needy, by acting in the face of injustice, and ensuring that groups of people, corporations, and governmental entities comply with the law. In many ways, the power, autonomy, intellectual challenge, access to other powerful people, and ability to change society is more available and accessible to lawyers than any other segment of society. Having said that, "law is not a happy-go-lucky profession."[43] You will often be dealing with people who are going through a great deal of pain. In order to make change and help people, you need to stand up for them and that means helping them with their problems. No one visits an attorney without a problem he or she can't solve alone. Being a lawyer is difficult work. Keeping your eye and focus on the positives can help you power through the negatives. So can a gratitude practice. See Chapter 18.

Dealing with People Who are Difficult to Love

Few things are more unpleasant than dealing with difficult people. We all know people like this.

LAW PAUSE

Think of a difficult person you know. Why is this person difficult? How is he or she difficult? What major differences do the two of you have? Is there a way to look at that situation without judging the other person?

Before we address how to deal with "difficult people," consider this story from Jack Kornfield's *After the Ecstasy*, in which he is discussing a nun's difficulty with two other nuns:

---

[42] *Ibid.*   [43] *Ibid.* at 65.

In my second community, there were only a dozen nuns. One was lazy and the other was self-absorbed. After my first year, I was in the kitchen complaining to a friend, who said, "You know these are really not bad people. What is it that gets to you?" I said "one is lazy and the other takes too much care of herself" and she replied, "Well you ought to be more lazy and take better care of yourself!"[44]

Little Pause: What does this story say to you?

Before we label someone as difficult, we should try to find our own part in the difficulty. It takes two to tango, as my mother-in-law used to say. For example, I am in sometimes in conflict with a colleague who is meticulous, detail-oriented and a strict follower of rules. I, on the other end of the spectrum, am flexible about almost everything, and am not a detail person, both sometimes to a fault. Is it a surprise that we are at odds?

Turning to your own situation, are you sure that the person(s) you are having difficulty with is / are the difficult one? Could you be the difficult person? Might you be part of the problem? Recall that fixing *part* of a problem is much better than fixing nothing at all.

LAW PAUSE

Pick out someone that you have had difficulties with at work, school, or in another setting. How do you two differ? Are there ways in which the problems are just a matter of style? Do others seem to get along fine with this person? Even if not, see if you can use this exercise to learn something new about yourself. Write a paragraph or two about these issues.

Sometimes people are just difficult for us to deal with, or for anyone to deal with, for that matter. Sometimes, admittedly rarely, it really is the other person and has nothing to do with you. In these situations, you should try not to be defensive in taking the other person's comments and actions personally. Try to differentiate between situations in which you are part of the problem and situations where the other person is just being difficult. Go back and reconsider the last Law Pause.

Assuming it is truly not you, and that the problem *is* the other person, consider these two questions:

1. What can you do to protect yourself without engaging in activity (or inactivity) that harms you or others?
2. Is there anything you can do to help the other person?

---

[44] JACK KORNFIELD, AFTER THE ECSTASY, THE LAUNDRY: HOW THE HEART GROWS WISE ON THE SPIRITUAL PATH 244 (BANTAM 2001).

Notice the order of the questions. Put your own mask on first before assisting others. If the answer to question two is no, and it is possible to limit your interactions with this person, disengage and don't look back.

Perhaps you cannot disengage because future interactions with this person are required. Try then to tell yourself that this person is difficult to love, but don't give up on them. Just don't spend much mental energy thinking about the person. Accept the situation for what it is and give it as little airtime as possible.

Dealing with Truly Difficult People

Perhaps you know someone that you cannot accept as he or she is, because the person is truly *harming* others, not just *annoying* them. Unfortunately, most of us know someone like this, a person so difficult and genuinely dysfunctional that no one gets along with him or her. Perhaps the person complains about most things, but will not work to improve anything. Perhaps the person is passive aggressive and even lies in wait, sabotaging situations by watching while mistakes are made, and not pointing them out until he or she can humiliate someone through the mistake. Know that most people who do these things are deeply unhappy, often lonely, people.

But suppose that you cannot simply disengage from this person because you need to have an ongoing relationship with him or her. You can control how you react. See if you can react with compassion. You have the capacity to react with the same unkindness that this person showed you, but then you have shown that you too are unhappy and lonely, or otherwise unsatisfied with your life. Alternatively, you have the capacity to react without much emotion at all, just with calm resolve. You can even reach out and match hostility with kindness. It is hard but you can do it.

One way to act with compassion is to help the person grow, while at the same time protecting yourself and your boundaries. This, however, requires calling out the person who is causing harm. I hate confrontation yet have found some degree of confrontation necessary in every job I have had. You cannot really succeed at anything until you can take on the bully. In *Coach Yourself to Success*, Talane Miedaner suggests calmly telling the bully that, "I am not sure if you realize it but you just raised your voice at me." In other words, politely call them out.

Miedaner actually has a whole system for taking on difficult people who make it a point to be challenging at work. She believes that if you implement the system, people will have more respect for you and also will stop making negative comments to you.[45] While this won't stop the person from doing negative things to others and

---

[45] Talane Miedaner, Coach Yourself to Success 15–19 (McGraw-Hill 2000). Miedaner does not call it a system, but it is one in my opinion.

being negative in general, a topic taken up below, her system for stopping the negativity directed at you is worth learning. She considers her "self-protection" system part of setting good boundaries, and suggests you use this system any time someone does something especially negative or hurtful.[46] Otherwise, she claims, you will waste a great deal of your time reliving that negative thing or comment. Miedaner suggests that rather than ignoring the slight, you gracefully and calmly do the following:

1. **Inform.** Say something like this: "Do you realize you are yelling?" "Do you realize that your comment hurt me?" "I really want to do my best work for you and I find that I work best when you point out my errors in a calm voice," or (and this one seems harsh to me but I share it anyway), "I didn't ask for your feedback." This step may put an end to the whole thing, but if not, move on to step 2.
2. **Request.** Ask the person to stop, by saying something like, "I ask that you stop yelling at me now," or "I ask that you give me only constructive feedback."

If that doesn't stop the behavior, move on to step 3.

3. **Demand or Insist.** Say "I insist that you stop yelling at me." If this doesn't work, move to step 4.
4. **Leave.** If step 3 does not work, leave without making any negative or snarky comments on your way out. Just say, "I can't continue this conversation while you are yelling at me. I am going to leave the room."

I don't know about you, but my own tendency is to leave without going through steps 1–3. In other words, I often just walk out, possibly pretending I have somewhere else to go. That approach lets the other person completely off the hook, puts the blame on me for acting childishly by not confronting the situation, and forces me to carry the burden for the exchange. The conversation plays and replays in my mind endlessly until even I get sick of it, but still can't get rid of it.

Miedaner insists that while you may think this direct approach will make people dislike you, it actually has the opposite effect. It makes people like and respect you more. She says that people know, on some level, when they are disrespecting you and do not want to get away with it. Also some people may not be aware of the effects their comments have on others, and that letting them know can actually help them.

Miedaner claims that her system is a powerful way to communicate. She asserts that communicating like this will make others want to be around you because they know exactly where they stand. She further claims that once people learn the technique, their boundaries are clear, they tend to get promoted and otherwise excel at work and life, while other people know and respect those boundaries.

---

[46] Miedaner actually suggests you use this system even for minor infractions. However, frequent use could be a waste of time and energy. If it is small, it might be best to let it go.

To make this practice work, however, Miedaner insists that you deliver the messages found in the four steps in a calm voice and that you allow the person you are speaking to a graceful exit. These two requirements are essential.

Calm Delivery

To deliver your message effectively, keep your voice calm and flat, and eliminate fire, judgment, or anger. Think of saying the four steps as ordinary facts, as if you were sharing something we all know, such as "the sky is blue." No excitement, no emotion, just neutrality. Miedaner also recognizes that tact is key. Try not to correct the person. Talk to him or her in private, rather than in a public meeting. Finally, be casual and don't make a big deal of it. Just be matter of fact.

As Part of Tact, Allow a Graceful Exit

Miedaner says that when you inform people, you need to allow them a graceful exit. This means that if they apologize, take it. Let them off the hook. If they don't apologize, go ahead and ask for one, but be sure to accept any apology you get.

Don't Wait, Do it Now

Again, bad news does not improve with time. The best time to have these conversations is now, in the present moment. Miedaner uses an example of a man who waited fifteen years to tell a cousin about a negative comment that bothered him. While catching the situation as it happens is by far the most effective, now is better than later, even if now is fifteen years after the fact. Without the conversation, the situation will never change.

LAW PAUSE

Think of a situation in which another person made a comment that really hurt you. Find a friend or family member and do a role-play. Pretend you are telling the person how you feel using steps 1–4. Use your calm voice and demeanor. If the role-play ends after step 1, which it likely will, ask your friend or family member to push a little harder until you have practiced more than one step. See how it feels to do this in a calm voice and to accept an apology.

Dealing with People Who Disturb and Harm Whole Workplaces

Difficult people who undermine an entire workplace are a breed unto themselves. In *The Successful Lawyer*, Gerald Riskin offers excellent advice for leaders dealing with difficult people who make a habit out of demoralizing others. He notes that often, in law firms, the difficult people are powerful senior partners at the top of the food chain. These bigwigs are tolerated (rather than removed from the firm) because they bring in so much money, meaning they contribute to the salaries of so many others at the firm. In some ways, these individuals can afford to be difficult because they do not need others to succeed. They feel they can do and say whatever they like, ignoring and demeaning others, and breaking rules.

Riskin found that these individuals sometimes fail to think before they speak, can be disruptive in meetings, and also demoralize other attorneys in the firm. They are often not collaborative, do not mentor or help others, and have horrible interpersonal skills. They may avoid group conversations where important decisions are made and then do what they like, even if this contradicts what the group decided.

Riskin suggests that another leader in the firm bite the bullet and communicate directly with the difficult person. There seems to be no other way. The leader should be patient, set aside extra time, and have these discussions with the difficult person before any important group meeting. The leader should ask directly if the difficult person has any concerns about the issues to be discussed at the upcoming meeting. Often the difficult person will open up with a huge number of concerns, which are good to know about in advance. These concerns will likely deal with threats to the difficult person's autonomy and fears that the group might curtail that autonomy. The person may be focused on their own needs alone, rather than the needs of the group.

Riskin suggests that the leader listen carefully and then agree that if a sensitive issue comes up, the leader will come back to the difficult person to check in and look for a mutually acceptable solution. After the leader makes that promise, he or she is in a position to exact a promise back in return from the difficult person. Riskin suggests this sort of conversation:

> You may not realize the persuasive power you have simply because of your seniority or by virtue of the practice you conduct. When you state a view or an opinion, it may have more force than if someone newer or more junior were to express the same opinion. Therefore I want to ask that you be careful not to express negative views or concerns in a way that might take the wind out of the sails of some of our junior people.

If the difficult person is senior, the leader might also add:

> Think back to when you were new. Think back to when a comment from a senior partner in the firm had a huge influence over you. Be guided by that as you think about what you say in the meeting.[47]

This might resonate even with difficult people. Some senior people may have forgotten what it was like to be junior and may not realize that what they say has tremendous influence. They may not know that their concerns or negativity could influence the group in a way that hurts everyone. The leader may need, however, to be even more blunt and say:

[47]   GERALD A. RISKIN, THE SUCCESSFUL LAWYER 151 (ABA 2005).

In exchange for the assurance I have given you, I'd like to ask that you refrain, if possible, from expressing negative views about where we are going as a group, because I think that may demoralize some of our junior people. I need their vigor, I need their best efforts, I need their peak performance, and candidly, I don't want anything to happen at the meeting that is going to detract from that. Is that fair?[48]

Some of these same techniques might apply to conversations you can have even when you are not the leader, especially when combined with Miedaner's four-step technique. Be calm and inform. Even if the difficult person does not need anyone's help to be professionally successful, he or she may be able to benefit from some enhanced interpersonal skills, especially if they have other relationships outside of work.

LAW PAUSE

Think about a truly difficult interpersonal situation. Ask yourself, "Who can do what today to move this conflict toward resolution?"[49] Write down a few words about your situation and your answer to the question.

Emotional intelligence matters, both at work and in other aspects of life. You do not want to be the difficult person. The difficult person is the one least sought out, the one least respected, and often, the difficult one has the least success. The good news is you can improve your emotional intelligence. Drawing again on the work of Carol Dweck in *Mindset: The New Psychology of Success*, emotional intelligence skills are not fixed but can grow and expand greatly.[50]

Recounting the stories in this sub-section, you'll note that very few junior people survive in law firms without emotional intelligence. Lawyers without these skills are let go. But that's not you. You may not be perfect but you are on the road to better interpersonal skills. Another one of these interpersonal skills is forgiveness.

Forgiveness

The weak can never forgive. Forgiveness is the attribute of the strong.

Gandhi

---

[48] *Ibid.*   [49] William Ury, Getting to Yes with Yourself 94 (Harper One 2015).
[50] Carol Dweck, Mindset: The Psychology of Success 7 (Ballantine Books 2006).

We are the primary beneficiaries of our choice to forgive. In *Getting to Yes with Yourself*, William Ury describes a situation in which a client claimed to get great pleasure from attacking an adversary. When Ury explored the issue a bit further, he saw that the client was being destroyed by his own anger, living in a resentful past, and behaving in self-destructive ways. When the client finally let go of the past and the constant temptation to keep reliving the injustices that he felt had been done to him, it completely changed his life. As Ury explains:

> Once my client was able to … settle his differences with his adversary, he told me he was a different man, feeling much lighter. Even his young children had noticed – and probably worried about – how much their father had been consumed by the conflict. When it ended, they saw, clearly relieved, a noticeable change in their father.

Failing to forgive is caustic. It interferes with our work, as well as our personal lives, yet there is a reason why forgiveness has been saved for our last conversation in this chapter. It is hard work to forgive. Like all negative emotions, a failure to forgive serves a purpose. Unforgiven acts allow us tell our story without taking full responsibility for our own actions, a form of denial that comes in handy. As long as it is someone else's fault, we don't need to address the problem. We can just let the blame lie elsewhere and live our comfortable lives, knowing "we have done our best." But have we?

In *After the Ecstasy, the Laundry*, Jack Kornfield describes a story in which soldiers rescue a man who was held in captivity during a war for decades by war criminals. The rescuers asked him, "Have you forgiven your captors?" and he said, "No, never." The soldiers then asked him, "So they still have you imprisoned then?"[51] Nelson Mandela said the same thing when, after his release from prison, then US President Bill Clinton asked Mandela if he hated his captors. Mandela said, "I felt hatred and fear but I said to myself, if you hate them when you get in that car, you will still be their prisoner. I wanted to be free so I let it go."[52]

Family situations are often the last ones we forgive. How many times have you heard people blame troublesome attributes of their adult self on their parents? Kornfield describes another situation in which a mindfulness teacher in an Indian ashram recalls his stepfather's harshness growing up. The teacher became aware that his stepfather's death was imminent and thankfully realized this about his stepfather:

> I realized that for all these years, he had tried to love me, but because of his own harsh father he could never let his feelings show; he was too afraid. In his own awkward way he had raised me as his boy. And in my own awkward way I forgive

[51] Jack Kornfield, After the Ecstasy, the Laundry: How the Heart Grows Wise on the Spiritual Path 47 (Bantam 2001).
[52] William Ury, Getting to Yes with Yourself 100 (Harper One 2015).

him. I went back to visit him. So much in my own life lightened up after that. Thank God for forgiveness.[53]

Some acts may seem so unforgivable that they do not deserve our forgiveness, but recall that the one hurt by this failure to forgive is not the enemy. It is us, drinking the poison and hoping our nemesis will die. Only we are hurt. This last tale (which is a true story) proves the point:

A fourteen-year-old boy killed another teen to prove he was worthy of gang membership. At the trial, the victim's mother sat impassively silent, until the verdict was announced. At that point she stood up and said to the killer, "I am going to kill you." The youth was then taken away to serve several years in a juvenile detention center, where he had no visitors, none except . . . the victim's mother, who began visiting him after six months or so. You see, the imprisoned boy had been living on the streets and had no friends or family.

The mother would visit, eventually bringing small gifts. Near the end of his term, the mother asked the imprisoned boy what he planned to do when he got out. The question confused the boy as he had no plans. She offered to help him get a job at a friend's company, and eventually, to let him live in her spare room. He lived there for eight months, eating her food, and working at the job she got him. One evening, she called him into the living room to talk and said, "Do you remember in the courtroom when I said I was going to kill you?" The boy said, "I sure do, I will never forget that moment." The mother continued:

"Well, I did [kill you]. I did not want the boy who could kill my son for no reason to remain alive on this earth. I wanted him to die. That is why I started to visit you and bring you things. That's why I got you the job and let you live here in my house. That's how I set about changing you. And that old boy, he's gone. So I want to ask you, since my son is gone and that killer is gone, if you'll stay here. I've got room and I'd like to adopt you if you let me."

She became the mother of her killer's son, the mother he never had.

Abe Lincoln said the same thing two centuries before, when he expressed sympathy for the plight of the south following the civil war. A Yankee patriot asked him how he "dared to speak kindly of our enemies when you ought to be thinking of destroying them." Lincoln responded by saying, "But do I not destroy my enemies when I turn them into friends?"[54]

LAW PAUSE

In *Getting to Yes with Yourself*, William Ury recounts this Lincoln story and then asks if there are "enemies" that we might be able to destroy by making them our friends.

---

[53] JACK KORNFIELD, AFTER THE ECSTASY, THE LAUNDRY: HOW THE HEART GROWS WISE ON THE SPIRITUAL PATH 50–51 (BANTAM 2001).

[54] WILLIAM URY, GETTING TO YES WITH YOURSELF 128–29 (HARPER ONE 2015).

Think of a couple of people like that and write a journal entry on how you might do this, if you chose to.

As important as it is to forgive others, it is even more important to forgive ourselves. We have all felt regret, shame, guilt, self-hatred, and self-blame, for breaking our promises and hurting others.[55] Once we can truly forgive ourselves, we are on our way to forgiving others.

CONCLUSIONS ABOUT ADVANCED EMOTIONAL INTELLIGENCE

Just as the Rumi poem says at the beginning of this chapter, this being human truly is a guest house. Emotions come and they go and we must experience them. After that, we have a choice about how to react to situations. We can choose to react in kind, we can do very little in reaction, or we can try to improve situations through our own insights and emotional intelligence. We will not have the energy to take on every battle, nor should we. Just know that, as long as we are mindful of the choices we are making, we each have the capacity to assess the situation and do what is best.

[55] *Ibid.* at 101.

11

Emotional Intelligence on the Page: The Writer's Life

Nathalie Martin

If you can find a lawyer job that does not consist primarily of writing, that is a rare job indeed. You are also missing out on one of the best things our profession has to offer. Just as children who read regularly in their formative years live easier lives, people who write well have a magic ticket in legal life.

Words are a lawyer's trade. Putting words on paper is a signature lawyering skill and likely our most meaningful societal contribution. Whether drafting or editing a bill for state or federal legislation, a letter for a friend or family member, or a complex buy/sell contract, lawyers must have a way with words. Lawyers also use words to prepare for arguments, negotiations, and meetings. We use words all day every day, many of them written. Lawyers deal in gray areas and difficult situations, making the particular words important. Intentional word choice is often the difference between winning and losing, succeeding and failing. This chapter focuses on how to write more easily, more effectively, and with greater emotional intelligence.

For many lawyers, writing things down is a way of thinking through legal problems. For this reason, we try to encourage you to write as much as possible in law school, in as many contexts as possible. As one clerk of US Supreme Court Justice Warren Burger said:

> For the Chief Justice, writing was not just a means of communicating. It was a necessary tool for thinking through the most difficult problems. For him, tough analytical thought and precise legal reasoning were not the product of oral disputation. Rather, the fundamental intellectual process of lawyering and judging occurred when the validity of an initial hunch or intuitive flash was tested by pen meeting legal pad. As the pen met paper, private musings and dialogue were transformed into solid analysis or discarded as useless as he searched for the appropriate outline of the opinion, the "best" phrase, the "right" words to convey a thought. After reading briefs, studying cases, and listening to oral arguments, he would often say "Let's see how this writes out."[1]

---

[1] Honorable Kenneth F. Ripple, *Legal Writing in the New Millennial: Lessons from a Special Teacher and a Special "Classroom,"* 74 NOTRE DAME L. REV. 925, 926 (1999).

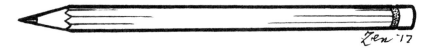

FIGURE 11.1 Pencil, Lawyer's Trademark Tool, created by illustrator, Pamela "Zen" Miller.

Learning to "write it out" means learning to hone your trade.

HONING YOUR TRADE

Words are the Lawyer's Primary Tool

Lawyers are often called wordsmiths. *Webster's Dictionary* defines a wordsmith as a person who works with words, or who is a skillful writer. Another source defines a wordsmith as:

> one with the ability to effortlessly string together words, no matter their actual meaning, in an instance and in such a way it brings a smile to the faces of those listening, sometimes often laughter or tears of admiration for having heard someone with such an amazing skill.[2]

To me, a wordsmith is a master of words, and most lawyers spend the majority of their time writing. As you get comfortable with your craft, life will become easier. The sustained practice of using words deeply hones the skill of wordsmithing. While it may take a while, you will soon marvel at your capacity to write.

This is purely intellectual work, with little physical or tactile activity to balance it out. This can cause lawyers to live inside their own heads more than many other people. Compared to lawyers, it is amazing to think about how much mechanics, potters, or traffic controllers use their whole bodies in their jobs. They use their hands, their backs, their feet, their full range of human capacity and experience in their jobs, while lawyers mostly use only their brains. No wonder most of us live from the head up.

Using Informal Writing to Build Your Writing Muscles

We can all improve our writing through various practices. Legal writing has its own peculiarities, but writing anything will help writing become second nature. Because writing anything helps you write everything, every type of writing can improve your skill. As Natalie Goldberg explains in *Writing Down the Bones*, you can make writing itself a practice, much like meditation or exercise.[3] The key to Goldberg's approach is doing it regularly, hopefully every day.

---

[2] *Wordsmith*, URBAN DICTIONARY, available at www.urbandictionary.com/define.php?term=wordsmith.

[3] NATALIE GOLDBERG, WRITING DOWN THE BONES 11 (SHAMBHALA 2016).

At first, the idea is to get used to writing regularly. Goldberg recommends that you take out a notebook and write. Just keep your hands moving, don't cross out, don't worry about spelling, grammar, punctuation, or even paragraphs, just write. Lose control, don't ponder, just get down to it.[4] Goldberg carries a notebook big enough to be substantial and small enough to have with her at most times. She writes until it is full, aspiring to fill a notebook per month. The idea is to clear the mind and write.

Similarly, in *The Artist's Way*, writing teacher and coach Julia Cameron suggests you start the day by writing a brain-clearing, three notebook pages of gobbledy-gook. This writing is like meditation to Cameron, who uses this approach to clear the mind of random thoughts and worries before she starts her formal writing. She says these "morning pages" have improved the focus of many of her clients and students, allowing them to be more successful and efficient in their art. The reason this approach may work for writers like you is because practice is what improves writing, nothing more, nothing less. Write, write, and keep writing.

I use a slightly different approach. For the past twenty years, I have used my first morning moments to help me efficiently and quickly write briefs, memos, articles, and books, and solve difficult life problems. Basically, I sit in quiet and write down my first morning thoughts. My purpose is to clear the mind as Cameron and Goldberg suggest, use my fresh morning perspective to quickly solve an intractable problem, or efficiently write a difficult document. Writing first thing in the morning (not always gobbledy-gook and not always three pages) helps me become more self-aware, get more work done, and improve my formal writing.

Writing down your first morning thoughts is not like writing a legal brief. First thoughts are special. They are unencumbered by ego, so at least for me, they have tremendous energy. To me, first thoughts are the most powerful thoughts. Try the approach described below and see if it helps, especially if writing is difficult for you. This approach will help fight perfection and procrastination, and get you in the habit of writing. Remember, the key to better and easier writing is to write.

LAW PAUSE

Experiment with these techniques. As Goldberg suggests, write a journal entry in which you write down whatever comes to mind for five to ten minutes. Don't try to make it say anything, just write. This is a form of written meditation.

In the next day or two, right after you get up, try my modified approach where rather than just gobbledy-gook, you write about something you are working on, but lightly and not in any particular way. Don't try too hard, just write something you need to write, with your clear, first morning thoughts.

---

4   *Ibid.* at 9.

Think about each of these techniques, and write a journal entry about which was more useful for you and why.

Legal Writing

Don't Fight the Formula

Now that we have talked about informal writing, we will touch on formal legal writing, the subject of one of the most critical classes in law school. You will learn a formula for formal legal writing. The formula never changes. Do not fight the formula. As explained in another way, by UNM Law Professor David Stout:

> the formula is critical to fulfilling a legal reader's expectations. Failing to follow the formula will frustrate the legal reader because your work will not provide the reader with the form he or she is expecting.[5]

Keep in mind that legal readers, particularly senior attorneys and judges, are voluntary readers. They can choose to stop reading your document and if this happens, you have lost your ability to communicate.

So what *is* the formula? In one iteration or another, you will basically be asked to state the legal rule and then carefully apply that rule to the facts of your case. You will make sure to spend more time, words, and space on the application or the way the rule applies to the facts than on stating the rule. The closer you stay with the formula for legal writing given to you by your professors, the easier life will be. State the legal rule, then apply the rule, and spend more time applying it than stating it. State another rule, apply, lather, rinse, and repeat. This is all I will say about this formula, which you will practice in various ways throughout your career. Consider the formula a gift and life will be beautiful. Fight the formula and you will suffer.

Fight the Perfect – Just Write and Revise

With legal writing, as well as the non-legal writing discussed above, practice is the key. If you write often enough to make it a habit, the writing becomes a mindfulness practice and flows. Don't try to control too much at first. Just write. Be willing to completely trash things you have written, but just keep on going. As William Faulkner noted, "Get it down. Take chances. It may be bad, but it's the only way you can do anything really good."[6] In other words, don't procrastinate and stare at a blank page. That has never helped anyone and won't help you. Write something down and revise it later to make it great.

The mere act of writing helps you to think, organize, analyze, and come up with new perspectives. Write ideas on paper to get your mind moving. You'll still need to

---

[5] Interview of David Stout by Nathalie Martin, July 15, 2017.
[6] Megan Willett, *17 Quotes On Writing That Every Wannabe Author Should Read*, BUSINESS INSIDER, Sept. 14, 2013, available at www.businessinsider.com/quotes-on-writing-from-famous-authors-2013-9.

revise and rewrite them, however. As articulated by US Supreme Court Justice Louis Brandeis and others, "There is no such thing as good writing, only good rewriting."

Brain Science and Productive Procrastination

Most of us can think of many ways to procrastinate, but law students often procrastinate on their written work. Neuroscientist Alex Korb, author of *The Upward Spiral*, suggests that procrastinating by doing other necessary tasks can actually stimulate the prefrontal cortex enough to get us to do the task we are avoiding.[7] Laundry, dishes, pulling weeds – doing all of these tasks will release dopamine into parts of the prefrontal cortex, which will in turn give you the motivation to do the task you have been avoiding.[8]

So go ahead and clean that fridge. It will help motivate you to get that memo done. Just make sure to give yourself a limited amount of time to do that side task.

More on Getting it Done

In the right frame of mind, and with the right research and reading beforehand, legal documents can write themselves. To stay motivated and not get psyched out, split your writing task into chunks so you can make a list of all you need to do. The chunks could be research on x, research on y, the facts, the point headings, a chunk for each subject matter, each section, etc. Break it down. The goal is to make legal writing less intimidating. Make a list, and check things off the list, chunk by chunk. The act of checking things off is motivating.

Mix the tough tasks with rewards. For example, write a section, go for a walk, write your point headings, cook dinner, write the facts, take a shower. In others words, use delayed gratification and a reward system to keep knocking out the chunks.

There are several other techniques you can use to get your writing done. Here are a few. No single technique works for everyone so it helps to know yourself and your own writing style. If you tend to procrastinate in bringing pen to paper, try each of the techniques below and see what works for you.

1. Use a little reverse psychology. I tell myself I cannot write a single thing until I have read a certain number of sources. Then by the time I have the sources read, I am dying to start writing. I have ideas in my head and cannot wait to write them down. If writing does not come so easily, you might want to tell yourself that you do not need to write anything down until you have read a certain number of sources. Chances are, by the time you have read those sources, you'll be ready to get some ideas on paper. By removing that initial pressure to write, you'll be able to read with focus and if nothing else, start a rough draft, based on the cases and theories you have read about. This will not work for those who get bogged down in research and never want to start writing.

---

[7] Alex Korb, The Upward Spiral: Using Neuroscience to Reverse the Course of Depression, One Small Change at a Time 135–36 (New Harbinger Publications 2015).
[8] *Ibid.*

2. Some people like to read similar or different types of writing before they start, to get in the right frame of mind. For example, my husband Stewart likes "to spend a couple minutes reading a couple of other similar types of writing, my own or others, so I get the format down before I start. I know what I am going to say but this reminds me how best to get there." My friend Pamela Foohey likes to read a different type of writing than she is attempting to write. As she says, "I read parts of a memoir before writing a law review article, for instance." Remember, know your own style and figure out which of these approaches might help you.

3. You can read very actively for quite a while, taking a lot of notes, marking possible quotes and themes, squirreling away information. You literally gorge on that information, thinking and questioning, until you are stuffed with it. Then put it all away and write your first thoughts, without any sources around. Just get it down, or as legal writing expert and author Bryan Garner has said, "Let the mad man loose for a while." Don't worry about the form. Write your themes down without doing your full citations. After the ideas are down, go back and fill in your sources, change the text to a more reader-friendly and active voice, shorten, condense, synthesize, and edit, edit, and edit some more.

In any writing project, it is absolutely normal to think your draft is not very good, especially about three-quarters of the way through. It happens to me all the time. You will be happy later; just keep going.

Give yourself tons of time to redo your work. Always give yourself early (or fake) deadlines and stick with them. You will feel amazing. Do not wait until the last minute.

---

4. Finally, know that a lot of good work starts with one really awful first draft. You can even look at websites with bad first drafts of popular books, such as: www.huffingtonpost.com/2014/05/05/shit-rough-drafts_n_5268269.html. Here is bestselling fiction author Stephen King's take on the subject of editing:

> Mostly when I think of pacing, I go back to Elmore Leonard, who explained it so perfectly by saying he just left out the boring parts. This suggests cutting to speed the pace, and that's what most of us end up having to do (kill your darlings, kill your darlings, even when it breaks your egocentric little scribbler's heart, kill your darlings) . . . I got a scribbled comment that changed the way I rewrote my fiction once and forever. Jotted below the machine-generated signature of the editor was this motto: "Not bad, but PUFFY. You need to revise for length. Formula: 2nd Draft = 1st Draft – 10%. Good luck."[9]

---

[9] STEPHEN KING, ON WRITING (POCKET BOOKS 2001).

Learning to Love to Write

Finally, always make it a point to *try* to enjoy writing, even if you feel like you hate it. Consider it a creative endeavor. Try to have fun and tell yourself it *will* be fun, even if it is sometimes painful. In *The Artist's Way*, Cameron describes her early life as a writer, writing the hard way. As she explains:

> I was creative in spurts, like blood from a severed carotid artery. A decade of writing and all I knew was how to make these headlong dashes and hurl myself, against all odds, at the wall of whatever I was writing. If creativity was spiritual in any sense, it was only in its resemblance to a crucifixion.[10]

Consider your writing to come from the divine, however you define the divine. This may be controversial to some of you, but doing this helped Cameron find a way to give up attachment to her witing and just get it down. As she explains:

> I learned to get out of the way and let that creative force work through me. I learned to just show up at the page and write down what I heard. Writing became much more like eavesdropping and less like inventing a nuclear bomb. It wasn't so tricky, it didn't blow up on me anymore. I didn't have to be in the mood, I didn't have to take my emotional temperature to see if inspiration was pending. I simply wrote. No negotiations. Good, bad? None of my business. I wasn't doing it. By resigning as the self-conscious author, I wrote freely.[11]

Jack Kornfield similarly describes a retreat in which he and a group of other authors were describing where they got their words, the inspiration for their words. Some said they received the ideas through music, others saw the words in written form in their heads others heard the words from an audible voice in their head, and still others got the words from dreams. As Kornfield humorously notes, it was clear that no one was writing their own material.

Little Pause: To remove the inner critic, author Barnet Bain suggests bringing to mind a time you felt judged and then re-experiencing that judged feeling in as much detail as you can. He then asks that you imagine the entire person or situation "vaporizing" through whatever means you conjure up. It can be a ray gun, an explosive, an ejection chair, whatever you choose – just make them go away. Now he asks that you note how your body feels now that the critic is gone.[12]

No matter what you do, if you need to write, then write. Keep going, keep writing, and keep trying to enjoy yourself along the way. Breathe, enjoy, and appreciate your gift, even if you are still developing it. After all, we are *all still* developing it. Writing is always a bit like driving a car at night. You can see only as far as your headlights,

[10] JULIA CAMERON, THE ARTIST'S WAY: A SPIRITUAL PATH TO HIGHER CREATIVITY XVIII (JEREMY P. TARCHER/PUTNAM 2001).
[11] *Ibid.* at xviii–xix.
[12] BARNET BAIN, THE BOOK OF DOING AND BEING: REDISCOVERING CREATIVITY IN LIFE, LOVE, AND WORK 107–108 (ATRIA 2015).

but you can make the whole trip that way.[13] As Ernest Hemingway said, "Once writing has become your major vice, and greatest pleasure, only death will stop it."[14]

Specific Words Matter: You've Got the Power

If I survive this life without dying, I will be surprised.

Mulla Nasrudin

The particular words you use can make a big difference in the outcome of a dispute. In the words of UNM Law Professor Emeritus Robert Schwartz, an expert on the "right to die" and physician-assisted suicide, using specific words can determine whether people believe a terminally ill person should be allowed to end their own life when they are sick. Words, the way you choose them, the way you use them, make the difference in whether you succeed or fail, win or lose, get what you want or fail to get what you want. Often the words from which you can choose mean the same thing but carry very different connotations. That is the incredible power of words. Here Professor Schwartz explains the power of particular words in the context of his field:

> Words make a big difference. No one likes to be involved in "killing," even "mercy killing," although the "mercy" somewhat ameliorates the "killing." Most people object to all forms of suicide (and, thus, assisted suicide) and euthanasia. On the other hand, everyone is in favor of "death with dignity," and no one would reject a "right to die," especially because that "right" is also a scientific necessity. We're not getting out of this life alive.
>
> Also, almost everyone agrees that patients should have options at the end of life. Thus, supporters of aid in dying (a physician's prescription of a lethal dose of medication for a competent, terminally ill person who is suffering) call their legislative proposals "Death With Dignity" Acts (that is the name in Oregon and Washington) or "End of Life Options" Acts (that is the name in California, DC and in the bill introduced in New Mexico).
>
> National polls find huge support for death with dignity, the right to die and end of life options, while there is serious opposition to any form of suicide or killing, even when death with dignity, the right to die, and end of life options refer to exactly the same medical process as assisted suicide and mercy killing.

Also realize that the content, tone, and means of communicating can make a big difference. For example, imagine you are renting out a ski house you own that allows pets. Which of these messages do you think would result in less pet damage to your house: "Never leave your pet alone in the house" versus "Treat our home as you would your own. Please do not leave your pet alone in the house unless you trust him or her completely"?

---

[13] E.L. Docotrow, *Goodquotes*, available at www.goodreads.com/author/quotes/12584.E_L_Doctorow.

[14] MATTHEW J. BRUCCOLI, CONVERSATIONS WITH ERNEST HEMINGWAY 114 (University Press of Mississippi, Jackson and London 1923).

Consider these two policies on mouse extraction and bird feeding, offered by two different pest control companies, both of which hired a lawyer to draft their contracts. One pest control company's policy provides that all elimination services include a ninety-day warranty, but the company will not provide mouse elimination services if the owner feeds birds within 100 feet of the house. Another company does not mention any warranty when you hire them, but after providing their services, hands the owner a sheet of paper entitled *Preserving Your 90-day Warranty*, which states that "We provide a 90-day warranty in certain instances." The sheet lists several things the customer can do if they would like the warranty, including refraining from feeding birds within 100 feet of the house. Assuming people like to feed birds in this area, which company is likely to get more customers based upon these terms, and why? I prefer to get the service and feed the birds even if the services are not under warranty.

The lesson in these examples is that it pays to get as much help as possible with your writing while in law school, to take every class that requires writing, and to get as much feedback on your writing as you can get.

EMOTIONALLY INTELLIGENT COMMUNICATIONS

Once you have begun to learn the power and persuasion of particular words, in terms of achieving the results you want, it is time to focus a bit more on how others will react to your writing. We all hope that people will read our work and also that it will convey what we intend in terms of information, persuasion, and tone. Because of the informality of some modern forms of written communications, however, getting the tone right can be tricky.

Email Communications

Emails, as well as text messaging, are particularly tricky ways to communicate. Many times, you will make your life easier and get a better result if you walk down the hall or pick up the phone. If you are speaking to someone, you are able to gauge their reaction to your words. Typed messages, especially short ones, are easily misinterpreted.

Dealing with Unpleasant Email
Just for fun, pretend you have received this email from the lawyer who represents the seller in a land sale where you represent the buyer. Imagine that earlier this week you had a meeting, after which you agreed to do the first draft of a purchase agreement:

Dear Josh:

As I am sure you know, this is not what we agreed to at all. I am actually pretty disgusted by the way you tried to get the upper hand for your client in this draft of our purchase agreement. Please redraft the contract in a fashion that better comports with our agreement.

When working with clinic students, I sometimes use the emotion wheel found in Figure 10.1 to help students identify the feelings they have upon receipt of such a lovely missive. Identifying these feelings and dealing with them at the outset, is the first step in dealing with a situation like this. After you know how you feel, you can neutralize those feelings, and decide when and how to respond to something like this.

Recall the poem at the beginning of Chapter 8, in which your mind can be visualized as a wild bull. It is bucking and you need to stop fighting it. When you stop fighting it, the mind quiets down. A natural extension of this poem is the idea that responding calmly is better than responding in kind. Even though you may wish to tell this person right where to stick it, if we calm down, we can control the bull. We need to control the bull, or the bull will control us.

We have the choice. We can blow up and escalate the situation or we can calm down and achieve the best possible result. You may decide to tell the person how you feel in Miedaner-style (see Chapter 10), or you might let it go and try to deal with the substance, but what should you actually do, in detail, step by step?

It is also important to ask whether it might be best to respond with a medium *other than* email? Most people prefer to respond to an email with another email, and may even wish to do so quickly, so that their name and work are not besmirched in the meantime, while the nastygram sits in your inbox. Waiting to respond to something particularly negative, however, is almost always best.

Any time you *really* need to respond to a nasty or sensitive email with another email, due to distance, time constraints, or unreliable phone service, it is best to draft your response, sit on it, and maybe even run it by another person, before you send it.

UNM Law Professor Stout recommends that you consider drafting a very angry response to a negative email to get all of your emotions out on paper, but then delete the draft and send a more civilized email.

There is a good chance, though, that you should not be responding by email. In these sensitive situations, which you will learn to spot, it is often best to pick up the phone or go visit. This might be the last thing you want to do, and perhaps you are sick of being the bigger person, etc., but this is what you need to do. Why? It will work better. You will be more likely to get your way, whatever that means, by matching hostility with cooperation. You may think responding to hostility with kindness or cooperation will have the opposite effect, but it usually will not. Being kind or collegial will make you the more reasonable person, may disarm the other person, and will almost always create a better result, which is your goal. Civility is also a hallmark of professionalism, both of which are increasingly important topics in the legal profession.

Studying A Few Lawyer Communications

Now let's look at some examples of things lawyers write outside the legal memo or brief, and how our words can influence a situation, good or bad.

1. Stretching The Facts

Last year, we had a neighborhood problem of sorts. Joanna Nesbitt, a much-loved elderly neighbor with seemingly limited financial means, was cited by the city for tree roots that had cracked the sidewalk and street in front of her home, making the sidewalk uneven and unsafe. The city sent an ominous letter, giving her sixty days to repair the street and sidewalk. The letter included a list of licensed contractors that she could contact to do the work. In addition to requiring Joanna to hire and pay a contractor, the letter claimed that the city would have to approve the work both in advance and on completion.

A few of us discussed how we could help, but were concerned that we might not be able to help enough. One neighbor who can do grading and paving said he could provide a quote, though he was not on the city's approved contractor list, and did not know what was meant by "plans approved." I offered to write a letter in response to the city, for her signature, hoping they would back off a bit. This was my first draft.

Joanna Nesbitt
1362 Temper Drive
Albuquerque, NM 87108
(505) 320–4401

City of Albuquerque
Department of Municipal Development
Construction Services Department
P.O. Box 1293
Albuquerque, NM 97103
March 8, 2016

Re: Notice to repair sidewalk, certified mail receipt no. 4014 2880

Dear City of Albuquerque:

I have received your notice dated February 19, 2016, asking me to fix the sidewalk in front of my house within 60 days. I understand that if needed I can take another 60 days to do it in addition to the first 60 days.

I have owned this home since 1972 and since I moved here, the city has done all the work on the sidewalks in front of my house. In fact, the trees that are apparently causing the sidewalk to buckle were there when I purchased the home 40 years ago. It is my position that, given the city's past pattern of practice in doing these repairs, and my reliance on these acts through the years, it would be unfair and likely unlawful for me to be charged for this work at this time.

I am a senior citizen with limited income and would be unable to pay for this work in any case. I respectfully request a letter back confirming that, given these facts, I am not liable for these sidewalk repairs.

Thank you for your consideration.

Sincerely,

Joanna Nesbitt

When I went to see Joanna to go over the letter, she gave me two eye-opening lessons. While she appreciated my help with the letter, Joanna expressed two major concerns. Lesson one, and I know this is obvious, you can't use your trade (words and wordsmith) to lie. The letter apparently contained a lie. Joanna had planted the trees. It was so interesting! I thought I was simply making a legal argument (reliance, estoppel, or some such). I guess I also figured, hearing about this fact for the first time, that it didn't really matter much what we said, since the planting probably occurred well outside the human consciousness of anyone alive today. In other words, for a few minutes or seconds there, it seemed OK to "stretch the facts," aka lie, if no one could check our facts.

She also pointed out another half-truth in the letter, namely that if she really had to, she might (we didn't know the price yet) be able to scrimp enough to be able to pay for this work. Goodness! That was my other ace in the hole, inability to collect even if they did cite her for something. But the fact that she couldn't pay wasn't technically true and I was willing (before this conversation) to say it anyway.

This made me wonder, how many things do lawyers say in daily documents and conversations that are not 100 percent true? I was starting to think that a lot of what we say was at least a stretch if not completely false, and it was worrying. Going back to the letter, it did not seem there was much we could say and my job was to do my best to get the city to back off. Note the ego here.

Then Joanna taught me lesson two. This was to be her letter, and my tone was off. It was not her voice. It was too aggressive, too impersonal. When I noted that the City's letter was downright threatening and certainly impersonal, she said that didn't matter, and that it would be bad karma to send a letter that could be perceived as rude. So we rewrote the letter together in her voice. I was pretty sure the letter would accomplish nothing, but we sent it anyway and she seemed pleased. Take a look:

Joanna Nesbitt
1362 Temper Drive
Albuquerque, NM 87108
(505)320–4401

City of Albuquerque
Department of Municipal Development
Construction Services Department
P.O. Box 1293
Albuquerque, NM 97103
March 8, 2016

Re: Notice to repair sidewalk, certified mail receipt no. 4014 2880

Dear City of Albuquerque:

I have received your notice dated February 19, 2016, asking me to fix the sidewalk in front of my house within 60 days. I understand that if needed I can take another 60 days to do it in addition to the first 60 days.

I have owned this home since 1972 and since I moved here, the city has done all the work on the sidewalks in front of my house. Now I am a senior citizen with limited income and wonder if there is a financial assistance program for this work. If so, can you send me information on that program?

Thank you very much!

Sincerely,

Joanna Nesbitt

A couple weeks later, we were out of town but heard from neighbors that city trucks had been working on the sidewalk outside Joanna's house, for days and days. Two weeks after sending this letter, the work was done. The City never asked Joanna for a dime. Joanna never got the letter I was hoping for, exonerating her from liability (note the fancy lawyer word), and she doesn't care. Somehow the kinder, more civil, more humane, letter worked.

2. Does Threatening Backfire?

Take a look at the two letters below and consider what you have learned about mindful communications. The letters were written to try to get a skilled rehabilitation center *not* to violate the law. The facility was threatening to release a patient from skilled rehabilitation earlier than the law allows. The patient had not yet set up her in-home follow-up care, making a release from the rehabilitation center premature and dangerous for the patient.

Can you tell what result the author is actually trying to achieve? Which letter do you think would get the result?

Letter 1

Dear Discharge Director:

I am Grace Byer's daughter and am writing on behalf of our whole family. My mother is in the Zapara rehab center and wishes to appeal the decision to discharge her on June 7, 2013. As you know, as a Medicare beneficiary, she has a right to a safe discharge, and also to stay in rehab for as long as she is making progress. She has never been told that she was *not* making progress. Also, as long as she is making progress, and since the law requires that she be discharged only if doing so is safe, she cannot be legally released from rehab if she does not have sufficient transfer or locomotion skills to be safe at home.

We anticipate that this request will be granted as the procedures required by law were not followed. For example, she was not provided with written documentation of her discharge within two days of the proposed discharge date. I tried to reach several people on your staff on the morning of Wednesday June 5, 2013 before any decision to actually discharge her was communicated to her. I left several messages which were not returned. I spoke directly to nurse Mel and left messages with George and Adam from the discharge department. I also left several messages with the charging nurse, Marla, on unit 1500, who never called back at all.

The stress imposed on our family has been palpable and is legally actionable. Please email me the QIO information and any other documents that led to your decision. Please send them to ll@trueld.com. If you decide not to honor our request, we have the absolute right by law to stay at the facility even if this means that the stay is ultimately deemed to be a stay paid for on a private pay basis, as you were informed by my mother and her husband Saul Fox on June 4, 2013.

Thank you,

Leslie Lawyer

Letter 2

FORMAL APPEAL OF DISCHARGE DECISION, DOB Oct. 27, 1936
Attn: George Kakoff

Dear Mr. Kakoff, Discharge Director, charging nurse, and therapists:

I am Grace Byer's daughter and am writing on behalf of our whole family. We are deeply grateful for the care you have provided to my mother over the course of two difficult back injuries, including a double back surgery. Your staff of therapists and caregivers has been top notch in every way.

My mother is in the Zapara rehab center now and wishes to appeal the decision to discharge her on June 7, 2013, if such a decision was indeed made. As you know, as a Medicare beneficiary, she has a right to a safe discharge, and also to stay in rehab for as long as she is making progress. She has never been told that she was *not* making progress, and just this morning I was told by an occupational therapist that she is indeed still making progress. Despite her progress, she also has not reached the point where she has sufficient transfer or locomotion skills to be safe at home.

My mother has already been in the rehab facility twice following her March surgery with Dr. Cheng of the Loma Linda surgery division, with very painful relapse. We think just another week will work wonders. I'd hate to see her go home, fall, and be back again in no time.

We anticipate that this request will be granted as it appears that some of the discharge procedures required by law were not followed. For example, she was not provided with written documentation of her discharge within two days of the proposed discharge date. As of yesterday early evening, she had received no information on how to contact her QIO. Indeed, as of last evening, she still had not received anything in writing about her discharge. I told her to ask for this paperwork, and a nurse handed her some papers around 7 p.m. She was alone and had difficulty reading them. The nurse also said these were subject to change.

As you know if she feels it is too early to be discharged, which she and her husband Saul Fox have been saying all week long, she must be given a written Notice of Medicare Provider Noncoverage (NOMPNC) within two days of the planned discharge, which was originally planned for tomorrow. It is clear that she cannot be asked to leave tomorrow.

I have tried to reach several people on your staff about these concerns over the course of two days, starting on the morning of Wednesday June 5, 2013, apparently before any decision to actually discharge her was communicated to her. I left several messages which were not returned. I spoke directly to nurse Mel and left messages with the discharge department.

Please email me the NOMPNC, with the relevant QIO information at ll@trueld.com. I would also be very grateful if someone would return my calls or email me to tell me that she will not be asked to leave tomorrow.

This is an issue of deep importance to me and my family, and the uncertainty of the situation is causing all of us a great deal of anxiety.

Thank you for your kindness,

Leslie Lawyer

Little Pause: Discuss these letters with two of your colleagues. See if you can agree on which letter will get the best result and why.

A Little Fun with Legal Writing

Eventually you can have some fun with your legal writing, as several poetic judges have found. In *Brown v. State*, 216 S.E.2d 356 (Ga. Ct. App. 1975), Judge Randall Evans wrote a poetic opinion because the lower court judge asked in a speech that if Evans "ever again was so presumptuous as to reverse one of [my] decisions, that the opinion be written in poetry." In a case in which Eminem was sued for defamation,

Judge Servitto wrote a fourteen-page opinion that ended with a rap. Find it at *Bailey v. Mathers*, Case No. 2001–3606-NO, slip op. at 13 n. 11 (Macomb County Circuit Court, Oct. 17, 2003).

Finally, in *Rimes v. Curb Records, Inc.* 129 F. Supp. 2d 984, 985–86 (N.D. Tex. 2001), country music singer LeAnn Rimes sought to void a recording contract on the basis that she was a minor when she signed it. Judge Jerry Buchmeyer upheld a forum selection clause in the contract and granted the defendant's motion to transfer the case to Tennessee, all to the tune of LeAnn's hit song, *How Do I Live?* The refrain went like this:

> Why did you sign, LeAnn Rimes?
> So long ago
> Off on that choice of forum?
> Your attorneys didn't know?
> They made lots of changes, but one thing survived . . .
> Forum clause, to that clause, what weight do we give?
> . . .

Final Words on Words

Some lawyers don't seem to understand that their goal is to communicate, to be mindful in their communications, and as a result, to get the best results. For some reason, they write in ways that are deeply mysterious, if not tragic. For example, check out these excerpts from Gary Kinder's Word Rake story about legal writing entitled *Your Honor, You are Stupid, You Suck, so Hold for Me*.[15] While acknowledging that lawyers work hard to be good at what we do, Kinder notes how common sense can go out the window when a client or colleague convinces us to say and do silly things. Kinder asks that we always remember that we alone are in charge of preserving our reputation, and asks if these three excerpts from formal legal briefs to a court are effective:

> This is a story of a legal system run amuck, a Kafkaesque demonstration of tyranny given free rein.

And then this:

> Importer's conduct in negotiating the "purchase" of these alleged liens was based on the syllogism employed by many Middle Eastern terrorists with a penchant for seizing airliners and their passengers to secure the righting of what they perceive to be wrongs.

And the last humdinger:

> The Defendant's actions can only be described as economic sodomy.

---

[15]   Gary Kinder, *Your Honor, You are Stupid, You Suck, so Hold for Me*, WORDRAKE, www.wordrake.com/writing-tips/your-honor-you-are-stupid-you-suck-and-please-decide-for-me/.

Did lawyers really write these things? This is the sort of thing that loses cases, Kinder notes, along with all sorts of great overstatements and exaggerations, use of exclamation points, and as one judge explained:

> vituperative language leveled against the trial judge . . . such as "the court systematically eviscerated plaintiff's case" or that "the judge created absurdity and injustice." . . . [P]laintiff was similarly highly disrespectful in his briefs to the trial court, as well. Such pre-planned advocacy by an attorney never arouses sympathy for his client.[16]

Professor David Stout elaborates further:

> Attorney expressions of ego, purely gratuitous, are exquisitely counter-productive. Not only is civility right, but it is the most effective way to persuade. In fact, it is almost certainly the *only* matter on which there would be a judicial consensus, I suspect unanimity, that harsh and ad personam attacks are an unnecessary distraction, a self-inflicted wound to the writer who wants to be a successful advocate.

Kinder notes that judges have two sure-fire ways to tell that a lawyer has no case:

1, Asks for more pages to continue rambling.
2, Gets shrill, haughty, cute, and feigns disgust.

Countering this poor writing are the words and thoughts of Abraham Lincoln, and repeated by Kinder: "When the conduct of men is designed to be influenced, *persuasion*, kind, unassuming persuasion, should ever be adopted. It is an old and a true maxim, that a 'drop of honey catches more flies than a gallon of gall'."[17]

Lincoln's advice is still good today. Use facts, the law, and your intellect to make your case, not over-active adjectives, ego, and slurs. Indeed, one bankruptcy judge told me that the habit he dislikes most among lawyers is the tendency to exaggerate.

CONCLUSIONS ABOUT MINDFUL WRITTEN COMMUNICATIONS

So what did we get from this chapter? Lawyers are wordsmiths and so will you be. Figure out how to make yourself a better writer. This can be through a writer's workshop or through reading a particular type of literature. Don't let your ego get to you – that is, don't bite off more than you can chew when you first start learning to write. Stick to the fundamentals before getting fancy. Become an excellent writer through practice. Above all else, words matter so pick them carefully. Have fun when you write, but remember that being a writer is empowering. Writing gives you the power of communication and change for the better, on behalf of yourself and the rest of society.

[16] *Ibid.*   [17] *Ibid.*

12

Giving and Receiving Feedback

Joshua Alt and Nathalie Martin

I never lose. I either win or learn.

Nelson Mandela

Experience is the name we give to our mistakes.

Oscar Wilde

Experts in attorney professional development believe that the ability to seek and receive meaningful feedback is one of the most critical attorney traits.[1] According to founders of the Holloran Center, Neil Hamilton and Jerry Organ, seeking out feedback is a key element in becoming a self-directed, professional attorney.[2] There is no doubt that receiving feedback gracefully is incredibly important to your career. In the words of law Professor Pamela Foohey, "Getting and receiving feedback is the ultimate part of any professional job. A person's ability to accept feedback depends on the circumstances of the job and what the feedback is about. Being able to recognize how to give feedback changes with context and is super-EQ."[3]

Yet feedback, and self-awareness in general, is not always pleasant. For example, not long ago, my husband and I (Professor Martin) helped a friend of a friend fill out the eHarmony questionnaire to help him find a good relationship. He had been slipping into harmful relationships for a long time, perhaps a lifetime. He is not much of a computer guy, so we helped with the initial form. As he filled out the questionnaire, he gave himself a six (the top score) in every category. The computer program eventually shut him down, deciding he was not an actual person. We do not know him well, but a lifetime of experience told us there had to be something for which he was not a six. We suspected it might be self-awareness.

---

[1]   Neil W. Hamilton, Verna Monson, and Jerome M. Organ, *Encouraging Each Student's Personal Responsibility for Core Competencies Including Professionalism*, 21 PROF. LAW. 1, 12 (2012).

[2]   *Ibid.*   [3]   Telephone interview with Professor Pamela Foohey, March 28, 2017.

As another example, I recently learned that I have a great propensity to start many things, but not much of a drive to finish them. I did not learn this on my own. Someone told me. Actually many people may have told me, but we all wait until we are ready to learn our own blind spots. This chapter is designed to help you learn yours. Once you do, life is easier.

To discover our blind spots, we need to look for feedback or listen carefully to the feedback we receive. We can seek out meaningful feedback from those we trust and engage in a self-awareness plan to meaningfully change those parts of our lives that are holding us back. This process is rewarding but can also be painful if we are not prepared.

LAW PAUSE

1. What feedback have you had that was useful, and why?
2. What was counterproductive, and why?
3. How did you react to receiving feedback, and why?

THE NEGATIVITY BIAS, AND RECEIVING AND GIVING FEEDBACK

With training, we can recognize that negative feedback initiates a bias in us that impairs our thinking. This is known as the negativity bias. Knowing a bit about brain science helps us prepare to receive feedback.

In general, we tend to focus on the bad news much more than the good, which is why Rick Hanson, in *Buddha's Brain*,[4] suggests that we focus on and highlight the good in our life as much as we possibly can. Try to take the negative feedback and act on it, but don't discount all the great things you do. When you receive a compliment, smile deeply inside and let yourself enjoy that feeling for as long as you possibly can, to counteract your over-active negativity bias.

The negativity bias causes us to keep replaying the bad in our minds, while downplaying the good. The negativity bias triggers circuits in our brain that are very sensitive – more sensitive than the circuits that handle the positive experiences.

If we are aware of our negativity bias when we receive criticism, we are better prepared for our emotional reaction and can better prepare to make good use of the feedback. Expect emotions to arise. Expect defensiveness. Then, calm the mind using the tips found throughout this book and in this chapter. Deep breathing is especially helpful when preparing to receive, and when receiving, feedback.

One law review article actually claims that law school can make one less able to graciously receive feedback, because law school causes people to feel insecure. It is

---

[4] RICK HANSON, BUDDHA'S BRAIN: THE PRACTICAL NEUROSCIENCE OF HAPPINESS, LOVE & WISDOM 41, 75–77 (NEW HARBINGER 2009).

difficult to receive feedback graciously when feeling insecure. As explained by Professor Deborah Borman in her article, *Fast Track Your Mindset: Engineering Confidence and Streamlining Feedback for Full Steam Success in Legal Practice*,[5] the insecurity caused by the law school process can also follow us into practice, where it impedes our growth and becomes much more of a problem. It is not just school and ourselves that are affected, but third parties such as clients.[6]

Professor Borman explains that confidence varies throughout life and is both innate and learned. She identifies three confidence busters that create inaction or paralysis:

- rumination (overthinking)
- hesitation (when fear keeps us from speaking up or contributing)
- a desire for absolute perfectionism (which keeps us from finishing anything).[7]

Professor Borman explains that fear and anxiety are experienced in the right side of the physical brain, and feelings of satisfaction, hope, and happiness, in the left side of the brain.[8]

Moreover, in her book, *The How of Happiness*, Sonja Lyubormirsky, explains that 50 percent of our feelings of satisfaction or well-being are wired at birth, and 10 percent is driven by our involuntary life circumstance, such as relationship status, health, etc.[9] This means that 40 percent of our well-being results from how we interpret and respond to what happens to us. In other words, 40 percent of how happy and satisfied we are depends upon attitude.[10] It is remarkable. Scientific studies confirm that up to 40 percent of our well-being is completely within our power to change.[11]

What is the key to which way your own 40 percent will go? You control it by adopting a growth rather than a fixed mindset. In her book, *Mindset: The New Psychology of Success*, Carol Dweck outlines just how powerful your mindset can be. If you believe that your basic qualities are things you can cultivate through your own efforts, your strategies, and your help from others, you will succeed in the things you put your mind to. If on the other hand you adopt a fixed mindset, and believe that your qualities are set in stone and cannot change, you will not find the motivation to reach your potential. This mindset is something you can control. You can take credit for your own hard work and use your success to catapult you through your next task. In many ways, your success in law school and in your career depends upon adopting a growth mindset. In other words, you have the power.

---

[5] *See generally* Deborah L. Borman, *Fast Track Your Mindset: Engineering Confidence and Streamlining Feedback for Full Steam Success in Legal Practice*, 49 University of San Francisco Law Review, 40 (2015).

[6] *Ibid.* at 40.   [7] *Ibid.* at 41.   [8] *Ibid.* at 42.

[9] Sonja Lyubormirsky, The How of Happiness: A New Approach to Getting the Life You Want 20–22 (Penguin Press 2007).

[10] *Ibid.*   [11] *Ibid.* at 21–23.

By adopting a growth mindset when it comes to feedback, you can take full advantage of every shred of feedback you receive. You can consider feedback as coaching advice from someone who cares about your growth, a fresh perspective that is helpful rather than hurtful. After all, more information is almost always better than less information. Since real feedback is rare, watch for it and see it as the gift that it is.

Finally, stay present and have compassion for yourself. Kristen Neff draws on scientific studies showing that how often people tend to focus on the future or past, as opposed to the present, predicts their happiness. People who focus on the future more than the present are less happy than those who spend quality time thinking about the present moment.[12] When the mind wanders, one can bring it back with self-compassion. It is our view that self-compassion, along with a growth mindset, are the traits that will most serve you as a law student and a lawyer, the most critical skills to success in law school.

TIPS ON TAKING FEEDBACK WELL

Learning to take and use feedback is an ongoing process. Few people like even the most constructive criticism, but seeing the feedback as an opportunity to grow makes the process of receiving it easier. Being able to graciously receive meaningful feedback will significantly enhance your career. You can improve easily by taking the advice.

On the other hand, without feedback and change, we all plod through life in the same old way. When receiving feedback, remember how hard it is to *give* feedback. This will help you have empathy for the giver and also help you see feedback as a gift. The person who can tactfully provide meaningful feedback is a rare treasure in any organization, so if you find one, latch on and get whatever advice you can.

A Law Firm Feedback Story

When I (Professor Martin) was an associate in a law firm, I recall a review in which one of the partners wrote, "She has a personality problem with some or all of the partners in her department." This was a big blow. All of the partners? A "personality problem?" I mean, come on, what can I do with that? Can we be a little more specific and helpful?

The truth is I did have a personality problem with some of the partners, but I did not have enough information from this comment to help myself improve. If this sort of thing ever happens to you, ask for more details. Be open to the possibility that the feedback could be true.

---

[12] Kristen Neff, Self-Compassion: The Proven Power of Being Kind to Yourself 85–88 (Morrow 2011).

Also be open to the possibility that if you are the junior person in a law firm and you don't get along with someone who is more senior, this will be seen as a problem with *your* personality, not the other person's. This is because it is your job as the more junior person to get along with the more senior people, regardless of how much this may be asking of you. In other words, you will be expected to be more emotionally intelligent than the people who are already working there.

In any case, the art of taking feedback comes down to our ability to temper our response to the situation, taking into account and being aware of our relationship with the giver, our emotions at that time, the time we have available, and even how much we've had to eat or sleep. However, there are some general things that help us receive feedback well.

1. Identify Your Relationship with the Giver

The relationship between the giver and receiver is important. This relationship often determines what will be said, how it will be said, and how it will be received. If your direct supervisor were to offer feedback, you might feel compelled to take the feedback and apply it, but you might also feel defensive if he or she criticizes you. If a friend is giving you feedback, you may be more receptive to hearing the feedback, but slower to actually apply it. You may even be thinking, "What does that person know anyway?"

LAW PAUSE

Write down the name of someone who recently gave you feedback and your relationship to that person. Was it a supervisor, colleague, friend, or maybe a spouse? What feedback did they give you? Write it down.

Now, honestly assess whether you have implemented the feedback. If so, write down how you implemented it. If not, write down the reason you have yet to do so. This may just be a timing issue, but you may have had the chance to apply it but didn't do it. Reflect on why not. Now, complete this process twice more.

Now, look back on what you wrote. What have you learned about your relationships and their effect upon how you take feedback? You may discover, upon further reflection or practice, that your reaction to feedback changes as your relationships change and develop. You can learn from how these relationships influence your ability to receive feedback. If you are aware, then you can better take stock of the situation when constructive feedback is offered.

2. Be Aware (and Beware) of Your Emotions

Be aware of your emotions when receiving feedback. This is one of the most important factors in determining your receptivity to feedback. When receiving feedback, we are vulnerable. Someone is criticizing our actions. No one likes to be told what to do or, no matter however lovingly, how to do something better.

Recognize this in yourself so you can step back and, as objectively and positively as possible, hear the comments. Trust that the person giving feedback has your best interests in mind, even if their skill in providing it is not optimal. Trust that the person is interested in your growth, and even if you suspect they may not be, see what you can learn. See it as a chance to be a better lawyer or lawyer to be.

In her article *Taking Constructive Criticism like a Champ*,[13] Nicole Lindsay recommends that you "stop your first reaction,"[14] which will probably be too emotional. She suggests you curtail defensiveness, avoid saying something sarcastic or cutting and don't get angry. Just note the emotion and let it go, moving on to see what you can learn from the feedback. Remember that getting feedback is a gift.[15] As Lindsay notes, "It can be challenging to receive criticism from a co-worker, a peer, or someone that you don't fully respect, but ... accurate and constructive feedback comes even from flawed sources."[16] Also, remember that giving feedback is hard work, so give the feedback giver the benefit of the doubt and assume good intentions.

For example, and along the same lines, try to give up pride of authorship in your writing. The whole point of providing drafts of documents to people is so they can provide feedback to improve the product. See what your teacher, supervisor, or colleague has to say about your product and make the product better. Lawyers deal with written feedback constantly and this will get much easier with time.

3. Take Notes

If the feedback is oral, take notes. Having something to do diverts defensive feelings. Writing down the feedback allows you to revisit the feedback when you are less emotional and more open to suggestions and advice. Taking notes is good advice in any setting in which one might become bored, distracted, or especially, defensive.

When given feedback, which also can be seen as criticism, it is natural to feel defensive, but it is best not to express that emotion. Whether or not we become openly defensive can depend on the relationship with the giver and other factors including content, tone, etc. We cannot always predict if and when we will be defensive, but if we are aware of the very human tendency to get defensive, we can better temper our reaction. Taking notes will help you temper your reaction and also create a record of the feedback that you can use as a guide for future actions and conversations.

---

[13]   Nicole Lindsay, *Taking Constructive Criticism Like a Champ*, FORBES, Nov. 7, 2012, available at www.forbes.com/sites/dailymuse/2012/11/07/taking-constructive-criticism-like-a-champ/#2b8a264f2c0c.
[14]   *Ibid.*   [15]   *Ibid.*   [16]   *Ibid.*

4. Be Actively Involved in Receiving the Feedback

Receiving feedback is not a spectator sport. It's like the lottery; you must play to win. You must be involved. Involvement is the key to understanding the feedback. To be involved, be a good listener, carefully listening for two things: understanding and deconstruction.

Starting with the understanding, you want to listen closely enough so that you can repeat what was said back to the giver. Focus on what is being said and try not to interrupt the giver. Listen closely.

Next, deconstruct by asking questions.[17] Choose your words wisely so you don't come off as defensive. Work with the giver to better understand the specifics. Asking questions allows the giver to elaborate on their comments and provide specific examples. If your relationship with the giver is comfortable enough, ask some challenging questions. It is empowering to have an active conversation while receiving feedback. Find out exactly how you can modify your behavior for the better.

5. Modify Your Behavior Based Upon the Feedback

Try to incorporate the feedback and act on it. Lindsay uses the example of a co-worker telling you that you get heated and lose your temper in meetings. In a situation like this, try to get some specific examples of the conduct, find out if this is an ongoing issue, and then ask for recommendations on how to fix it. Then try to change your behavior.

6. Say Thank You

As difficult as it might be, especially if you are defensive, tell the giver that you appreciate his or her feedback. Giving feedback is difficult, even if the feedback isn't particularly helpful. This doesn't mean you have to implement the feedback, but acknowledge the giver's time and effort.

7. Request Time to Follow Up

Lindsay suggests you finish the whole process off by asking for a good time to follow up. This may be overkill but if the feedback relates to something critical to your success, it may make sense to follow up.

In her article, *Receive Feedback with Grace and Dignity*,[18] Susan M. Heathfield shares similar advice, but incorporates some of the emotional intelligence tips discussed throughout this book:

1. Try to control your defensiveness. Fear of hurting you or having to deal with defensive or justifying behavior make people hesitant to give feedback.
2. Listen to understand. Practice all the skills of an effective listener including using body language and facial expressions that encourage the other person to talk.

---

[17]   *Ibid.*
[18]   Susan M. Heathfield, *Receive Feedback with Grace and Dignity*, Oct. 17, 2016, available at http://humanresources.about.com/cs/communication/ht/receivefeedback.htm.

3. Try to suspend judgment. By learning the views of the feedback provider, you learn about yourself and how your actions are interpreted in the world.

4. Summarize and reflect on what you hear. Your feedback provider will appreciate that you are really hearing what is said. You are affirming that you are really hearing.

5. Ask questions to clarify. Focus on questions to make sure you understand the feedback.

6. Ask for examples and stories that illustrate the feedback.

7. Just because a person gives you feedback, doesn't mean their feedback is right. They see your actions but interpret them through their own perceptual screen and life experiences.

8. Be approachable. People avoid giving feedback to grumpies. Your openness to feedback is obvious through your body language, facial expressions, and welcoming manner.

9. Check with others to determine the reliability of the feedback. If only one person believes it about you, it may be just him or her, not you.

10. Remember, only you have the right and the ability to decide what to do with the feedback.[19]

GO ON A FEEDBACK SCAVENGER HUNT

When someone gives us unsolicited advice, even if it's good advice, we tend to reject it.[20] However, if we actively seek this advice, on our own terms and our own timetable, we are much more receptive to the feedback. Because sought-out feedback is more used and useful, take matters into your own hands – go out and actively seek feedback from people whose opinions you value.

Do not seek feedback only from people with whom you have a good personal relationship. Look also for people you may not like on a personal level, but whose insight you value. That way, you can get honest advice. By seeking out feedback on your timetable, you are more in control of the situation, which will help reduce the negativity bias. Many students and executives describe this process of seeking feedback as career-changing. When asking for feedback, make it easy on your source, by asking an easy question such as "What's one thing you see me doing (or not doing) that is holding me back?"[21] By the way, just seeking the feedback creates a more favorable impression of you. Overall, people who actively seek feedback get higher performance ratings, which could either be because they took the feedback, or simply because they created a favorable impression by asking for it.[22] Those who seek feedback are seen as confident, humble, respectful, and passionate about excellence.

[19] *Ibid.*   [20] *Ibid.*

[21] Sheila Heen and Douglas Stone, *Find the Coaching in Criticism*, HARV. BUS. REV. Jan.–Feb. 2014, at 7, available at https://myhbp.org/leadingedge/d/cla?&c=30794&i=30796&cs=1df4d26c09afe3198c57 f6ea786e3f2a.

[22] *Ibid.* at 8.

Design a feedback-solicitation plan based upon these steps:

1. **Choose your sources and seek feedback.** Identify between three and five people who know you well from different walks of life, and ask them to write a story about a time when you were at your best. Also ask for a time when you missed an opportunity or held yourself back through your behavior. Diversity is key. You want work colleagues, family, friends, and even businesses you and your family frequent.
2. **Spot patterns.** Once the feedback arrives, look for the common themes that appear in multiple stories. Make a list of the themes, the key examples that support each of them, and what they suggest about your strengths.
3. **Create your self-portrait.** Using this information, write out a brief profile of who you are when you're at your best. Then make a short list of traits you'd like to improve.
4. **Put your strengths into action.** Create an action plan for how and when you'll utilize your strengths, and also how you'll improve on some of your weaknesses.

GIVING FEEDBACK

You may be young in your career, but even so, there may be times that you need to give feedback to another person. We end this chapter with the topic of giving feedback, something that Joshua is quite good at and Professor Martin is not (yet). See Figure 12.1 for a fantastic recipe for giving good feedback.

I (Joshua) was a manager at a phone service company, where I was trained in giving feedback. Based on my experience in the work world, here is some advice for giving feedback:

1. Always lead with questions, such as, "How do you think you're doing?" It gives the recipient joint ownership of the evaluation and helps him or her feel included, not excluded.
2. Unless it is part of your formal job description, don't give criticism unless it's been invited. Unsolicited negative feedback only provokes annoyance and will be discounted.
3. Make sure you are seen as having the authority to give corrective feedback. Criticism from those perceived as peers or otherwise unqualified to give it often creates resistance and rebellion.
4. Never give feedback when you're angry. Anger will alienate the listener. Expressing disappointment is more productive.

FIGURE 12.1 Criticism Sandwich Cartoon, by Tom Fishburne, licensed from *Marketoonist Cartoons.*

5. Consider the mental state of the person to whom you are giving feedback. Narcissists take any criticism as a personal attack. Those who are insecure lose self-esteem.

6. Know yourself too. If you're relatively insensitive to criticism, curb the tendency to be heavy-handed when delivering it.

7. Expect some defensiveness as a first response to criticism and be prepared for it. A change in performance may come later.

Try to give feedback when you can, knowing it is a gift and that useful feedback can change lives. It has the potential to promote positive change and enhance their work and life. Hopefully, you can see it in that light. It is much easier for the giver of feedback not to say anything and, thus, not to help the receiver improve. It is also safer. The giver doesn't need to worry about taking time to prepare for the conversation, hurting the other person's feelings, or spoiling the relationship, etc.

Giving helpful feedback takes time and effort. Helpful feedback is appropriate for the time, place, relationship, and on a topic the receiver can actually do something about.

Little Pause: Think of a time when someone was honest with you about something you were doing but not aware of, and the honesty really improved your ability, skill, attitude, perception, or "know how." It may have been pleasant or unpleasant at the time, but in retrospect it was worth learning about. How was that feedback given, and what made it worthwhile?

Recall my (Professor Martin's) story where I was told that I had a personality conflict with *all* of the partners in my firm? In my scenario, I was perceived *not* as the one who was forced to work with the bully, but rather the one who could not manage the bully. Because I was more junior, the problem was mine. And it really was mine. If I had followed Talane Miedaner's advice about calmly confronting the bully, I would likely have been all set. (Quick side note, I might not have become a law professor because I literally left this firm to become a professor, in order to get away from the bullies. Sometimes the culture at a workplace can be so different from your own culture that you need to look for other opportunities.)

Now let's consider a situation from the other point of view, when I (Professor Martin) failed to give feedback to a former student. I recall a situation in which a good student had alcohol on his breath at 10.30 in the morning. I would have recommended this student for jobs but decided not to because of this. If I had just asked him about this, there may have been an explanation. If not, I may have been able to get him help. Instead I decided to butt out and be a coward just to avoid confrontation and appearing foolish. I think about this often because I could have helped and didn't. Since then, I have tried to do what I can, learning from my mistake.

Summarizing the Art of Giving and Receiving Feedback

To summarize, consider these tips when receiving feedback:

1. Prepare yourself emotionally. Feedback invokes a negativity bias, which may make us partially or completely resistant to feedback. We need to get over this because we can use the feedback.
2. Feedback is so important. We are able to learn from our supervisors, peers, instructors, and others qualified to teach and develop us in a certain skill set. Without these people we fail to grow.
3. If the person giving you feedback is acting aggressively or angrily, and it is possible to do so without jeopardizing your job, reschedule the feedback so you won't be defensive and incapable of receiving the feedback.
4. Take notes, particularly if you cannot overcome an emotional response otherwise. You can revisit the notes to see if the feedback makes more sense once you are not under the sway of defensive emotions.
5. Don't be a spectator to your feedback. Interact by asking clarifying questions about the feedback. In other words, make it a conversation, not a speech. If you don't understand, make sure you ask questions until you do understand.

6. Follow-up on feedback. You may think of questions later. You may want to approach the giver with actions you have taken to see if the actions resolve the concern.
7. Encourage feedback by being thankful for effective feedback. Always be grateful for feedback, but make sure to identify the pieces that particularly helped you. This can be done in a follow-up conversation or email.

If you want to become a real feedback connoisseur, read Sheila Heen and Douglas Stone's book, *Thanks for the Feedback: The Science and Art of Receiving Feedback Well*,[23] or their very accessible article, *Find the Coaching in Criticism*.[24]

As you'll see from these sources, taking feedback is much more art and self-awareness than science. Feedback takes practice, both in giving and receiving. Be patient and develop your relationships. Ultimately, we benefit from feedback, no matter how hard it is to take it. As we discussed in Chapter 11, practice humility. Receiving feedback is a gift, part of your job, and part of being human. It is an opportunity for growth that could improve your life significantly.

Now consider these tips when giving feedback:

- Try to pick a good time.
- Prepare your remarks.
- Make the results constructive.
- Make them specific.
- Do it now. Bad news never improves with age.
- Only give feedback about things the other person can actually change. Give this concept quite a bit of thought. Some things really can't or won't change.
- Mix good feedback with bad feedback; never just give bad feedback.

---

[23] DOUGLAS STONE AND SHEILA HEEN, THANKS FOR THE FEEDBACK: THE SCIENCE AND ART OF RECEIVING FEEDBACK WELL (VIKING 2014).
[24] Sheila Heen and Douglas Stone, *Find the Coaching in Criticism*, HARV. BUS. REV. Jan.-Feb. 2014, available at https://myhbp.org/leadingedge/d/cla?&c=30794&i=30796&cs=1df4d26c09afe3198c57f6ea786e3f2a.

13

Empathy

Nathalie Martin

If you find yourself saying "But I'm just being honest," chances are you've just been unkind. Honesty doesn't heal. Empathy does.

Dan Waldschmidt

Empathy is an understanding of and an interest in the human condition. It is a personal trait that allows each of us to identify with the thoughts and feelings of another person and then respond appropriately.[1] Legal scholars describe empathy as the sense, emotionally and cognitively, of knowing what it is like to be the other person, and becoming "attuned to the emotional resonance of another person."[2]

Legal employers expect young attorneys to arrive at their first law jobs with well-developed interpersonal skills, as well as the ability to be self-aware. Empathy ranks highly among those desired skills. Clients also crave empathetic lawyers and may prefer these over the smartest and best technicians. Unfortunately, some scholars note that traditional legal education "systematically eliminate[s] empathy from law students."[3] Here we try to reverse this process and bring empathy back.

This chapter discusses how to improve empathy skills. After discussing empathy in general, it explores the importance of empathy in developing cultural competence. This chapter then examines the role of empathy and cross-cultural competence in the attorney decision-making process.

Learning to "think like lawyer" in the traditional sense is all well and good, and you will have three intense years to learn to think like a lawyer, but remember, the

---

[1] DOUGLAS O. LINDER AND NANCY LEVIT, THE GOOD LAWYER 6 (OXFORD UNIVERSITY PRESS 2014).

[2] HEIDI BROWN, THE INTROVERTED LAWYER 39 (ABA PUBLISHING 2017), citing Professor Joshua Rosenberg of University of San Francisco School of Law and Emily Gould of the Vermont Disputer Resolution Section of the Vermont Bar Association.

[3] Ibid., citing Joshua Rosenberg, Teaching Empathy in Law School, 36 U. SAN. FRANCISCO L. REV. 621, 632 (2002).

core of the profession is serving others and the first step is empathy.[4] Empathy is critical to good lawyering for at least four reasons, and you can probably think of more:

1. Empathy allows us to acknowledge and respect other people's thoughts, so they feel heard and valued.
2. Empathy reduces the likelihood of miscommunication and misunderstanding, which could otherwise lead to wasted efforts and counterproductive results.
3. Empathy allows us to discern other people's reactions so we can make adjustments when we are having a negative or unintended effect on situations or other people. In other words, if people think we are acting inappropriately, we can pick up that cue, stop, adjust our behavior, and move back into the problem-solving role.
4. Empathy for adversaries and clients, in particular, allows us to better understand and tell their stories.[5] It improves an attorney's results.

LAWYERS AND EMPATHY

Empirical data show that overall, many lawyers lack the empathy needed for the job. Research by the American Bar Association, the association that accredits law schools across the country, shows that 60 percent of clients polled had negative reactions to their lawyers, even though clients felt their lawyers were smart and knowledgeable.[6] Think about that for a minute. Sixty percent, more than half of all clients, hold animosity toward their own lawyers. Perhaps even more disturbingly, the more contact the client had with his or her lawyer, the lower the client's opinion of that lawyer.[7] When asked why people had these negative views of their lawyers, a common explanation was that lawyers seemed to lack care and compassion. They had no empathy. Remarkably, clients reported caring more about feeling listened to and cared for than about the traditional legal skills of the lawyer. In other words, "caring is as much a part of the legal profession as intelligence."[8]

A Dichotomy

As you continue in your legal education, especially when you represent clients in a live client setting, you will need to balance empathy for clients with the regulation of your own feelings. You don't need to jump into the emotional morass with the client – you must stay separate enough to be of value, measured and thoughtful, all while feeling their pain. This requires walking the fine line between having empathy, yet not falling apart, and remaining objective enough to provide the legal assistance needed. This is where mindfulness practices, including a long walk, a run, or any exercise to clear the mind, can really help you stay balanced. This is just another version of that airplane adage: "Put your own mask on first before assisting others."

---

[4] DOUGLAS O. LINDER AND NANCY LEVIT, THE GOOD LAWYER 21 (OXFORD UNIVERSITY PRESS 2014).
[5] *Ibid.* at 7. [6] *Ibid.* at 7. [7] *Ibid.* [8] *Ibid.* at 21.

CAN PEOPLE LEARN EMPATHY?

Empathy is an advanced emotional intelligence skill, and if you could choose just one lawyer superpower, this one just might be it. There are many figures in history that model empathy, but is empathy something you can actually learn? Yes, you can. Many scientific studies show that people can learn empathy skills and improve their responses to others.[9]

The Empathetic Brain

Due to recent scientific studies, we now know quite a bit about empathy and the brain. In 2013, a study published in the *Journal of Neuroscience* used brain imaging to study the parts of the brain affiliated with empathy.[10] Researchers studied the cerebral cortex and, in particular, a smaller region on it known as the right supramarginal gyrus, which helps us "distinguish our own emotional state from that of other people and is responsible for empathy and compassion."[11] Though other parts of the brain are affiliated with similar emotions, this little spot is the center of our empathetic brain.

The gray part in Figure 13.1 shows where the supramarginal gyrus is.[12] It is located at the junction of the parietal, temporal, and frontal lobes. The right supramarginal gyrus apparently allows us to "decouple our perception of ourselves from that of others."[13] Scientists found that when the neurons in this part of the brain were disrupted in the course of a research task, the participants found it difficult to stop from projecting their own feelings and circumstances onto others. The participants were also less accurate when forced to make particularly quick decisions related to what *another* person would want.[14] This study confirms that we can observe and measure the empathetic part of the brain.

Scientists have also studied the anterior rostral prefrontal cortex and temporal poles. This is the area of the brain related to understanding other people's emotions and intentions. Studies show that when people interact with others in a compassionate way and make decisions involving a moral issue, in other words when they experience empathy, this area is activated.

---

[9] Roman Krznaric, Empathy: Why It Matters and How to Get It 27 (Perigree 2014). A quick Google search will bring up dozens of books on the subject. Moreover, tens of thousands of children are taught empathy in schools through the Roots of Empathy Program, which is a useful resource for tackling bullying.

[10] Christopher Bergland, *The Neuroscience of Empathy*, Psychology Today, Oct. 10, 2013, available at www.psychologytoday.com/blog/the-athletes-way/201310/the-neuroscience-empathy.

[11] *Ibid.*

[12] *Ibid.* Gray726 supramarginal gyrus.png, Wikimedia commons, available at https://commons.wikimedia.org/wiki/File:Gray726_supramarginal_gyrus.png.

[13] Christopher Bergland, *The Neuroscience of Empathy: Neuroscientists identify specific brain areas linked to compassion*, Psychology Today, Oct. 10, 2013, available at www.psychologytoday.com/blog/the-athletes-way/201310/the-neuroscience-empathy.

[14] *Ibid.*

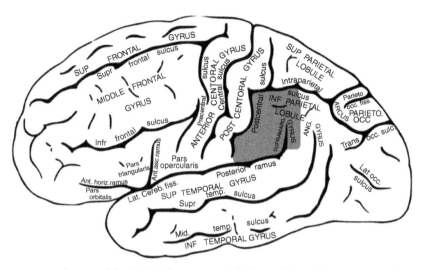

FIGURE 13.1 Image of the Brain's Supramarginal Gyrus, Gray726 supramarginal gyrus. png, Wikimedia commons, available at https://commons.wikimedia.org/wiki/File: Gray726_supramarginal_gyrus.png (released into the public domain, worldwide).

Finally, scientists have found that damage to these areas of the brain is linked to a lack of empathy. Indeed, taking this idea to the extreme, scientists have compared the brains of psychopathic criminal offenders to those of non-psychopathic offenders, and found that the psychopaths had significantly less gray matter in the empathy centers of the brain.[15]

Because our brain's physical structure (to be more specific, neural circuitry) is malleable and can change, a person's capacity for empathy can also change. This means we can increase our empathy by changing our brains, primarily by putting ourselves in someone else's shoes. Practices that help us do this reinforce and strengthen our brain's capacity for empathy.

Changing Your Brain Through Meditation

Meditation is one way to rewire the brain, according to Dr. Dan Siegel and others. Siegel is a pioneer in the field of interpersonal neurobiology and executive director of the Mindsight Institute, which educates health professionals, educators, business professionals, coaches, parents, and others on brain science and mental health. A large body of scientific research now shows that mindfulness meditation

---

[15] Robert Waugh, *Born to Kill? Psychopaths have different brains to normal people – and current "therapies" for killers may be useless: Psychopaths have less grey matter in areas of brain used to "understand" other people*, Daily Mail, May 8, 2012, available at www.dailymail.co.uk/sciencetech/article-2141160/Born-bad-Rapists-psychopathic-murderers-physically-different-brains-normal-people.html#ixzz4WLeQaaZm.

stimulates the growth of integrative fibers in the brain. The most famous study of neuroplasticity, or the brain's ability to rewire itself, was carried out on Buddhist monks. University of Wisconsin Professor Richard Davidson conducted MRI brain scans on Tibetan Buddhist monks and found that loving-kindness meditations produced measurable changes in the brain. Davidson measured the monks' gamma wave electrical signals and found that when they were asked to meditate on "unconditional loving-kindness and compassion," their brains generated powerful gamma waves indicating a compassionate state of mind. This study is but one example of the scientific evidence showing we can cultivate deeper empathy.[16] Also recall the studies by neuroscientist Eleanor Maguire of University College London showing that London taxi drivers had larger-than-average hippocampi because to get licensed, they need to memorize a labyrinth of 25,000 streets within a ten-kilometer radius.[17] We have the capacity to change our brains.

EMPATHY AND THE SERVICE PRACTICE

Learning about empathy allows us to better understand our clients. Even before you graduate from law school, you can look for moments in your day-to-day life to exercise and improve your empathy skills. Start by noticing how everyday people react to the law and often fear it.

From the first day you enter law school, you will likely have family members asking for advice, and through these interactions you will be able to see firsthand how stressful most people think dealing with the law is.

While working on the first draft of this chapter, a colleague was trying to figure out how to reassign the beneficiary of a family life insurance policy from a trust held by a defunct bank. His mother told him, "I do not want to go to court no matter what, regardless of what we get or don't get in terms of money." Around the same time, I was trying to help a family member with identity theft (getting the paperwork together), and also trying to reinstate health insurance cancelled due to no fault of yet another family member. Everyone wanted to avoid court and even the law if possible. Another friend's family member was trying to avoid litigating over a class action settlement in which she was one of the *plaintiffs*, meaning a person in line to

---

[16]   Another 2013 study from Harvard and Northeastern Universities found that meditation can improve compassion and altruistic behavior. The researchers found that participants who had meditated were more likely than non-meditators to lend a helping hand to an actor with crutches who was pretending to be in pain. Another 2012 Emory University study suggested that compassion training derived from ancient Tibetan mindfulness practices may boost empathy, and other research has found that loving-kindness meditation could increase positive emotions and lead to more positive relationships over time. ROMAN KRZNARIC, EMPATHY: WHY IT MATTERS AND HOW TO GET IT 21–26 (PERIGREE 2014).

[17]   Ferris Jabr, *Cache Cab: Taxi Drivers' Brains Grow to Navigate London's Streets: Memorizing 25,000 city streets balloons the hippocampus, but cabbies may pay a hidden fare in cognitive skills*, SCIENTIFIC AMERICAN, Dec. 8, 2011, available at www.scientificamerican.com/article/london-taxi-memory/.

get money without doing anything except mailing in a postcard. This person told my friend that "under no circumstances do I wish to get involved with any courts," even though all she had to do to receive the settlement was fill out a postcard!

> Most people hate paperwork, red tape, and especially litigation and courts. Those things are, in a word, scary! Remembering this fear will help you have empathy for all those scared people out there, who seek your help because they cannot help themselves.

EMPATHY VERSUS SYMPATHY

There is a big difference between empathy and sympathy. While empathy involves imaginatively stepping into the shoes of another person, understanding their perspectives, challenges, and limitations, and using that understanding to guide your own actions,[18] sympathy involves sadness, pity, and sorrow. If you still can't quite picture the difference, watch Brené Brown's video on empathy versus sympathy at www.youtube.com/watch?v=1Evwgu369Jw.

Sympathy is a solitary emotion. It does not involve trying to figure out how the other person feels. Empathy on the other hand is a shared emotion, what Austrian philosopher Martin Buber calls an "I and Thou" connection.[19] Researchers often note the human capacity for empathy by noting that when one baby in a nursery cries, the others soon join in. Author and social philosopher Roman Krznaric has taken this observation further, noting that before his daughter turned twenty-four months, when her twin brother would cry, she would offer him her own toy dog. At age twenty-four months she learned that to really make him feel better, she could hand him his own toy cat rather than her toy dog. Her brother was comforted by what *he* liked best, not by what *she* liked best!

Through this and other examples Krznaric explains why the golden rule, "Do unto others as you would have them do unto you," is not as good as what he calls the "platinum rule." Under the platinum rule, you do unto others what *they* would want you to do, *not* what you would want done to you. Krznaric quotes George Bernard Shaw as saying "Do not do unto others as you would have them do unto you. They may have different tastes."[20] The key is to somehow, some way, determine how the person with whom you are engaging would like to be treated, and see if you can do so.

LAW PAUSE

This is a hard one. Try to write an empathy note or an empathy card, as opposed to a sympathy card. Remember to keep the subject on the other person and not on you. Hard, but give it a try. It will be worth talking about what makes this difficult.

---

[18] *Ibid.* at x.   [19] *Ibid.* at 51.   [20] *Ibid.* at x.

THE PRACTICE OF EMPATHY

An Easy Empathy Exercise: Loving-kindness or METTA Meditation

Because studies repeatedly show that loving-kindness meditation, also known as METTA, has a profound effect on the part of the brain responsible for feelings of empathy, we start our "empathy training" with a loving-kindness meditation. An exercise like this, even over a sustained period, can be easier than actually expressing empathy to others but it is a start. To some of you, this exercise will seem strange, but it works.

In a calm place, sit upright and quietly, and say to yourself:

- May I be safe.
- May I be happy.
- May I be healthy.
- May I live with ease.

Now think about a person or a pet you love deeply and bring them to your heart or the forefront of your thinking, and offer that person or pet these wishes:

- May you be safe.
- May you be happy.
- May you be healthy.
- May you live with ease.

And now bring to your heart and mind someone about whom you feel neutral – neither disliking nor liking them, and offer that person these wishes:

- May you be safe.
- May you be happy.
- May you be healthy.
- May you live with ease.

Now, bring to your heart and mind a person with whom you have had difficulty, perhaps not *the most difficult* person, but a person who is annoying or with whom you often disagree. Hold that person in your awareness and offer that person these wishes:

- May you be safe.
- May you be happy.
- May you be healthy.
- May you live with ease.

You can continue this until the whole universe is involved, working through family, community, city, country, etc., but we'll stop there for now.

After a while, it can become second nature to give these silent wishes to each person. Chade-Meng Tan, author of *Search Inside Yourself* and mindfulness trainer at Google, regularly does this around his office. That's right, while you are walking around formulating those point headings or revisiting last night's ball game, and we are working on our four-count breathing, Meng Tan is wishing the universe well, one person at a time.

Eventually, this loving-kindness meditation exercise can be extended. You can imagine that you are each of the people you chose. Imagine yourself first as your loved one that you meditated on. Just visualize and imagine that person's life, dreams aspirations, fears, and failures. This should not be too difficult. Next, imagine yourself being the neutral one and living that person's life, visualizing that person's life, dreams, aspirations, fears, and failures. Finally, try to imagine living the life of the difficult one, visualizing what it is like to live that person's life, dreams, aspirations, fears, and failures.

LAW PAUSE

Try either the loving-kindness or the extended empathy exercise a few times, and write down your reactions to it.

Developing Empathy Through Daily Living

Besides meditating, there are at least three other established ways to develop basic empathy for others. You can experience a similar situation yourself, get to know others who are different from you, and read about the lives of those who are different from you. These approaches all work to some extent but are presented here in the order of effectiveness. In other words, it is easier to empathize with someone who has had a similar experience to you than one you read about in a book.

1. Live a Similar Experience

The *most effective and direct* route to empathy is to actually go through what the person with whom you would like to empathize has gone through. For example, I lost my father, to whom I was very close. My husband was very close to his mother who died some years back. Until I lost my father, I had no idea what my husband actually went through with his loss. In fact, once my father died, I felt badly that I did not do a better job "sitting with" my husband during his pain. I just had no idea how painful his loss really was. Now I know. Now I empathize with all who have lost a close parent, or any parent. As a good friend explained, "When you lose a parent, sometimes you are close and you mourn that relationship. Sometimes you are not, and you mourn the loss of the possibility of someday getting close. Either way, you mourn." I can now better empathize with those who have suffered a similar loss.

2. Get to Know Others Who are Different from You

The *most common* way to experience empathy is to personally get to know people who have had experiences that you have not. According to Susan Fiske, author of *Envy Up Scorn Down: How Status Divides Us*, it is especially helpful to get to know people who are less privileged than you are, because privilege almost always creates judgment and scorn.[21] Regardless of your background, it won't be difficult to find less privileged people because you are a law student or lawyer, which is a privilege in itself.

My husband, for example, is a white male from New England, who works with undocumented people. He feels their pain and knows quite a bit about what it is like to live undocumented in the United States. He hasn't been there personally but he does experience and exhibit empathy every day through the lives of those around him.

You can often find these empathy "opportunities" all around if you stay open to them. Oskar Schindler was not Jewish but saved many Jews during the Holocaust in World War II, because he felt for them. His friendship with his Jewish accountant Itzhak Stern provided an opportunity to see life through the eyes of another.[22]

While getting to know people different from you is not the same as actually living through their experiences, it is an effective empathy-builder and by far the most common way to experience empathy. Mahatma Gandhi was not from the Dalit caste (known in India as the untouchables), but he had deep empathy for people of this caste. Mother Teresa never experienced the poverty she saw in the world, but that did not stop her from empathizing deeply with the world's poorest people.

3. Read About People With Lives Different from Your Own

A third way to build empathy is through reading about and watching others who are different from you. In *Empathy: Why it Matters, and How to Get It*, Roman Krznaric chronicles the way in which many book and screenplay authors have brought empathy to the world through their media. For example, he strongly recommends that we watch the 1930s version of the movie, *All Quiet of the Western Front*, based upon the book by the same name. In the story, a feverishly patriotic German foot soldier drops into a trench for cover, only to be followed by a French soldier doing the same thing. Without thinking, the German soldier stabs the Frenchman. However, the Frenchman does not die, and they remain there together overnight. At first the German soldier is annoyed at the Frenchman's wheezing, but eventually deep empathy sets in, as his compatriot in war becomes humanized in his eyes. The German soldier states:

> I didn't want to kill you. I tried to keep you alive. If you jumped in here again,
> I wouldn't do it. You see, when you jumped in here you were my enemy . . . and

---

[21] Susan T. Fiske, Envy Up, Scorn Down: How Status Divides Us ix (Russell Sage Foundation 2012).

[22] Roman Krznaric, Empathy: Why It Matters and How to Get It, 47 (Perigree 2014).

I was afraid of you. But you're just a man like me, and I killed you. Forgive me comrade. Say that for me. Say you forgive me! . . . Oh no, you're dead! Only you're better off than I am. They can't do any more to you now . . . Oh, God! Why did they do this to us? We only want to live, you and I. Why should they send us out to fight each other? If they threw away these rifles and these uniforms, you could be my brother.[23]

This single literary work is said to have turned millions of people worldwide into anti-war sympathizers and peace activists.[24] In other words, people were able to empathize. The more modern movie, *Moonlight*, about a kid growing up black, gay, and poor in Miami, had a similar effect on me. It was depressing but good to see a sliver of life that was otherwise outside my consciousness.

It is not just fiction writers who increase empathy through their writing. In their book *Scarcity*, Sendhil Mullainathan and Eldar Shafir discuss managing scarcity of all kinds. They define scarcity as having less than you think you need. For some it is money, for others time, for others space, love, attention, confidence, and so on. One of the authors' primary goals in writing their book is to create an empathy bridge through which upper and middle class people can experience what it is like to be poor.[25]

An Advanced Practice: Expressing Empathy When Someone Experiences Trauma or Death of a Loved One

While the golden rule claims that we should treat others as we would like to be treated, we learned above that it is even better to treat others as *they* would like to be treated. But how are we supposed to figure out what would be good for the other person? The difficulty in doing so might explain why the golden rule prevails but this other tougher task, the platinum rule, should prevail.

Many of our clients experience unbelievable trauma. Many have experienced the loss of a loved one. Some have even lost entire families to death and other tragedies. It is always hard to know what to say. What should we say when the parent, spouse, or, heaven forbid, child of someone you represent, dies? When a family member or loved one dies, it is as if a vital life parachute disappears. It is good to know what to say or not to say. A few things that are not very helpful include:

- It's for the best (decidedly the all-time worst thing to say).
- He's in a better place.
- At least he is not suffering.
- This is God's will.
- The Lord wanted to take him.

---

[23] *Ibid.* at 135–37. [24] *Ibid.* at 137.
[25] SENDHIL MULLAINATHAN AND ELDAR SHAFIR, SCARCITY, WHY HAVING TOO LITTLE MEANS SO MUCH 150 (TIME BOOKS, HENRY HOLT & COMPANY, LLC 2013).

But what *do* you say? Sometimes a simple "I am so sorry" and a hug is best, followed by either "Can I do something or help?" or better yet, "Let me bring you some food. I can just drop it off if you prefer," or "Let's grab a coffee or go for a walk." Be specific. When my father died, I did not know what I needed or how anyone could help. I would go to work but was not really doing anything. A haze set in so thick that it seemed as if life was literally gone from me too. I felt dead myself and sometimes still do. But some things did help. Some things to say that are good, if true, might be:

- The way you took care of him inspired me to take care of my own father.
- You were a wonderful son, daughter, wife, father, etc.
- I am in awe of your relationship with your _____.

An elderly friend who has buried his parents, his brother, and virtually everyone else around him told me this and it helped: "All the things, the trees, the flowers, each one has its time." Sad but a lovely, universally applicable thought.

Things from the heart are generally good even if they come out wrong. My close friend and neighbor is a man who has a completely open heart and would never hurt anyone. He told me, about two weeks after my father died, "Every time I see you I just think of your dad and feel so depressed." Trying to be a considerate person, I wondered if I should hide from him so he would not feel depressed, but then I realized what he was trying to say, that he could understand how I felt. As was described in his autobiography, when Robert Kennedy was grieving the death of JFK, a young boy came up to Robert and blurted out, "Your brother died." It was just so raw and honest, similar to my neighbor's comment, that Robert just picked up the boy and hugged him. If it is heartfelt, it is also empathetic.

More Help with Empathy

If you would like to become even more empathetic, here are some suggestions from a post on the Greater Good Science Center's wonderful web page:[26]

1. Practice active listening, by approaching conversations with a genuine desire to understand the other person's feelings and perspective, without judgment or defensiveness. Tune in to what the other person is saying without interrupting and pay attention to his or her body language and facial expressions. Mirror back what the person is saying to make sure you understand. Research shows that practicing active listening can increase empathy and improve relationships. Perhaps this is too obvious to require a study, but it is still good to know.

---

[26]   Roman Krznaric, *How to Fight Stress with Empathy*, GREATER GOOD SCIENCE CENTER, available at http://greatergood.berkeley.edu/article/item/how_to_fight_stress_with_empathy?utm_source=Newsletter+Jan +11%2C+2017&utm_campaign=GG+Newsletter+Jan+11+2017&utm_medium=email.

2. Share in other peoples' joy, not just sorrow. There is an old Jewish saying: "Sorrow shared is half sorrow, joy shared is double joy." Empathy is not just about commiserating. Research confirms that sharing good news is as important to relationship-building as sharing bad news. Again, this is no big surprise, but nice to know.

3. Seek commonalities with other people, such as the same car, same food, same sports team, whenever you can. Find that connection. We all know people who can talk and listen to anyone. They know how to find the connection.

4. Learn to read faces and non-verbal cures. There is a great quiz found on the Greater Good Science Center's web page, entitled, How well do you read people. Take it by clinking here: http://greatergood.berkeley.edu/ei_quiz/.

5. Do some deep breathing to get ready to focus on the other person.

Fight Stress with Empathy

Finally, another Greater Good Science Center article suggests that empathetic behavior comes back around and lowers your own stress. Psychologist Arthur Ciaramicoli describes a Center for Disease Control study in which 66 percent of American workers reported lying awake at night because of stress. Ciaramicoli argues that stress can be reduced by finding meaning or purpose in our work (the subject of Chapter 16) and also by practicing empathy. When we give and receive empathy, he claims, we produce the neurotransmitter oxytocin, which "creates a sense of trust and cooperation—keys to negotiating and resolving conflict, whether between couples, communities, states, or countries. Leading with empathy can help those around us to be sources of support in our lives and reduce the likelihood of interpersonal conflicts."[27]

In short, whether you are a scientist, author, lawyer, gardener, or doctor, all agree that practicing empathy can be learned and can reduce stress.

A Few Words About Law School and Empathy

You may recall that in Chapter 5, we learned that one of the main things people want in an attorney is empathy. Learning to practice empathy while starting law school may be a bit more difficult to do than if you were, say, studying to be a psychologist or a pediatrician. You can do it, however. There is no doubt that many, if not most, incoming law students have good empathy skills when they arrive.

---

[27] Arthur P. Ciaramicoli, *How to Fight Stress with Empathy: Psychologist Arthur Ciaramicoli argues that empathic listening may be the key to reducing stress in our lives*, GREATER GOOD SCIENCE CENTER, Jan. 11, 2017, available at http://greatergood.berkeley.edu/article/item/how_to_fight_stress_with_empathy/success (discussing Arthur P. Ciaramicoli's book, THE STRESS SOLUTION: USING EMPATHY AND COGNITIVE BEHAVIORAL THERAPY TO REDUCE ANXIETY AND DEVELOP RESILIENCE (NEW WORLD LIBRARY 2016).

Unfortunately, traditional legal education, which emphasizes critical thinking, analysis, finding holes in arguments and identifying problems with cold, unemotional facts and theories, tends to de-emphasize the personal side of law. In *Riding the Waves*, Law Professor and Dean Emeritus Charlie Hapelrin explains his own initiation to law through the first-year curriculum:

> We were learning the language and the tough demeanor of lawyer discourse. Our vocabulary became skewed. Being tough-minded, hard-nosed, and thick-skinned were virtues; there was little talk of altruism or kindness. During a contract negotiation, for example, our job as lawyers was to imagine all the negative outcomes that might possibly happen and draft contract language that would protect our clients' interests in the event of fraud or chicanery by the other contracting parties. The law presented a Darwinian world, and the possibility that people would act out of selfless or generous motives was considered highly unlikely. I found it alarmingly easy to slip into this mindset—suspicious, lawyerly, and aggressive.[28]

Perhaps it is no wonder that toward the end of law school, students' interpersonal skills suffer. Law students and lawyers read many stories about people's lives in the form of cases. Yet in class, as well as in practice, we tend to focus only on the rule, the reasoning, and the "determinative" facts. Through the exercise the professor is using, you are learning the connection between the holding and the facts that led he or she there. This is important to know. The facts drive the law. This connection is at the heart of learning to think like a lawyer.

Nevertheless, focusing on the feelings, understandings, perspectives, and expectations of the people in those cases can help us think of clients as real people and not just hypothetical scenarios designed to teach us legal rules. Learning to think like an empathetic person is not one of the stated goals of most law school classes, so we will indulge a bit here and reawaken your empathy, the empathy you likely came in to law school with, by using a case from class in a different way. Choose a law school case of your choice and do this exercise:

LAW PAUSE

You are reading about the lives of many people in your cases. Because learning legal analysis, methodology, and vocabulary is so foreign and because there is a lot to learn, your other professors will use most of their limited class time to teach legal rules and identify the particular facts that led to the court's decision.

Here, we invite you to think about a case in a different way. Step into the life of one of the people you've just read about. Describe what life might be like for this person, the questions, confusion, and uncertainties he or she must be experiencing, and how he or she might be dealing with or feeling about their legal problems. What

---

[28] CHARLES HALPERN, MAKING WAVES AND RIDING THE CURRENTS 58 (BERRETT-KOEHLER PUBLISHERS 2008).

questions, fears, and hopes might that person have about his or her case or the legal system?

Keeping this exercise in mind will help you become an empathetic lawyer.

As you may recall from Chapter 5 on essential lawyer skill sets, empathy is one attribute all lawyers need. Empathy is enhanced by training in cultural competence. Empathy helps us make better, more ethical, and more client-centered decisions. Empathy smooths the way for better results in our legal professions and our lives in general. As a result, empathy is one serious attorney superpower. Fortunately, we can all improve our capacity for empathy and need not rely solely on the empathy that comes naturally to us.

14

Cross-Cultural Lawyering

Kendall Kerew[1]

The real voyage of discovery consists not in seeking new landscapes, but in having new eyes.
Paraphrased from Marcel Proust, *Remembrance of Things Past: The Captive*, Volume III

As a member of the legal profession, you will engage with others of diverse cultural backgrounds – clients, other lawyers, judges, and jurors. To be an effective lawyer, you "must be able to recognize, and appropriately respond to, [your] own and others' cultural perceptions and beliefs because these often play a central role in lawyer-client communications."[2] Therefore, it is important to become aware of how your cultural background affects your "perceptions, beliefs, and actions"[3] so as to avoid "cultural misunderstandings [that] may impede lawyers' abilities to effectively interview, investigate, counsel, negotiate, litigate, and resolve conflicts."[4] You will need not only to recognize the "cultural lens"[5] through which you see others, but also employ methods to facilitate your ability to "see the world through the eyes of others."[6]

CULTURAL SELF-AWARENESS

Let us begin with a word about nomenclature. While many legal scholars use the term "cultural competence" to describe the ability to engage in effective cross-cultural lawyering, I will use the term "cultural self-awareness"[7] for two reasons.

---

[1] I developed much of my thinking about cross-cultural lawyering and the exercises within this chapter in collaboration with my colleague, Professor Kinda Abdus-Saboor, and from the scholarship of my colleague, Professor Andrea Curcio.
[2] Andrea A. Curcio et al., *A Survey Instrument to Develop, Tailor, and Help Measure Law Student Cultural Diversity Education Learning Outcomes*, 38 NOVA L. REV. 171, 192 (2014).
[3] Ibid. at 189.   [4] Ibid. at 192.
[5] Ibid. at 207; *see also* Carwina Weng, *Multicultural Lawyering: Teaching Psychology to Develop Cultural Self-Awareness*, 11 CLINICAL L. REV. 369, 381 (2005).
[6] This is one of the Shultz-Zedeck Lawyering Effectiveness Factors discussed in Chapter 5.
[7] Carwina Weng, *Multicultural Lawyering: Teaching Psychology to Develop Cultural Self-Awareness*, 11 CLINICAL L. REV. 369, 372 (2005).

First, some legal scholars have objected to the term "cultural competence" because "it is impossible for anyone to become *competent* in another's culture."[8] Second, effectively managing cross-cultural interactions begins with self-awareness. You will need to develop an awareness of your own cultural identity and implicit biases in order to determine how your cultural lens impacts the way you see and interact with others.[9]

Little Pause: What do you believe are your strengths and weaknesses in dealing with cultural differences (when a person is of a different race, ethnicity, religion, generation, etc. from your own)?

The Impact of Culture

Culture can be based on "ethnicity, race, gender, nationality, age, economic status, social status, language, sexual orientation, physical characteristics, marital status, role in family, birth order, immigration status, religion, accent, skin color or a variety of other characteristics."[10] Because culture is so broad and diverse, a person can ascribe to more than one cultural group, each of which has a set of attitudes, values, and norms of behavior.

As a result, an individual's cultural identity can be layered and complicated not only because a person is likely to identify with more than one cultural group, but also because that same person may not subscribe to all of the norms and values of that culture.

Little Pause: Think back to when you identified your core values in Chapter 1. Were the core values you chose influenced by your culture? If so, how so? If not, why not?

Geography and education are two examples of culture that can influence how we view ourselves and others in ways we may not realize. Consider, for example, the cultural differences between and within the regions of the United States (Northeast, South, Midwest, and West). Where you live or have lived in the United States[11] impacts attitudes, social norms, and language – in particular, the primary language spoken in your community, the specific words used to describe common objects,

---

[8] *See* Andrea A. Curcio et al., *A Survey Instrument to Develop, Tailor, and Help Measure Law Student Cultural Diversity Education Learning Outcomes*, 38 Nova L. Rev. 178 (2014). at 186 (emphasis in original) (reasoning that one cannot become competent in another's culture because "culture is a complex, multi-faceted concept, and because all people have multiple cultural backgrounds and experiences that influence the lenses through which they see the world"); *see also* Antoinette Sedillo Lopez, *Beyond Best Practices for Legal Education: Reflections on Cultural Awareness — Exploring the Issues in Creating a Law School and Classroom Culture*, 38 WM. Mitchell L. Rev. 1176, 1178 (2012) (asserting that it is impossible for a lawyer to become "cross-culturally competent" because of the many different cultures in the world).

[9] Susan Bryant, *The Five Habits: Building Cross-Cultural Competence in Lawyers*, 8 Clinical L. Rev. 33, 20 (2001) ("To become good cross-cultural lawyers, students must first become aware of the significance of culture on themselves.")

[10] *Ibid.* at 39.

[11] If you are an international student, this same analysis can be applied to your country of origin.

and the pronunciation of those words. In this way, culture can influence how we categorize where a person lives or grew up based simply upon language.

Take the *New York Times* Dialect Quiz, "How Y'all, Youse and You Guys Talk," available at www.nytimes.com/interactive/2013/12/20/sunday-review/dialect-quiz-map.html?_r=0.

We often don't think of education as a cultural category. But consider the attitudes, social norms, and values associated with law school. Law school is a transformative experience and one you are likely not aware of as it is happening. You are learning a different way of thinking, a professional set of values, and a new way of communicating. And you might find that the only people that truly understand your law school experience are your fellow law students, your professors, and practicing lawyers.

Little Pause: Think back to the first day of law school. How has your world view changed, if at all?

These two small examples illustrate how cultural experiences may influence our perceptions and interactions. Until we consider the wide array of cultural experiences we have had throughout our lives, we may be unaware of how our cultural backgrounds and experiences intersect to form the lens through which we see the world, interpret what we observe, and interact with others.

The Intersection of Culture and Identity

Identity is inextricably intertwined with culture. Yet, as discussed above, we may not always be cognizant of the way culture shapes our identity. This is why, in order to achieve cultural self-awareness, we must peel back the layers of our cultural identity to determine what cultural forces influence our world view. Thus, in exploring your cultural identity, it is important to identify those cultural influences that have the greatest impact on how you see yourself and the world around you. And because culture is influenced, in part, by life experiences, the elements of culture with which you identify may change.

List the top ten cultural attributes with which you identity – not as defined by others, but as you see yourself.[12] As described above, culture can involve ethnicity, race,

---

[12] *Cultural Awareness, Learning Module One*, FREE RANGE RESEARCH, available at https://freerangeresearch.files.wordpress.com/2012/10/cultural-awareness-learning-module-one.pdf.

gender, nationality, age, economic status, social status, language, sexual orientation, physical characteristics, marital status, role in family, birth order, immigration status, religion, accent, skin color or a variety of other characteristics. Now, consider what percentage of your identity you attribute to each cultural attribute.

In considering your cultural identity and that of others, you need to be conscious of your own attitudes (evaluative feelings that are positive or negative) and stereotypes (the traits or characteristics we associate with a cultural category)[13] and those held by others. Being aware of how you perceive others and how others perceive you is necessary to your ability to effectively manage cross-cultural interactions.

Little Pause: Think about your experience with stereotypes. Fill in the following sentence with a stereotype that is inconsistent with who you are: "I am _____, but I am not _____."

Now, consider this experience of a law student doing an externship at a non-profit agency:

> The following day a new employee and I were told to obtain our ID cards so we could access the building. I had no problem going with her and was looking forward to getting to know more about my new colleague. After I obtained my ID and returned to the waiting area to reunite with her, I overheard her talking on the phone about how she was having to travel around with this "little blonde girl." She did not sound pleased. It seemed to me that I was an inconvenience and she did not take me seriously as a professional.
>
> She did not know that I overheard the conversation and continued to act kindly towards me. However, I found myself struggling with the stereotype. It made me feel as if my appearance gave off the impression that I was not smart or a hard worker. I did not hear the entire conversation and it could have been taken out of context, but the comment made me feel that she had judged me before even getting to know me very well. I now feel as if I have to work extra hard to show her that despite my appearance, I do have something to contribute to the office. I am an intelligent, hardworking individual and I do not fit into the stereotype of a "dumb blonde." (She did not call me a dumb blonde but that is how I interpreted the comment.)
>
> I think this experience taught me a number of things. First being that not everyone is going to like me right off the bat, and it may take a little extra time and effort to develop a sound professional relationship. I will have to prove myself to be more than just a "little blonde girl" and I am determined to do so. The color of my hair or my age and stature does not determine the type of employee that I am capable of being. I also have to learn that not everybody is going to like me, and as long as I am fulfilling my employment duties and doing the best I can, that is all that I can do.
>
> The second thing that I learned from this experience is to not judge a book by its cover. I have learned from the other side how it feels to be stereotyped and it is not

---

[13] Jerry Kang, *Implicit Bias: A Primer for Courts*, Aug. 2009, available at http://wp.jerrykang.net.s110363 .gridserver.com/wp-content/uploads/2010/10/kang-Implicit-Bias-Primer-for-courts-09.pdf.

a good feeling. We all have personal biases embedded in our makeup and it is our responsibility to not let those biases affect our work environment. I learned how it felt to be judged by my appearance and how wrong the stereotype was that was placed on me. The best thing that I can do in the future is to not do the same thing to someone else. It is hurtful and most of the time incorrect. In the future, I will work to not have preconceived ideas of people and to let the person show me what kind of person they really are.

Little Pause: What is your reaction to this student's experience? How, if at all, is your reaction influenced by your own attitudes and stereotypes?

AWARENESS OF IMPLICIT BIAS

Although it is difficult to acknowledge, we all have implicit biases. This may be particularly dissonant for millennials who, as a generation, believe they do not see color.[14] Yet implicit bias exists despite our best intentions and without our realizing it. It is important to recognize implicit biases because these biases, and racial biases in particular, have a significant impact on the justice system.

To be clear, implicit bias is not the same as prejudice, which results when a person acts on known, explicit biases. Rather, implicit bias results from schemas – unconscious mental shortcuts our brain has developed to make sense of our interactions with others. These schemas are often based upon visible characteristics and result from both direct (personal interactions) and indirect (books, movies, pop culture, etc.) experiences with others.[15] Because these mental shortcuts are unconscious, we can develop and act on stereotypes and biases without being aware of it. Because most people want to think of themselves as being free of bias, or at least not acting upon biases, recognizing and acknowledging our biases often results in discomfort. Nevertheless, it is critical to identify our biases because, if we do not, we cannot address the real-world problems those biases create.

LAW PAUSE

Watch Yassmin Abdel-Magied's TED Talk found here: www.ted.com/talks/yassmin_abdel_magied_what_does_my_headscarf_mean_to_you?language=en. Stop the TED Talk at 6.39 (right after she says, "Because that's my day job."). Did the TED Talk facilitate your understanding of implicit bias? Did it expose any of your implicit biases?

[14] Jamelle Bouie, *How Millennials Perpetuate Racism by Pretending It Doesn't Exist*, SLATE, May 17, 2014, available at www.businessinsider.com/how-millennials-perpetuate-racism-by-pretending-it-doesnt-exist-2014-5?IR=T.

[15] Jerry Kang, *Implicit Bias: A Primer for Courts*, Aug. 2009, available at http://wp.jerrykang.net.s110363.gridserver.com/wp-content/uploads/2010/10/kang-Implicit-Bias-Primer-for-courts-09.pdf.

In one-on-one encounters, our implicit biases may affect our eye contact, how often we smile, how close we sit to someone, and many other subtle cues that communicate messages we may not intend.[16] Within the legal system, implicit bias can impact a lawyer's "professional relationships with case stakeholders (i.e. opposing counsel, witnesses, judges, etc.); in developing case strategy; and in interactions with the client and other parties invested in the case's outcome."[17] In addition, it can play a role in the decisions judges[18] and jurors[19] make. Thus, to effectively manage cross-cultural interactions, lawyers must become aware of the hidden biases that may influence the decisions they make and their interactions with others.

Because people are often unaware of them, implicit biases can be difficult to identify. That said, the Implicit Association Test (IAT), a reaction time test that asks the test taker to sort categories of pictures and words under time pressure, has been the most thoroughly tested and validated in measuring implicit attitudes and beliefs.[20]

LAW PAUSE

Visit https://implicit.harvard.edu/implicit/index.jsp. Take the IAT for: 1) Race; 2) Age; and 3) A test of your choosing.

NOTE: The IAT is an educational tool designed to develop awareness of implicit preferences and stereotypes. It does not measure whether you accept, agree with, or act in furtherance of any implicit bias. Your results are personal and confidential. The next question asks for your reactions to the test. There is no expectation that you disclose your results.

Did the IAT results align with what you expected your implicit preferences to be? Explain.

THE BEGINNING OF THE JOURNEY

Just as individual cultural identity is multi-layered and complex, so too is the journey to develop cultural self-awareness. Having examined your cultural identity and implicit biases, you have only just begun that journey. It will take continued conscious effort to develop a sense of how your cultural lens impacts the way you see and interact with others. For lawyers, this understanding is essential but it, alone,

---

[16] Andrea A. Curcio, *Addressing Barriers to Cultural Sensibility Learning: Lessons on Social Cognition Theory*, 15 Nev. L. J. 537, 551 (2015).

[17] *Ibid.*

[18] Jeffrey J. Rachlinski and Sheri L. Johnson, *Does Unconscious Racial Bias Affect Trial Judges?*, 84 Notre Dame L. Rev. 1195 (2009); Pamela M. Casey et al., *Addressing Implicit Bias in Courts*, 49 Court Rev. 64–70, available at http://aja.ncsc.dni.us/publications/courtrv/cr49-1/CR49-1Casey.pdf.

[19] Art Markman, *Juries, Lawyers, and Race Bias*, Psychology Today, Jul. 22, 2016 ("In reality, people's biases affect their evaluation of what they see and hear.").

[20] *Project Implicit*, Harvard University, available at https://implicit.harvard.edu/implicit/takeatest.html.

is not enough. Rather, lawyers must strive to become aware of how their own cultural identities intersect with those of their clients, other lawyers, judges, and members of the larger community – individuals with equally complex and layered cultural identities and implicit biases.

You don't need to wait until you enter the legal profession to begin to develop cultural self-awareness and a consciousness about how your cultural experiences affect your perceptions. There are some things you can do now and throughout your law school career. For example, as you read cases and discuss them in class, think about how culture plays a role – not only in how you read and interpret the case facts, but how you view the parties to the case, the law, and the legal system. Take advantage of experiential courses that provide real-world experience in interacting with clients and judges. And as has been discussed in the preceding chapters of this book, work on developing empathy and active listening skills, which will help you to identify potential miscommunication and assumptions.

Lawyers and judges recognize how important cultural self-awareness is to good lawyering, and many attend seminars and trainings to learn more about this complex issue. You, too, may wish to do that. If, throughout your professional career, you continue to develop an awareness about the effect culture has on your own and others' perceptions and interpretations, you will become a better communicator and a more effective lawyer.

15

Making Mindful, Client-Centered Decisions

Nathalie Martin

Good decision-making, particularly in a service profession where decisions are made for the benefit of another, is critical to good lawyering. While claims ultimately make their own decisions, in many complex legal settings clients can only decide with the thoughtful help of their clients. In reality, lawyers make hundreds of decisions a week, many on behalf of clients. Yet research shows that most lawyers prefer to rely exclusively on order, structure, and reason when making decisions, particularly when compared to the general population.[1] Other people, including clients, may not appreciate this fact-based, highly structured approach. In fact, good decision-making requires cultural competence, the subject of the last chapter, as well as good listening skills. More balanced, empathetic decision-making skills can also help us in our personal lives.

Before making an important decision on behalf of a client, engage with the three preparatory steps below. Then use the practices in step 4 to actually make the decision.

1. Get yourself in order, go up to the balcony, and take an inside look. What are you thinking or feeling? Use your mindfulness techniques to check in and see where you are and what you are up to, what you are thinking and feeling.

2. In client matters, put yourself in your client's shoes. Before making big decisions for a client, use your listening skills and your cultural competence to consider the similarities and differences between you and your client. For similarities, bring back a time in your life when you felt similarly, based upon a previous situation in *your* life that mirrors in some small way what the client has experienced. Then chart the ways in which you and the client are different, perhaps on gender, race, age, sexual orientation, disability, or economic status,

[1] Jeff Foster, Larry Richard, Lisa Rohrer, and Mark Sirkin, *Understanding Lawyers: The Personality Traits of Successful Practitioners*, 2010, at 1, available at www.thresholdadvisors.com/wp-content/uploads/2011/04/Understanding-Lawyers-White-Paper-Oct-2010-revised.pdf.

or even more subtle cultural issues of some kind. Do not overlook one difference that will be present in most representations. You know the legal system and the client does not. The client is likely scared and worried about accessing the system through a third party, you, who are essentially still a stranger to him or her.

3. Go back and examine your own motivations.

Little Pause: Think back to a time when you were making a decision on behalf of another person. What might you personally have been trying to get out of the situation, out of the decisions? What part of your ego was at work there? Were you seeking fame, fortune, a promotion or better job, a good grade, or perhaps a way to get back at a nemesis, show him or her who's boss? When making future client decisions, do not proceed until you are sure that you are actually doing what your client wants and needs. Make sure you have explored these questions in detail with the clients.

In other words, make sure you are doing whatever you're doing *for the client*, not for some other reasons.

4. See what the experts say about how to improve lawyer decision-making. As University of Colorado Law professor Peter Huang explains, one source of lawyer misconduct is mindlessness.[2] Scientific studies show that the practice of mindfulness can improve ethical decision-making.

For example, one study found that people who scored highly for mindfulness reported a higher likelihood to act ethically, were more likely to value the upholding of ethical and moral standards, were more likely to use a principled approach to ethical decision-making, and cheated less than people who scored low for mindfulness.[3] Another study found that ethical decision-making and moral reasoning improved, two months after training in Mindfulness Based Stress Reduction (MBSR).[4]

As Professor Huang explains, mindfulness provides lawyers with "real options" for preserving valuable resources such as a lawyer's reputation, a client's goodwill, and the market value of a lawyer's business. Mindfulness also helps lawyers gather more complete, accurate information about facts, possible outcomes and their likelihoods or probabilities, while recognizing that we always have limited information.

USING WRAP TO DECIDE

The WRAP technique, developed by Chip and Dan Heath in their book, *Decisive*,[5] combined with mindfulness, reduces susceptibility to cognitive biases and improves

---

[2] Peter H. Huang, *How Improving Decision-making and Mindfulness Can Improve Legal Ethics and Professionalism*, 21 J. L. Bus. & Ethics 35 (2015).

[3] *Ibid.* n. 39.   [4] *Ibid.* p. 40.

[5] Chip Heath And Dan Heath, Decisive: How To Make Better Choices in Life and Work (Crown Business Books 2013).

the quantity and quality of information used to make decisions. These combined approaches fight the cognitive biases that interfere with good decision-making and help us act on unbiased information.

Both Professor Huang[6] and Executive Coach Michael Melcher[7] have used the WRAP decision tree created by the Heath brothers to train lawyers in better decision-making. The elements of WRAP are:

1. Widen your options.
2. Reality test your assumptions.
3. Attain distance before deciding.
4. Prepare to be wrong.

Each of these steps counteracts a common cognitive bias. These cognitive biases include

1. Narrow framing of a decision.
2. Confirmation bias of collecting skewed and supportive information.
3. Temptation from short-term emotions.
4. Overconfidence about the ability to predict how the future will unfold.

According to the Heaths, WRAP applies to many business and personal decisions, including litigation, mergers, optimal pricing, romantic break-ups, and relocation. In *How Improving Decision-making and Mindfulness Can Improve Legal Ethics and Professionalism*,[8] Professor Huang demonstrates how these principles can be used by attorneys to improve decision-making, and meet or exceed attorney ethical and professionalism obligations.

WIDEN YOUR OPTIONS

Just widening options improves decision-making markedly because a common decision-making error is framing the available options too narrowly. A study of decisions by businesses, non-profit organizations, and government agencies found that a large percentage of decision makers considered just a single alternative when making decisions. This study also found that the failure rate of one option "whether or not" decisions was 52 percent, compared to 32 percent of decisions with at least two alternatives, because "whether or not" decisions frequently cause decision makers to become vested in their one alternative, so much so that they do not even consider the possibility of other and possibly better alternatives.

---

[6] Peter H. Huang, *How Improving Decision-making and Mindfulness Can Improve Legal Ethics and Professionalism*, 21 J. L. Bus. & Ethics 35, 35 (2015).
[7] Michael Melcher, The Creative Lawyer 241 (2nd Edn. American Bar Association 2014).
[8] Peter H. Huang, *How Improving Decision-making and Mindfulness Can Improve Legal Ethics and Professionalism*, 21 J. L. Bus. & Ethics 35, 35 (2015).

Little Pause: Train yourself to recognize "whether or not" alternatives you have created for yourself or your clients.

To practice, ask yourself: "If I choose option A, what am I giving up?" Anyone who has ever planned a vacation can relate to this idea. If we choose Belize, then we can't go to Tulum Mexico, right? This is a lost opportunity cost, though the dollar cost is the same. Also try the Vanishing Options Test, in which you ask what you would do if the current option vanished.

Too many choices can also lead to decision paralysis, which can be addressed through the following Law pause.

LAW PAUSE

Take a tough decision in your life and pretend you chose one option. Ask yourself: "How will I feel about making this decision in ten minutes, ten months, and ten years?" In other words, pick a choice. Pretend you have actually done it. How do you feel? How will you feel in ten months? How about ten years?

> Decision-making styles differ greatly from person to person. For example, my husband and I have totally different decision-making modes. I like to decide quickly based upon intuition and some but never all of the facts. Stewart likes to continue researching for as long as possible and put off deciding for as long as possible. I also dislike going back and reconsidering. Perhaps that last sentence was a bit of an understatement. I virtually refuse to reconsider and particularly do not want to do the legwork to unravel the work and redo it. We reach a compromise by making detailed analytical charts. We did this when we picked our cabin in the mountains outside Philadelphia. Pros, cons, check, check, check. Then it all fell into place.

REALITY TEST YOUR ASSUMPTIONS

Confirmation bias is our natural tendency to seek out information that confirms our initial and possibly biased or self-serving "beliefs, ideologies, or preconceived worldviews."[9] For example, people have told me they are happy they hired a certain financial advisor, for example, despite piles of evidence that the market in general (index funds and exchange traded funds) beat their expensive advisor. Once a decision has been made, people tend to listen only to information that proves that they were right, which confirms their positive views of themselves and their decision. To fight this tendency, ask for feedback that is not necessarily in agreement with your conclusions. Be bold and get out there and do it.

[9] *Ibid.* at 46.

One example of reality testing used by the Heath brothers involves a law student considering a job in a particular law office. The Heath brothers suggest that, rather than taking at face value what an employer says about that office, find two or three people who have left that law office and find out why. Ask them why they left, what they are doing now, and whether life is better now that they made this change.

You can also ask yourself, "If I were looking at this situation from the outside, as a neutral third party, what would I see?" Few of us will get as good a result using this method as the method in which you actually ask third parties. Most of us are just not that evolved.

♦

ATTAIN DISTANCE BEFORE DECIDING

Try to determine if emotions are driving your decisions. All decisions are ultimately the client's to make, but in a large number of instances, the client will be relying heavily on your expertise in trying to figure out how exactly to implement decisions. The best way to attain distance is to put time and space between the decision and any lingering emotions you may be feeling. In other words, sleep on it. You can also ask yourself, "How would I advise a friend making this decision?" Studies show that people find it easier to focus on the single most important aspect of a decision when they gave decision-making advice to others, but weighed too many not-so-important factors when making decisions for themselves. According to Huang:

> [another] way to attain distance before deciding is to identify, reflect upon, and enshrine your personal core (meaning in part, long-term) priorities. One way to honor your core priorities is to create an annual "stop-doing list" of what you will concretely give up doing so as to create the additional time that is required for you to devote to your core priorities. Another way to honor your core priorities is to set a timer to beep hourly and when it beeps to ask yourself these two questions: (1) are you currently doing what most needs to be done, and (2) are you currently being who you most want to be.[10]

PREPARE TO BE WRONG

To fight overconfidence in your predictions about what will happen next, imagine that it actually worked out differently than you predicted. Conduct an after-the-fact analysis of the situation, assuming that you made the wrong decision. What bad, though not horrible, things ensued?

Another way to prepare to be wrong is to prepare against unknowable contingencies by simply assuming that you are going to be overconfident and correct for that

---

[10] *Ibid.* at 50–51.

overconfidence. As Huang explains, you can do this by providing yourself with a generous built-in cushion or margin of error. Huang elaborates:

> Examples of this type of preparing to be wrong are the safety factors that engineers build into their designs of airplanes, bridges, dams, elevators, ladders, and space shuttles. Other examples of this kind of preparing to be wrong are the buffer times that software companies add to developers' overconfident underestimates about how long projects will take to complete or the buffer amounts that accounting firms add to accountants' overconfident underestimates about the amount of time, money, and other resources that projects will take to complete.[11]

In conclusion, good decision-making is part of good lawyering. Making better decisions improves our work lives and our personal lives, by creating better results and fewer regrets. A system for making good decisions also reduces stress and worry, and enhances productivity.

---

[11]   *Ibid.* at 51.

PART III

You and Society: Finding Greater Purpose

16

Purpose, Creativity, and the Practice of Law

Nathalie Martin

This chapter describes the relationship between purpose, creativity, and satisfaction in your career. It begins once again with awareness of each of our unique strengths and weaknesses, as well as an examination of our passions. The chapter ends with ideas about how to transform our experiences with the law to create the most meaning in life.

WHO AM I?

Who am I?
Am I spirit or flesh?
Am I sacred or secular?
Am I irrevocably shaped by the circumstances of my
    personal history, or am I still free to move and
    grow, to uncover a new and brighter path?
Am I fragile or strong?
Am I broken or am I whole?
When I listen deeply to my inner life, what do I hear?
What is the substance of my soul?
What is the core of my being?
What is my true nature?

Wayne Muller[1]

If you are more self-aware, people will respond more favorably to you. As a result, self-awareness is your ticket to better relationships and a happier and healthier life in the law. Self-awareness serves an even more critical function, however, as it helps you learn what is important to you. With self-awareness, you will be drawn to what is important to you, consciously and unconsciously.

---

[1]   WAYNE MULLER, HOW THEN SHALL WE LIVE? 3 (BANTAM BOOKS 1994).

In her book with Karen Gifford, *The Anxious Lawyer*, Jeena Cho explains that throughout the majority of her career, she worked harder with each passing year, but never gave much thought to why she was working harder or what she was working toward. She changed jobs a few times and worked harder at each successive job. Cho felt certain that becoming a partner, climbing the ranks, and having more and more clients would make her feel fulfilled.[2] As she explains:

> I wasn't exactly unhappy. I just felt lost. I felt overworked, and constantly exhausted. Then I returned to a practice I had abandoned since law school: *meditation.* Through meditation, I was able to calm my mind, which was constantly operating in overdrive. Once I found stillness, I had space to examine my life.
>
> Why are you here? What makes you feel alive? What is the unique gift of yourself that you are bringing to all of us?
>
> When my friend Kit Newman asked me these questions, I cried. I cried because no one had ever asked me those questions. More importantly, I cried because I had never asked myself those questions.
>
> These critical questions unlocked something inside of me – the part of myself which had been hidden, suppressed, and neglected all my life.[3]

While Cho waited many years to ask herself these questions, we hope that by posing these questions now, you can avoid the purposeless life so many of us in the profession have experienced. We hope that instead you can find a sense of meaning and purpose from the beginning of your career and thus be more fulfilled over your entire lifetime.

In a way, finding our purpose is easy. We just need to each ask ourselves this: What are the people, projects, and aspirations that make me want to get up in the morning? What gives my life meaning? As William Ury explains in *Getting to Yes with Yourself*:

> For some, a purpose may be to raise and care for a family; for others, it may be to play music or create art. For some, it may be to build something that has never been built; for others it might be to care for a garden. For some, it may be to give service to customers or to mentor younger colleagues; and for still others, it may be to help people who are suffering. If we can discover a purpose that makes us come alive, it can not only be a source of inner satisfaction, but also an excuse to give to others around us and to strengthen the giver in us.[4]

How Can I Become More Authentically Me?

One way to find purpose is to figure out what makes you unique and then capitalize on the real you. Becoming more authentically you will make you happier and more

2   JEENA CHO AND KAREN GIFFORD, THE ANXIOUS LAWYER 228 (ABA 2016).   3   *Ibid.* at 229.
4   WILLIAM URY, GETTING TO YES WITH YOURSELF 156 (HARPER ONE 2015).

successful. Again, you can never become someone else. The best you can do is to become more you.

All lawyers are not the same. Each one has different skill sets, goals, life aspirations, and desires. My close friend at work, another law professor, would rather feel than think. I would rather think than feel. She would rather visit, engage with, laugh with, and console an elderly neighbor being asked by our city to pay a fine. I would rather write a letter to the city explaining the situation and asking for assistance. We both bring necessary skills to the field of law and we both serve different but necessary functions.

What unique traits and skills do you bring to the table? Before saying "nothing," I guarantee that you bring a long list of skills to the profession. You would not have come this far otherwise. What do you most enjoy? In other words, what in your day strikes you as work, and what strikes you as play?

As you know, attorneys spend a lot of time with other people, many of whom are suffering in some way. Self-awareness helps us deal with other people's feelings too. As Wayne Muller, Santa Fe author, minister, therapist and founder of the non-profit Bread for the Journey, says, we create our own image of ourselves, and our description of ourselves becomes our reality. As he explains, "Whether we call ourselves father or mother, lover or friend, weak or strong, Democrat or Republican, our descriptions of ourselves set the course of our lives, determine what we love, how we live, and what gifts we will bring to the family of the earth."[5]

LAW PAUSE

From Wayne Muller's book,[6] try journaling a list of your traits or skills, including obvious aspects such as male and female but also adjectives that best describe you, then spend a few minutes narrowing the list down. Keep narrowing until you are down to one long phrase that describes your essential nature.

Now let's try the same task from a different angle. Pull out an old-fashioned piece of paper and write "I AM" at the top. Then complete that sentence in as many ways as you can for a set amount of time, perhaps ten to fifteen minutes.

Use adjectives and feelings and parts of your past. Include words and images you affiliate with yourself. Examples might be afraid, exhausted, a female, a weight lifter, a daughter of an alcoholic, son of a mechanic, college graduate, youngest of seven. Never censor or judge, just keep the list going as long as you can and eventually, once exhausted, stop. This sort of task makes reading for torts or contracts fun, I know, but don't give up. Stick with it.

Now go back and once again, whittle your list. Are there certain themes or words that keep coming up? Which of these things would you choose if you had to define

---

[5] WAYNE MULLER, HOW THEN SHALL WE LIVE? 5 (BANTAM BOOKS 1994).   [6] *Ibid.* at 40.

yourself through just a few? Note how many attributes are permanent, such as I am short and female, versus changeable, such as I am a tennis player or a smoker.

Now identify a single phrase describing yourself. Pick one that seems most potent.

Muller suggests you take a few moments to reflect on the phrase and become aware of what it may say about your current sense of self. Note that some of the attributes you ascribed to yourself could be inaccurate, and others may be true now but could later change. Be open to that change. Think about who you are now, who you once were, and who you want to become. As a famous US Supreme Court case proclaimed, "A judicial oak ... has grown from little more than a legislative acorn."[7]

The point of all this asking is to figure out who we are in regular ordinary life, perhaps even labeling each interaction, such as student, teacher, helper, leaders, PTA mom, performer, reader, or spectator.[8] With each change in role, we see how words, hopes, dreams, and postures change as our identities shift. Who are you in each situation, and which words or descriptions are most accurate? Which words represent the most precise sense of your deepest nature, and which reflect your goals and aspirations?[9]

Once you know yourself you can make choices that honor that true self. For example, Muller tells the story of a young man named Jeff. Jeff came to Muller for a therapy session and reported being quite depressed, which was somewhat common for Jeff. He planned to take medication. When Muller explored the problem, it seems that Jeff had recently been at a party where he was unable to make small talk and decided that he was a failure. As it turned out, Jeff just liked to spend a lot of time alone. Growing up, he was socialized to think that people who enjoyed being alone were weirdos, but Jeff enjoyed his solitude.

What if, Muller asked him, it was considered OK to lead a quiet life without guilt or insecurity? What if living that type of life was considered OK? It turned out that living more or less in solitude was part of Jeff's fundamental nature, and once Jeff could believe that this was fine, he happily lived the life he wanted without medication, depression, or self-hatred. Basically, without outside judgment, Jeff liked being Jeff.

Muller says you can gain self-awareness by talking to yourself the way you would talk to a therapist. Just listen for the words you use to describe your own feelings and yourself. Describe what you are going through, read the words, and find the problem. For example, after listening to another seemingly depressed client, Muller discovered that she was really just exhausted from caring for other people. She needed some of that care back. It was not a case of clinical depression, as Muller observed, but a cry for help that would put this client back in working mode.

---

[7] *Blue Chip Stamps v. Manor Drug Stores*, 421 US 723, 737 (1975).
[8] WAYNE MULLER, HOW THEN SHALL WE LIVE? 24 (BANTAM BOOKS 1994).   [9] *Ibid.*

FOUR SELF-ACTUALIZING QUESTIONS TO ASK THROUGHOUT LIFE

In Chapter 1, we promised that these final chapters would help you find and sustain the most meaningful life possible. A meaningful life results from finding your ultimate purpose. Muller suggests we ask ourselves four questions to find this purpose.[10]

Muller notes that the rush of everyday life often distracts us from these questions until we are confronted with something that wakes us up. Then we begin to listen to how things really are in our lives. The something could be a death, a divorce, a change of jobs or location, or simply a subtle feeling that something isn't right, that something we loved to do is no longer satisfying. Muller asks us to meditate on these four questions, and if you like, you can write about each one, considering each to be a Law Pause.

1. Who Am I?

Beneath all the stories of our past, beneath our joys and sorrows, beneath our challenges and successes, we each have an essential nature that is whole and unbroken. What is this essential nature, and how do we find it? If we can take nourishment from this inner nature, we can find great strength, peace, and courage.

We have worked with this question in one form or another throughout this book, but offer one more exercise here in self-awareness. Looking at the past can often help us see the crucial moments of our lives that have made us who we are, and also help us recognize these moments as they occur in the future.

LAW PAUSE

This task is adapted from Drexel University Kline School of Law Associate Dean, Susan Brooks' Stepping Stones exercise:[11]

Pull out a blank piece of paper and pen. Put your name in the far left corner and draw a stepping stone some way out. In that stone, write down an event in your early life in which something significant happened. At the time, it could have been a small thing, but as you look back, you can see that it was big. Perhaps you met someone who gave you a new idea or who became a mentor in an unexpected way.

[10] *Ibid.* at 3. These are obviously not the four questions Jewish people ask on Passover, but perhaps they should be.
[11] Susan L. Brooks, *Using A Communication Perspective to Teach Relational Lawyering*, 15 Nev. L. J. 477, 508 (2015). As Professor Brooks explains:

> the students . . . reflect back and identify decision points/critical moments/influential people in their lives that have led to the present moment, and chart them for themselves or depict them in some other visual way. The students then share their stories with a classmate of their choosing, who is encouraged simply to listen and not ask questions right away. After they each take turns, the listener in each pair introduces his or her partner to the class, and the other student has the chance to "edit" the introduction afterwards. I also share my own chart.

Perhaps you faced a crossroads and made a crucial decision. Perhaps you met a mentor who guided you to another step or journey in life, which turned out to be very important to your future, and to where you are today.

Now draw another stone, and another, creating a maze of stones filled in with life-changing events or crossroads in your life so far. Leave plenty of room between the stones.

Then go back and near each one, note how that event came about. Was it through hard work, extensive planning, personal connections, good deeds, or pure serendipity? Also note how you made the choice to proceed in the way that you did.

Then spend a bit of time reflecting on what resulted from the exercise.

2. What Do I Love?

In the second question, Muller asks what we love. What we love will shape our days and provide the texture for our inner and outer life. How can we plant what we love in the garden of this life? Where we place our awareness is where we put our energy. What we focus on is what we ultimately attain, so focus on what you really love and make sure you really love what you focus on.

3. How Shall I Live, Knowing I Will Die?

Every moment in this life is a precious gift. In your brief time here, what qualities do you wish to cultivate? What deeds, relationships, and other aspirations do you most want to accomplish? If you are aware of your own mortality, you will live less by accident and with more clarity and purpose. You can develop clarity, purpose, and enhanced focus with conscious awareness.

In his book, *Happier*, Tal Ben-Shahar describes the incredible clarity of purpose that cancer patients finally achieve when they are close to death.[12] Many move into a form of existence that is richer than the one they experienced prior to their illness. Many report a dramatic change in perspective and better communication with others. Over and over they say, "Why did we have to wait until now, till we are riddled with cancer, to learn how to appreciate life?"[13]

4. What Is My Gift to the Family of the Earth?

Each of us has a gift to bring to the table, that others want and need. How can we uncover our true gifts? How do we balance giving and receiving? And where can we find the confidence to offer our gifts freely and happily?[14]

---

[12] TAL BEN-SHAHAR, HAPPIER: LEARN THE SECRETS TO DAILY JOY AND LASTING FULFILMENT 147–48 (McGRAW-HILL EDUCATION 2007).

[13] *Ibid.* at 148.   [14] WAYNE MULLER, HOW THEN SHALL WE LIVE? xii (BANTAM BOOKS 1994).

Muller explains that the answers to these four questions can change over time. Like most of the questions posed in law school, there are no right "answers" to these questions. However, by asking these questions and spending time trying to answer them, we can find what brings us meaning and purpose in life.

LAW PAUSE

In one paragraph or less, answer each of the last three questions. Consider revisiting the answers to all four questions (these three and the question in the previous Law Pause) from time to time.

PURPOSE

Creating a Lifetime of Meaningful Work

Our happiness depends most upon our sense of purpose. According to psychologist Abraham Maslow's hierarchy of needs, which you perhaps studied in undergraduate psychology, once our basic survival needs are met, we seek safety and security, then love and belonging, and then self-esteem. Once all of those needs are met, finding life's true purpose or meaning becomes our goal. We reach for self-actualization, defined by Maslow as morality, creativity, spontaneity, acceptance, purpose, meaning, and inner potential. Figure 16.1 shows Maslow's theory in picture form, but the idea is that we

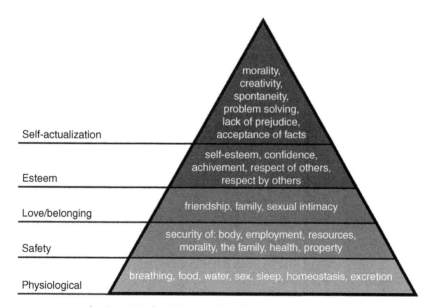

FIGURE 16.1 Abraham Maslow's Hierarchy of Needs, Abraham Maslow, Maslow's Hierarchy of Needs.svg, WIKIMEDIA COMMONS, available at https://commons.wikimedia .org/wiki/File:Maslow%27s_Hierarchy_of_Needs.svg.

move up the pyramid until we are in a position to look for life's deeper meaning. To be our best selves, we each hope to spend time examining the top part of this pyramid.[15]

The most satisfying legal careers involve all of the self-actualization skills listed at the top of the pyramid. Morality is a cornerstone of all legal practices, and the most fulfilling legal jobs require constant creativity and spontaneity, and continual learning and growth. Meaning and inner potential are goals we all have, and are also the best predictors of job satisfaction and overall happiness.

Throughout our lives, we never stop looking for meaning or purpose. I recently saw the new "business" card of an acquaintance. Here is what it said across the middle of the card:

No job
No office
No appointments
No commitments
No hassles

While the card did have a picture of a person in a hammock off to the side, drinking a fancy cocktail, the card didn't appeal to me. It might just as well have read "no purpose." From resilience, to physical health, to mindfulness, to emotional intelligence, to just plain happiness, without a sense of purpose in our lives, we are not really living the dream. Perhaps we are not really living at all.

Little Pause: Think about the maximum time period in which you could just relax, with no job, no volunteer work, no obligations to family or friends. How long could you go?

Perhaps you really *could* enjoy six months or a year off, but I doubt many people could enjoy that much time off with no purpose. I know from experience that my maximum amount of vacation time with no purpose and no work is about three weeks. I just don't do well without some purpose in life, even for short bouts. My first sabbatical in Chile ended in a deep depression and while I am doing better this time, writing this book in Oregon and Colorado, I have learned that my very best days rank like this:

BEST DAY: A day with no work after a series of successive busy and productive days.
NEXT BEST DAY: A day in which I do some quality work and also take time to play and relax (to the extent I can relax; I am not a big relaxer).
NEXT BEST: A day in which I work literally all day, with very few breaks, under a deadline.
WORST DAY: A day in which I don't do any work and don't feel I deserve the day off. This one here is in last place.

[15] Abraham Maslow, Maslow's Hierarchy of Needs.svg, Wikimedia Commons, available at https://com mons.wikimedia.org/wiki/File:Maslow%27s_Hierarchy_of_Needs.svg (licensed under the Creative Commons Attribution-Share Alike 3.0 Unported license).

I am not alone in finding the most happiness and peace through purposeful work. News stories abound about people who die right after their retirement or who fall into poor health the minute they have nothing left to work toward. We never outgrow the need to feel needed. I know a ninety-eight-year-old celebrity yoga teacher, Täo Porchon-Lynch, and look at Warren Buffet. The billionaire is still working at age 86!

Perhaps not surprisingly, then, elderly people have better health outcomes when they have a purpose. In one nursing home study, all patients were given a plant. Half were told that the plant would die if they did not care for it. The other half were told that they need do nothing to help the plant. One year later, the death rate was drastically lower in one of the two groups. Can you predict which one?[16] HINT: Having a purpose keeps us happy and healthy. Having no purpose leads to depression and despair.

While Socrates may have said that the unexamined life is not worth living, the same is true of the purposeless life. As ill and aging author Reynold Price explains on the last page of his book, *A Whole New Life*:

> I write six days a week, long days that often run till bedtime; and the books are different than what came before in more ways than age. I sleep long nights with few hard dreams, and now I've outlived both my parents. Even my handwriting looks very little like the script of the man I was in June '84. Cranky as it is, it's taller, more legible, with more air and stride. It comes down the arm of a grateful man.[17]

Reynolds had been a wheelchair-user for decades before writing this paragraph. He knew what it was like to live a life of purpose, even when life was difficult.

LAW PAUSE

Make a list of three to five happy people you know. What are some of their traits? What do their days looks like? What things do these people have in common?

One of my happy people is my neighbor Trude, who is a retired massage therapist in her 80s. Each day she meditates, reads, listens to inspiring music, cleans up around her house and her yard, pets and cares for her cat, does some volunteer work, visits with friends. She is not retired, not in the traditional sense. Her goal is to learn a little bit each day and leave the world a better place. Not bad goals, if you think about it.

---

[16] JON KABAT-ZINN, FULL CATASTROPHE LIVING: USING THE WISDOM OF THE BODY AND MIND TO FACE STRESS, PAIN, AND ILLNESS, 219 (2ND EDN. PIATKUS 2013).

[17] REYNOLDS PRICE, A WHOLE NEW LIFE (BANTAM BOOKS 1991), *quoted in* WAYNE MULLER, HOW THEN SHALL WE LIVE? (BANTAM BOOKS 1994) at 229.

As we discussed at length in Chapter 3, on managing energy as well as time, one of the energy stores we can use to build efficiency is spiritual energy. This comes from living life with purpose. When we believe that we are living with purpose, in line with our core beliefs, our lives are more positive. In Chapter 3, we discussed how to develop rituals around our core beliefs and access the energy of the human spirit, by:

1. doing what we do best and most enjoy while at work;
2. consciously allocating time and energy to the areas of our lives – work, family, health, service to others – we deem most important; and
3. living our core values in our daily lives through our particular behaviors.[18]

I have no doubt that you can find purpose in virtually *any* law job that you truly enjoy. Because lawyers change jobs many times throughout a career, this purpose can be found (and refound) in many successive law jobs.

In their book *The Happy Lawyer*, Professors Nancy Levit and Douglas Linder describe purpose as the key cornerstone to a fulfilling life in the law. Their book is jammed with interesting stories about fulfilled lawyers, including a young attorney named Bill Colby.[19] Colby serendipitously found himself representing a *pro bono* client in Missouri's first right-to-die case, a case in which the woman in the case would never recover any sense of a normal life and was attached to feeding tubes against her family's will. Even more serendipitously, the case became the first right-to-die case to reach the US Supreme Court, *Cruzan v. Director, Missouri Department of Health*. Through Colby's services, Cruzan's family was permitted to remove her feeding tubes. Colby left his law practice to write a book called *Long Goodbye: The Deaths of Nancy Cruzan*. Afterward, Colby became a senior fellow at the Center for Practical Bioethics. He has since dedicated his life to making sure that other families will not have to suffer anguishing legal battles at the end of a loved one's life. Colby currently serves as general counsel at a large inner city hospital.[20]

I tell this story to demonstrate the fluidity and variety of legal opportunities out there, as well as the serendipitous ways in which career paths change. Many opportunities present themselves, if you are open and watching for them. Also, if you keep an optimistic perspective and believe good things will come, they often will. If you think change will be bad, that will be true as well. In other words, stay positive and look for opportunities. Be sure to leave space in your day and your mind so those serendipitous things can find you. As explained by Levit and Linder, Colby appears to have been "lucky" in landing this right-to-die case and winning it, but Colby's "luck" probably had more to do with his outlook that anything else. The case

[18]　Tony Schwartz and Catherine McCarthy, *Manage Your Energy, Not Your Time*, Harvard Business Review, Oct. 2007, available at https://hbr.org/2007/10/manage-your-energy-not-your-time.

[19]　Nancy Levit and Douglas O. Linder, The Happy Lawyer: Making a Good Life in the Law 228–30 (Oxford University Press 2010).

[20]　*Ibid.* at 228–29.

was obviously a peak experience for Colby, one that changed the entire course of his purpose-filled life. The same thing can happen to you if you are open to it and expecting it.

Meaning Expressed Through Peak Professional Experiences

Levit and Linder describe many lawyer stories that can be called peak professional experiences.[21] All of them involve work that aligns with core values. These experiences need not involve taking a case to the US Supreme Court. Indeed, many are rather mundane in terms of the legal issues, but the significance of these services to clients is monumental.

A family law attorney from North Carolina tells a story that still brings tears to her eyes. She was representing a couple in a collaborative divorce. Typically in a divorce, each party to the marriage has his or her own lawyer because they have conflicting goals and needs. In a collaborative divorce, one lawyer can represent both parties, because their interests are aligned. The lawyer here was representing both the husband and wife collaboratively, but this did not mean the situation was without acrimony. Though both people wanted the best for their children, they were in bitter dispute about other things. The lawyer explains:

> This was not the lovey-dovey case that most people imagine collaborative divorces to be, but they worked very hard and we came up with a deal that suited both of them. We gathered for a signing ceremony and were waiting for the notary to arrive. Someone suggested that we ought to sit and have a beer while we waited and our host happened to have some in the fridge. The husband and the wife decided they didn't want a whole beer and decided to share one. It was an intimate moment that seemed to bring back memories of many times shared. The notary arrived, the papers were signed. As we stood up to leave, the husband and wife looked at each other and hugged. As they held each other, he tenderly petted her hair and each thanked the other for everything that had worked in their marriage and for working so hard to reach agreement.[22]

Another lawyer recalled an adult guardianship case in which the lawyer represented a woman who was temporarily placed in a psychiatric institution because her long-term partner could no longer care for her due to his own illness. The lawyer's job was to obtain an adult guardian for the woman, who would otherwise be unsafe living outside an institution because she could not manage her medication. After successfully obtaining the guardian, the lawyer was leaving the courthouse when she was approached by the long-time partner. As the lawyer tells the story:

> He had tears in his eyes. He was frail and very thin, and was coughing up blood into his handkerchief. He told me he was dying of AIDS and could no longer take care of his beloved. He had managed her medication for many years, but his doctor told

---

[21] *Ibid.* at 222–24.   [22] *Ibid.* at 222.

him that he would die very soon, so he decided it was time to find someone else to take care of her. He took my hand, looked into my eyes, and thanked me for obtaining a guardian for his one true love. He explained that he could now die in peace because he knew she would be taken care of.[23]

Note how incredibly generous the man was with his praise at an incredibly tender time near his own death, and also how meaningful this representation must have been for the lawyer.

While many lawyers have noted that representing individual people is usually more meaningful for them than representing corporations or organizations, here is another take on that topic, from a lawyer for the non-profit, The American Civil Liberties Union (ACLU):

Every day that I go to work at the ACLU, I strive to advance values that make this country great: freedom, democracy and equality. I work on a wide range of constitutional rights issues, including freedom of speech, freedom of assembly, freedom of the press, religious liberty, privacy, the right to be free from unwarranted police intrusion, the right to counsel, racial justice, gender equality, student rights, reproductive freedom, lesbian and gay rights, voting rights, and prisoners' rights . . . those who work at the ACLU and other public interest organizations are not motivated by the desire to get rich, but rather by the desire to achieve the greater good. I believe that this difference helps to create a wonderful, collaborative, and supportive atmosphere in the office. Though we often work long hours, we do so because we want to and without resentment. Our work to preserve civil liberties and civil rights is a labor of love.

Finding purpose and your unique gift involves finding out what interests you and then combining that knowledge with your signature strengths, as well as your reflections on past peak experiences. Go back and look at the results of your VIA Survey of Character Strengths and other tests from Chapter 1. You might also retake some of them to see if anything has changed.[24]

Finding Your Purpose, Not Someone Else's

The key to finding purpose is to follow your own purpose and not someone else's. As one law professor told Levit and Linder: "Follow your heart in choosing your career path. It's the most important advice I give my students each year. Such simple advice, yet so hard to follow. If you get it wrong the first time, which you are likely to do, don't be afraid to change course."[25]

Stated even more strongly, a New Orleans environmental attorney had this to say:

I know so many people who feel stuck in jobs they don't want. In the beginning, they knew it was not for them, but said, I'll work here, advocating positions I don't like

[23] *Ibid.* at 223. [24] These tests can be found here: www.authentichappiness.sas.upenn.edu/testcenter. [25] NANCY LEVIT AND DOUGLAS O. LINDER, THE HAPPY LAWYER: MAKING A GOOD LIFE IN THE LAW 225 (OXFORD UNIVERSITY PRESS 2010).

and working 2000+ hours a year for just a while. Once I make lots of money, I will move on. They get in and find themselves vested and unable or unwilling to take the risk. Years of their lives will get by them with little reward except perhaps the money, and that does not compensate them for having no life. I say, take a job that satisfies you and allows you to embrace your interests now, not later . . . working for people, and undertaking causes and cases, you believe in. I call that Tikkun Olam, leaving the world a better place.[26]

Oddly, many of the lawyers in Levit and Linder's book left "big law" to find work that was more meaningful to them, and found that the new jobs paid better too.[27]

Research on Happy Lawyers

Levit and Linder also report on some rather surprising empirical research on which lawyers are happiest. Overall, a few things they found do not surprise me, such as that small firm and solo practitioners are happier than large firm lawyers, government lawyers are happier than lawyers in private practice, people enjoy the intellectual challenges of law very much, women are less happy in the practice than men, you are happier if your work aligns with your values, you are happier if you get feedback at work, and you are happier if you do not work with unethical lawyers.

One finding that did surprise me was that you are somewhat less likely to be happy if you graduated from a top tier law school than if you graduated from a fourth tier law school. If you are attending one of those top schools, perhaps you could ask yourself why this might be. One finding that pleased me was that at the end of their careers, most lawyers were happy they chose law.

FEELING THE FLOW

As articulated in Chapter 1, you can determine where some of your strengths lie by reflecting on a time when you were in flow, when everything clicked and you worked efficiently and effectively with minimal effort and maximum focus.[28] What made it so easy? What were you doing at the time? Was this you at your best?

Most of us have been "in the zone" or in "flow" before, where we lose track of time in a task or activity. Flow is that state of mind where we become so engrossed that the time slips away and we virtually become one with the task. Sometimes described as being "in the zone," this state of mind can be experienced almost as a "high," or as one in which the task at hand completes itself.[29] You, the actor, almost disappear.

---

[26] *Ibid.* at 225. Tikkum Olam is a Jewish concept meaning acts of kindness performed to perfect or repair the world. The phrase is found in the Mishnah, a body of classical rabbinic teachings. It is often used when discussing issues of social policy, insuring a safety net for those who may be at a disadvantage in society.

[27] *Ibid.* at 228.   [28] *Ibid.*

[29] *See* DANIEL GOLEMAN, EMOTIONAL INTELLIGENCE: WHY IT CAN MATTER MORE THAN IQ 91 (BLOOMSBURY 1990); JEANNE NAKAMURA AND MIHALY CSIKSZENTMIHALYI, *Flow Theory and Research*, in OXFORD HANDBOOK OF POSITIVE PSYCHOLOGY 18, 195–206 (SHANE J. LOPEZ ET AL. EDS. OXFORD UNIVERSITY PRESS 2009).

In general, flow involves harnessing emotions so that they are "in service" to the task, channeling all positive energy to the task. When we are in flow, we achieve singular focus on the task.[30]

FLOW → COMES WHEN FOCUSING ON ONE THING AT A TIME
Once again, we are rewarded if we can focus on one thing at a time. Mindfulness practices develop that skill.

For writers, including lawyers and legal scholars, the author in flow becomes the written work. There is no separation between the author, the work, the words, or hopefully, the reader.

Flow was named by modern psychologist, Mihaly Csikszentmihalyi.[31] Csikszentmihalyi studied flow in surgeons, artists, mountain climbers, and other high achievers, noting the relationship between effectiveness and this magical state of focused concentration. In studying flow, Csikszentmihalyi found that this state of mind could be so enjoyable that the mind becomes completely absorbed in the task.[32] He also found that flow could release otherwise dammed-up solutions into consciousness.

According to Csikszentmihalyi, flow is achievable only when we understand the ultimate goal involved, when the task is challenging but not beyond our skills or capacity to grow, and when we believe that the situation will respond to the quality of our actions.[33] Tedium, inability, or anxiety are buzz kill or "flow kill," as are external motivations that focus only upon pleasing others.[34] This "antiflow" includes all activity that is "meaningless, tedious [and] offers little challenge; is not intrinsically motivating; or creates a sense of lack of control."[35]

Law Professor Stefan H. Krieger associates flow with creativity and describes it as:

> Artists, athletes, composers, dancers, scientists, and peoples from all walks of life, when they describe how it feels when they are doing something that is worth doing for its own sake, use terms that are interchangeable in their minutest details. This unanimity suggests that order in consciousness produces a very specific experiential state, so desirable that one wishes to replicate it as often as possible. To this state, we have given the name of "flow," using a term that many respondents used in their interviews to explain what the optimal experience felt like.

---

[30]   DANIEL GOLEMAN, EMOTIONAL INTELLIGENCE: WHY IT CAN MATTER MORE THAN IQ 91 (BLOOMSBURY 1990).

[31]   *Ibid.* at 364, 374.

[32]   Richard K. Neumann, *Donald Schon, The Reflective Practitioner, and the Comparative Failures of Legal Education*, 6 CLINICAL L. REV. 401, 422 (2000) (citing MIHALY CSIKSZENTMIHALYI, FLOW (HARPER & ROW 1990); MIHALY CSIKSZENTMIHALYI, BEYOND BOREDOM AND ANXIETY: EXPERIENCING FLOW IN WORK AND PLAY (JOSSEY-BASS 1975)).

[33]   *Ibid.*   [34]   *Ibid.* at 364, 374.

[35]   *Ibid.* at 422–23 (citing MARIA T. ALLISON AND MARGARET CARLISLE DUNCAN, WOMEN, WORK, AND FLOW, in OPTIMAL EXPERIENCE 118, 120 (MIHALY CSIKSZENTMIHALYI AND ISABELLA SELEGA CSIKSZENTMIHALYI, EDS. CAMBRIDGE UNIVERSITY PRESS 1988).

Flow – the enjoyment that comes from surpassing ourselves, from mastering new obstacles, from making new discovery – motivates us to engage in creative activity.

To experience flow, Csikszentmihalyi found, a person must become totally immersed in the activity. Flow transports us to a "new reality," to a more complex self. To accomplish this transformation, a person must pay close attention to her actions so she can monitor feedback and concentrate on achieving her goals.

Moreover, she needs to enjoy herself by staying close to the "boundary between boredom and anxiety." When there are too many demands, options, and challenges to handle, a person feels anxious and becomes paralyzed; when there are too few, she becomes bored. That point between boredom and anxiety allows for "convergent" thinking (conventional intelligence oriented to finding the one "correct" answer) but also "divergent" thinking (the ability to produce a number of possible answers based on the available information). The tension between these types of thinking evolves into a creative idea: holding on to what is accepted but being open to new viewpoints and ideas.[36]

As Krieger notes, strong domain or substantive knowledge is needed in order to be in flow. Otherwise anxiety takes over and makes the right frame of mind impossible.[37]

Did you know that Michael Jordan, Shaquille O'Neal, and Kobe Bryant all share the same meditation teacher, George Mumford? When Mumford first talks to top athletes about the benefits of meditation, he discusses these benefits in terms of being in the zone and achieving flow. Mumford describes how one can slow time down and create space between stimulus and response, thus improving performance.[38]

To be in flow, the task must be hard enough to be interesting and challenging, but not impossible. That is just frustrating. What I have found in my own law practice, as well as in academia, is that flow starts to happen when I finally feel like I know what I am doing. In *The Happy Lawyer*, Levit and Linder tell a story of a lawyer in flow, despite very challenging work conditions. This New York tax attorney regularly had

---

[36] Stefan H. Krieger, *Domain Knowledge and the Teaching of Creative Legal Problem Solving*, 11 CLINICAL L. REV. 149, 173–74 (2004).

[37] *Ibid.* at 175; *see also* Owen Shafer, *Crafting Fun User Experiences: A Method to Facilitate Flow*, 3–4 in HUMAN FACTORS INTERNATIONAL (2013), available at http://web.cs.wpi.edu/~gogo/courses/imgd5100/papers/FlowQuestionnaire.pdf. Shafer claims that these seven conditions create flow:

1. Knowing what to do;
2. Knowing how to do it;
3. Knowing how well you are doing;
4. Knowing where to go (if navigation is involved);
5. High perceived challenges;
6. High perceived skills; and
7. Freedom from distractions.

[38] Lauren Effron, *Michael Jordan, Kobe Bryant's Meditation Coach on How to Be "Flow Ready" and Get in the Zone*, April 6, 2016, http://abcnews.go.com/Health/michael-jordan-kobe-bryants-meditation-coach-flow-ready/story?id=38175801.

difficult and mysterious tasks dumped on him by other attorneys in his firm. He reported:

> I started to get the chance to feel like I knew what I was doing. I'd be the one that knew the most about the case, from reviewing all the documents and doing the legal research, and it's a good feeling to feel like you're on top of things and contributing. It's just like when you are a child – it feels good to master things, and it's unpleasant when you don't know what you're doing and no one is helping you.[39]

On the other hand, once the intellectual challenge is gone and the work becomes rote, flow goes out the window. At that point, it is time to find another role in the current job or to find that next job or purpose. Most lawyers change their jobs, and even careers, several times to continue challenging themselves, and to continue maximizing their efforts in flow.

One thing that never gets boring is serving other human beings or serving society at large, whether in private practice, local politics, law teaching, or wherever your path takes you. Law school teaches you to think in meaningful ways and give back in meaningful ways. Often, each client or situation is different, which keeps things interesting and novel. For all of the demands of the job, being of real use to others is what many lawyers describe as their primary source of flow.

Little Pause: Think about a recent situation in which you were in flow, focusing on the feelings and also what you were doing. How did you know that you were in flow? Now think about a situation in which you were in flow and also in service to another person or cause. How were those situations and your feelings about them similar or different?

As Levit and Linder explain in *The Happy Lawyer*, "The luckiest lawyers in the world are those who each morning can't wait to head into the office and find themselves asking from time to time, 'How is it that I actually get paid for doing work that I love so much?'"[40] While acknowledging that the practice of law is not always a bowl of cherries, Levit and Linder have collected many stories of lawyers who are so happy and in the moment in their practice that they regularly achieve "flow" at work. Flow is achievable for each of us, so go find yours!

Check out the job waterfall, or "Job Lawterfall", in Figure 16.2.

GOING WITH A DIFFERENT KIND OF FLOW
TO LIGHTEN YOUR LOAD

Flow cannot happen, nor can purpose, creativity, or meaning, when we are constantly fighting ourselves. For example, Wayne Muller tells a story of an artist named

---

[39] NANCY LEVIT AND DOUGLAS O. LINDER, THE HAPPY LAWYER: MAKING A GOOD LIFE IN THE LAW 220 (OXFORD UNIVERSITY PRESS 2010).

[40] *Ibid.* at 217.

FIGURE 16.2 Job Waterfall created by author, Nathalie Martin.

Jack who became very depressed. He drank alone at night and became suicidal, claiming that he was going crazy. He believed that artists had to be struggling, hard-drinking, and misunderstood, and that to be a worthy artist, you needed to suffer for your work.

Jack also taught painting. He loved to "paint" versus "creating art." When he taught and painted, Jack felt light. He was able to quiet himself down, listen for the correct colors to use, and follow the brush as it found the space between things. He listened for the tiniest of indications of what was needed. He taught his student to "be easy" and "let the colors tell you where to go." Jack was known as a master teacher who could help students find the best in themselves.

Jack was torn between becoming a famous artist and being a painter and teacher. The teaching and painting were light and easy, but the creation of art was miserable. One day Muller asked Jack, "What if for one day you allow yourself to live your life and your career in the same way that you paint. To push less, to allow what is necessary to emerge from the canvas of each day?"

Jack was stunned at the suggestion and also skeptical, repeating that a great artist has to suffer. Muller reported that the very next week, however, Jack was much lighter and happier when he appeared for his appointment. He told Muller:

> I have never felt this good. For all of these years, I have lived with the burden of thinking I had to work against my grain and suffer to be successful. Now that I feel how easy it is to just listen to myself and trust my own rhythm, I feel cheated out of the last twenty years. But now, I have the next twenty. And it feels great.[41]

When I read Muller's book, *How Then Shall We Live*, I realized how much of my own life I have spent swimming against the current rather than with the current. Lawyers tend to default to a fighting mode. If you become a fighter, a warrior, say against predatory loan practices, for justice or for peace, you can begin to internalize mostly fighting. Fighting becomes your nature. You can begin to fight everything because it is in your nature to fight. Be careful. While it is worthy to fight when you need to, it is equally worthy to *not* fight when you don't need to. Otherwise, you may just fight automatically. You may even fight for things you already have, or for things that are actually the opposite of what you really want. Knowing when to fight and when not to fight requires that you first know yourself and your motives.

Little Pause: Think of a time when you fought hard for something but it turned out not to be what you actually wanted. Why do you think you fought so hard? What does this teach you about yourself?

Slow Down for Yourself and Your Dreams

When our days are complicated and fast, things get lost, including precious things such as a sunset, a walk, a gentle wind, or an opportunity to help someone in need.[42]

---

[41] WAYNE MULLER, HOW THEN SHALL WE LIVE? 177–79 (BANTAM BOOKS 1994).   [42] *Ibid.* at 211.

TAPPING INTO CREATIVITY

There are many times in a lawyer's life when intense creativity is required, for example, writing a complex argument for a brief, looking for a negotiated resolution to a complicated dispute, or finding a solution to a sticky problem for a client or one's self.

We are very fortunate to have jobs that require creativity. The most rewarding tasks in life require creativity, as do the most difficult tasks. We have all been there. We need a solution badly but cannot find one. Then boom, we come up with it in the shower, while watching a movie, or while working in the yard. One way to really excel at creativity is through mindful practices. A clear mind is a creative mind.

Generally, then, nothing fancy is required in order to call on the creative energies. In my experience, creativity is most powerful after a good night's sleep, while taking a mind-clearing walk or run, having my first cup of tea in the morning, or following my morning meditation. Letting the mind lie fallow often does the trick. Working the body first makes it even better because exercise improves brain function.

> For maximum creativity, work your body and rest your mind. Walk, run, or do other exercise, then sit and do nothing. Creativity will hit. Give it time and space.

In addition to giving the mind space, there are other ways to enhance creativity. One way is to embrace opposites, dichotomies, and paradoxes. Embracing opposites provides an antidote to linear, logical thinking, which can limit the brain's capacity to "think outside the box." As creativity expert Barton Bain explains, embracing paradox loosens the grip of the logical mind, which can be the enemy of creativity:

> We commonly think of paradox as something that exhibits a contradictory nature ... and we tend to leave it at that. End of story. But paradox is much more than a contradiction. Paradox is the holding of two or more separate frequencies of idea and/or action simultaneously without any loss of attention ... from either task. More importantly, it is a *channel of communication* through which our ultra-creative selves reach out to us from beyond logic and reason.[43]

You are likely wondering if I am actually asking you to think about two opposite things at the same time, given that we have spent 240 pages discussing the importance of learning to focus on just one thing at a time. Yes, and this is an exception to that rule. By now you are familiar with one of the law's most frustrating attributes.

---

[43] BARNET BAIN, THE BOOK OF DOING AND BEING: REDISCOVERING CREATIVITY IN LIFE, LOVE, AND WORK 141 (ATRIA 2015).

Every rule has one or more exceptions. Bain's ultra-creativity practice is the exception to the "focus on one thing" rule.

Bain's ultra-creativity practice can be incredibly helpful to lawyers, given that we must live with life's dichotomies every day. We first described some of these dichotomies in Chapter 1, which include:

1. Living in the present versus preparing for the future.
2. Accepting things as they are versus doing something to fight injustice.
3. Refusing to judge others versus calling out reprehensible acts.
4. Being still versus being active.
5. Being calm versus getting things done.
6. Practicing non-attachment versus caring enough to achieve your goals.

In Chapter 1, we also discussed how frustrating it can be to constantly ponder questions that have no answers. It is this precise aspect of the law that makes lawyering so creative. The questions, not the answers, provide the meaning. Your ability to connect seemingly unrelated facts and circumstances, as well as to navigate complex situations, is your professional muse, so creativity is paramount.

We also need to be able to balance conflicting goals and live with the realities of paradox in our lives and in our practice. We need to see opposites as sides of the same coin, and know that without evil there is no good, without cold, there is no hot, and without darkness, there is no light.

Bain's practice of calling on opposite concepts and focusing on them intently at the same time helps us make sense of these dichotomies and paradoxes, which we must do in order to successfully practice law. After all, if we cannot see one side, we surely cannot see the other.

Little Pause: In *The Book of Doing and Being*, Barton Bain suggests this exercise for increasing creative energy, which he calls the Space Between.[44]

Close your eyes and imagine your most joyful future, your heart's desire regarding what you hope to do for yourself, others, and the world at large. Move that image to the right side of the inner screen behind your eyes.

Now imagine your worst terror, your darkest fear. Do not be afraid, just see it and feel it. Move that image to the left side of the screen behind your eyes.

Now step into the space between these extremes and imagine yourself there, with your biggest desire to one side and your deepest fear on the other. Spend a couple minutes there in the middle, really experiencing what it feels like to be there in the middle, and when you have had enough, let go. Go about your day, but come back to this from time to time to develop inner, non-linear creativity and thinking.

[44]   *Ibid.* at 148–49.

TRANSFORMING THE PROFESSION
SELF-AWARENESS AND VISION

We ask now that you do something radical, by imagining yourself in your most successful career.

LAW PAUSE

Picture yourself having the most significant impact on society that you can currently imagine. Picture that you are doing whatever constitutes your highest and best use of your talent, skills, and life.

Write down that vision of yourself, first in broad terms and then in more specific ones. What do you actually do in this life? At work? Not at work? What is your life like? How do others see you? How do you see yourself? Who benefits from your work? Write about that impact and that life at length.

Now visualize a world in which you are at the helm of something bigger and larger than yourself, and how, through that image, the world is able to change in meaningful and dramatic ways. Write that down.

Keep this piece of paper. Post it. Tack it up. Read it daily as often as possible. See it and become it.

17

Responsibility to Society, Professional Identity, and Access to Justice

Nathalie Martin

At the end of the last chapter, you were given the chance to imagine your wildest dream for your life in the law. You had the opportunity to vividly picture yourself having the impact you want on society and the opportunity to write about that impact at length. You even got a chance to visualize a world in which you were at the helm of something bigger and larger than you, and how, through that image, the world could change in meaningful and dramatic ways. We promised that in this last full chapter, we would explore how to create that place, which we will do now.

But first, we ask you also to imagine law school and the legal profession as a place in which you feel at home and of use to society as a whole.

TRANSFORMING LAW SCHOOLS TO SERVE OUR INTERESTS AND THOSE OF SOCIETY

Think back to the feeling you had when you first entered the law school building? Did you feel out of place? Did it seem like you did not fit in?

If you felt out of place, perhaps it is because law school did not embody your ideas of justice or your dreams for yourself as a lawyer. Perhaps that uneasy feeling of being out of place had more to do with the place than with you. Perhaps it was the formality, the lack of formality, the values, the lack of values, or just the way the building looked.

LAW PAUSE

Take ten minutes to write a few paragraphs on the following:

What would it take to make the law school climate just right for you? What would it take to change that climate to fit you, rather than you changing to conform to it?

Put another way, imagine what the profession would look like if you could build it from the ground up. How would it be different, in terms of training, focus, and emphasis? How about the teaching and the learning? Imagine what the profession could look like if law school was really good not just for you but for the people you want to serve.

Each of us is a small part of that reconfigured reality, a small but critical part. Which part are you? Who are you in creating that new law school and new legal profession?

Now think about how we build that new place. Think about the concrete steps and write them down.

Just as we can eliminate our enemies by turning them into friends, we can change the law school environment and the legal workplace from the inside out. The law school where you belong is one that reflects your values, your purpose, your meaning, your goals, and your respect and understanding of and for others. We can each help create that place. In this chapter we explore how to do so, both in school and in the profession as a whole.

ACCESS TO JUSTICE AND PERPETUATING THE LEGAL LABYRINTH

Is There a Scarcity or a Glut of Lawyers?

To begin imagining a better law school and legal profession, we first need to face a few tough realities. One of those realities is that the vast majority of Americans cannot find a lawyer to meet his or her needs. Numerically, there are plenty of lawyers to go around. Yet as with money and power, lawyers are concentrated at the high-income end of society. Most of them represent big corporations, insurance companies, and powerful governmental entities.

An astounding 80 percent of the population has reported being unable to afford an attorney, which means the poor and the middle class generally go without legal services. And those are just the people who realized they needed an attorney! According to Law Professor Rebecca Sandefur,[1] most of these people assume that their problems are not "legal" ones, even though they relate to a myriad of common

---

[1] Rebecca Sandefur, *The Importance of Doing Nothing: Everyday Problems and Responses of Inaction*, in TRANSFORMING LIVES: LAW AND SOCIAL PROCESS 112, 116–17 (PASCOE PLEASENCE ET AL. EDS., STATIONERY OFFICE 2007). As Sandefur explains, many poor people's problems are less institutionalized as legally solvable, meaning they cannot necessarily be remedied through the law. Poor people may lack resources, such as transportation, that would allow them to benefit from the remedy, and some problems result from the poverty itself, which the law does not rectify. *Ibid.* As Sandefur explains:

> Many of the problems faced by low-income people are not of the sort that the law is presently designed to remedy. For example, through the legal remedy of evictions, landlords may deny shelter to tenants who can no longer pay their rents; poor people have no corresponding legal right to shelter. Through taking legal action or seeking legal advice, tenants facing eviction may be able to achieve a delay in their exit from shelter or a reduction in the back rent they owe, but they cannot achieve the kind of decisive resolution in their favor that is available to the landlord who moves to evict them.

legal problems such as debt collection, problems with insurance claims, credit reporting and scoring, eviction, tax problems, environmental hazards, wage and employment issues, personal injury, family law meaning divorce and custody, and wills and trusts. Many people just hope that if they wait long enough, the problems will go away. You may have heard about food deserts, parts of the country where healthy food is unavailable. We also have lawyer deserts, places where there are lawyers but they are not available to help the vast majority of people.

Lawyer deserts are most dramatic among people with the fewest resources. Many poor people in the US lack access to lawyers when they confront major life challenges, including eviction, deportation, custody battles, and domestic violence. People with legal representation naturally fare better in housing, immigration, and domestic violence cases, but there's no right to counsel in civil disputes in the US, only in criminal cases.[2] In other countries, for example, most countries in the European Union, free lawyers are provided for civil disputes as well as criminal proceedings, for those who cannot pay. This makes access to justice less of a problem elsewhere than in the US.[3] Indeed, on June 8, 2015, the Human Rights Policy Center at the University of North Carolina issued a report confirming what many have long known, namely that equal justice remains elusive for millions of poor and low-income Americans.[4] Although the legal system is premised on the idea of a level playing field, this is a fiction because so few Americans can afford counsel.

Perpetuating the Labyrinth

Regular people in the US are often flummoxed by the sheer complexity of the US system, which my former student Deian McBryde and I like to call "the labyrinth." The legal labyrinth is the complex web of procedural and substantive rules that comprise our legal system. This labyrinth is a self-perpetuating web that leaves the law outside the reach of the average American. Included in the labyrinth is the active perpetuation of a legal system favoring confrontation and adversity over collaboration and cooperation. Without some sort of correction, the labyrinth is slowing the evolution of our legal system into one that better suits society.

The labyrinth, combined with no access to affordable attorneys and the intimidating chaotic nature of courts, creates a widening justice gap.[5] This lack of access and

---

[2] Carrie Johnson, *Rights Advocates See "Access To Justice" Gap In U.S.*, March 10, 2014, available at www .npr.org/sections/thetwo-way/2014/03/10/288225649/rights-advocates-see-access-to-justice-gap-in-u-s.

[3] *Ibid.*, citing a study from the National Center for Access to Justice at Cardozo Law School, Lauren Carasik, *Equal Justice Remains Elusive for the Poor*, June 29, 2015, available at http://america .aljazeera.com/opinions/2015/6/equal-justice-remains-elusive-for-the-poor.html.

[4] *Ibid.*

[5] For examples of how technology can help those without lawyers help themselves, see Dan Jackson, *Human-Centered Legal Tech: Integrating Design in Legal Education*, 50 L. TEACHER 82, 93–94 (2016); *see also* NULawLab Website, *RePresent: Online Game for Self-Represented Litigants*, available at

intimidation means that the poor stay poor and the marginalized stay marginalized. Those who find their way to court are often there over disputes threatening their livelihood, safety, or housing, so the stakes are high:

> Losing housing to foreclosure or eviction can lead to loss of employment, a change of school districts for children and can even affect custody determinations. For a tenant who cannot afford rent, a lawyer can sometimes negotiate time to find suitable housing or even rental debt forgiveness. An attorney can empower a domestic violence victim who would otherwise find the court process daunting or help maintain income by enforcing workplace rights.
>
> By contrast, those with resources can afford legal representation to vindicate their rights. This two-tiered system of justice is eroding the legitimacy of the U.S. legal system.[6]

The US has long recognized that the poor need access to counsel, and as a result, in 1974, President Richard Nixon created the Legal Services Corp. (LSC), a non-profit corporation that provides grants for civil legal assistance to low-income Americans as part of Nixon's war on poverty. The LSC now supports 134 programs nationwide, but is deeply underfunded. When LSC was formed, only 12 percent of Americans were eligible for LSC assistance. Today the situation is graver. Nearly 20 percent of Americans are eligible for LSC help, meaning over sixty-four million people. Yet the organization has little money and other legal aid organizations are in the same boat. LSC funding has decreased in real dollars since the program's inception, all while the need for lawyers has increased. The result is that the most marginalized and disempowered remain largely unrepresented.

How will legal assistance for the poor and middle class be provided in the future? What will be your role in providing it? One of the reasons we had you dream big in the last chapter was to see where your dream could take you.

"Big Law" is the term we give to jobs in huge corporate law firms. There is nothing wrong with the prestigious high-paying jobs but they are not for everyone, or for the majority of lawyers.[7] When I went to law school, I did not know there were jobs other than Big Law so I got a Big Law job. I do not recall any public interest jobs being mentioned at all during our exposure to career services.

Indeed, many law school placement offices around the country, thankfully not my own, act as though high-paying firm jobs are the only law jobs worth getting. Fall and

---

http://nulawlab.org/view/online-simulation-for-self-represented-parties; https://ctlawhelp.org/repre sent. While resources like this will never be a substitute for actual representation, they are helpful in the absence of actual live legal assistance. These resources also highlight how much a technology background can help in the field of law.

[6] National Center for Access to Justice at Cardozo Law School, Lauren Carasik, *Equal Justice Remains Elusive for the Poor*, June 29, 2015, available at http://america.aljazeera.com/opinions/2015/6/equal-justice-remains-elusive-for-the-poor.html.

[7] For a fascinating, tongue-in-cheek look at how "Big Law" can trap people into having no life at all, *see* James C. Spindler and M. Todd Henderson, *Corporate Heroin: A Defense of Perks*, 93 Geo. L. J. 1835 (2004–2005).

spring recruitment at most law schools focuses on Big Law jobs. All the while, public interest jobs, such as jobs in non-profit and legal aid offices, barely get mentioned.

What are some ways in which you could see yourself helping to solve the access to justice problem? Think outside the box. Big Law attorneys can also help in a big way. What is your path? Write a brief journal entry on this topic.

Wherever you work, there will be two general ways for you to contribute to solving the access-to-justice problem. If you work in a private law firm, you will use some of your free time to help those who cannot afford a lawyer. As alluded to above, you can also make solving the problem part of your regular job, by pursuing a job in a non-profit, in government, for a religious organization, or in some other public interest capacity. You might also provide private law services for low-income communities at low rates, which is sometimes called low-bono.

PROFESSIONAL RESPONSIBILITY AND IDENTITY FORMATION

As we discussed in Chapter 5, law firms and other law offices expect their young attorneys to start work ready to practice law. In particular, these employers expect starting attorneys to have excellent people and communication skills. A big part of being ready to practice law is preparing to serve others. Law is a service profession. We exist to serve society, not ourselves. Most law students know this when they come to law school, but many forget it by the time they leave.

As a result, at UNM, we ask each first-year student to write their own creed of professional responsibility. The creed can be a poem, letter, memo, essay, whatever the students choose. The creeds help students stay focused on what matters most to them as they become lawyers and professionals. The creeds are also sometimes pulled out and revisited in other subsequent classes such as clinic and legal ethics.

LAW PAUSE

Write a creed of your own for your life as a lawyer. Your creed may be expressed as an oath, poem, letter, affirmation, creed, prayer, ethical code, promise, contract or any other statements by which you intend to live as a lawyer. Write one page or less.

HELPING OTHERS HELPS US

Most of us know that giving feels great. It wards off depression, anxiety, stress, and even feelings of inferiority. Giving also helps our careers. According to Wharton

Business School Professor Adam Grant, in his book *Give and Take*, the most successful people are givers rather than takers. According to Grant, business people who are a little more generous with employees and partners have more opportunities and ultimately make more money than those who are less giving. Sales people who focus on providing exemplary customer service sell more products and services. People who give more to charity are happier and wealthier than those who give less or don't give at all.[8]

Giving need not be all about money. Professor Grant interviewed a manager named Sherryann, who spent many hours mentoring young women in her field. As the manager explained, "I'm not looking for quid pro quo: I'm looking to make a difference and have an impact, and I focus on people who can benefit from my help the most."[9]

Similarly, I recently interviewed community leaders fighting payday loans. One community organization was named Youth Leadership Institute or YLI. YLI uses high school students to fight for community reform in Northern California. By doing so, YLI simultaneously improves the community and builds leadership skills in the youth. When asked if he needs to be careful to choose particularly responsible young people to head his projects, project leader Fahad Qurashi said he does just the opposite. As he explains:

> Some of the youth have so many problems to deal with that it is hard for them to engage in community action. But those are the ones we want the most, the ones we go after the hardest. And so in the cases where we see a young person that might be not sure or not available or maybe a little checked out, we push even harder and we try to give them a leadership role.[10]

Making a difference in the lives of others is what makes our lives meaningful. As William Ury explains in *Getting to Yes with Yourself*, if we focus only on ourselves, no matter how much we get, it is never enough. Our neediness can never be satisfied if we meet only our own needs.[11] When we discover giving for pleasure, however, "a virtuous circle of giving and receiving begins."[12]

Everyone has the ability to give, even those with very little. In *How Then Shall We Live*, Wayne Muller recounts the stories of many people who have been through immeasurable pain, including those who have lost a child or suffered other life tragedies. Over and over again, despite their own pain, Muller has witnessed these people's strong desire to share their gifts with the world. Indeed it is through this

[8] WILLIAM URY, GETTING TO YES WITH YOURSELF 145, 155 (HARPER ONE 2015), citing ADAM GRANT, GIVE AND TAKE (W&N 2014) at 74.
[9] *Ibid.* at 153.
[10] *See* Robert N. Mayer and Nathalie Martin, *The Power of Community Action: Anti-Payday Loan Ordinances in Three Metropolitan Areas* (Jan. 24, 2017), http://fcs.utah.edu/_documents/ MayerMartinPaydayOrdinances.pdf.
[11] WILLIAM URY, GETTING TO YES WITH YOURSELF 155 (HARPER ONE 2015).   [12] *Ibid.*

sharing and giving that many have been able to come back from the deepest of tragedies.

One client of Muller's was Roger, a Northern New Mexico man from a relatively poor community known for its apple growers. Roger was suffering from AIDS. Roger's father, José, was frightened and confused by his son's diagnosis. Muller heard that José wished to speak to him and Muller went to see him. Of course, Muller assumed that the topic of conversation would be Roger's diagnosis. To Muller's surprise, José wanted to talk about something else. "I want to talk to you about apples," José said. Muller was surprised. What did Roger's diagnosis have to do with apples? José continued:

> A few of us up here have been seeing pictures on the news, all those poor children in Rwanda. I know a lot of apple growers around here, and we thought we could send some of our apples to them. We organized some elementary school children to help us peel and dry the apples so we could send them to the children in Africa. But we cannot figure out how to get them where they need to go. Do you think Bread for the Journey could help us?[13]

Muller reports:

> At first I could not respond. I was so touched by his generosity. This was a man whose son was infected with HIV, someone who had every reason to feel angry and bitter. Yet this seemingly unquenchable impulse to be generous flourished even in the midst of his sorrow. Even more, I know that José would never have named this as generosity at all, but rather as a simple and necessary response to the suffering of children. He saw a need and knew he had something that could help fill that need. He did not think twice about offering his gift of apples – even though I knew that apple growers had had a bad season, with heavy losses from the frost. From what they had, they wanted to give.

Muller notes that it is likely not stinginess or selfishness that keeps people from sharing their gift but rather, a fear that their gift will not be good enough or big enough. People feel ashamed that their gift might be insufficient, and afraid that it will be rejected.[14] They are frightened that they are not good enough or strong enough or smart enough. In reality, the smallest gifts are often the most appreciated. Things like a kind word, a smile, a meal, a compliment, a comforting visit, a gentle touch, or a few minutes of assistance, can be immensely important to another person.

We can each give something, but what? As Muller explains:

> If we have apples, we give apples, if we have a sense of humor, then laughter is our gift. If we can cook, then food is our gift. If we can make music or hold a hand or listen or build or love well, these are our gifts. The currency of our kindness flows from what we are, what we love.[15]

---

[13] Wayne Muller, How Then Shall We Live? 235–36 (Bantam Books 1994).   [14] *Ibid.* at 236–37.
[15] *Ibid.* at 239.

Sometimes, even our sorrows and challenges become our gift. Alcoholics help others in recovery, withdrawn people with huge imaginations share their stories and become role models for similarly withdrawn children. Any way you look at it, helping others helps us. As an example, Muller tells the story of an abused runaway child, Maria, who was emotionally traumatized from a horrible childhood. When Maria was taken in at Muller's farm, she saw some bigger chickens ganging up on a smaller chicken and it opened Maria up. She began trying to protect the little chicken, and developed a bond with it. Soon she began to heal through her found sense of compassion for others.[16] True healing came from watching chickens! No gift is insignificant and some are truly life-changing for the receiver *and* the giver.

We do not do things for others in order to get something in return, but we will get satisfaction and meaning from these deeds. The pleasure is ours because sharing is a gift in itself.

> Doubting that one person can make any sort of difference in this world? Think about this. Young teens who participated in a Big Brothers/Big Sisters program were less likely to have drug or alcohol problems, had more success in school, and had better relationships with their parents than were similar young people not involved in the program.[17]

WHAT IS YOUR GIFT?

Now imagine that your highest and best gift is not money at all. It is your time. While we can't solve world hunger, we can help one person or group at a time. As Albert Camus once said, "Perhaps we cannot prevent this world from being a place where children are tortured. But we can reduce the number of tortured children. And if you don't help us, who in the world will help us do this?"[18]

LAW PAUSE

Visualize a problem you see in the world and how a person, a group, or a government entity might help ameliorate that problem. Be specific about what the person or group would do.

Now imagine how you would find clients or people to help create this change. If it is a non-profit you picture, imagine raising money for this organization. Where would you find others who are like-minded, and would also want to help solve this problem? What would you call the organization? If it is a government entity,

[16] *Ibid.* at 225.
[17] Big impact – proven results, BIG BROTHERS BIG SISTERS: A COMMUNITY OF CARING, available at www .bbbsmi.org/site/c.7pLFLSPzEeLUH/b.6715989/k.A38C/Big_impact8212proven_results.htm.
[18] Albert Camus, statement made at the Dominican Monastery of Latour-Maubourg in 1948. CAMUS, RESISTANCE, REBELLION AND DEATH, trans. JUSTIN O'BRIEN, p. 73 (ALFRED A. KNOPF 1961).

imagine what the agency would be called and how it would implement change. Write out what you see.

Now think about what is stopping you. Write down the names of a few non-profits you'd like to give money to, existing or made up.

Many people all over the world start non-profits because they see need and they also see others who want to help fill that need. For example, Jenny Landau of the Immigrant Law Center started her non-profit right out of law school and has since provided legal assistance to hundreds of immigrant families. Pat Stelzner started the Senior Citizens Law Center in Albuquerque and has served hundreds of low-income seniors who would otherwise have no had legal assistance at all.

Similarly, Wayne Muller started Bread for the Journey so he could donate some of his private psychotherapy back to the community. He felt that by doing this, he could remind himself and his clients that we are all connected to the sorrows of our community. He felt that this giving bestowed a different kind of integrity on the counseling relationship, because he and his clients were working together to help those in need. He raised just $200 in the first year of his non-profit, but felt great when he wrote out two $100 checks, one to a local food bank and another to a soup kitchen. Bread for the Journey has grown and grown, and sometimes even offers cash to people who are a little short, addressing a deep need that is often filled by the most predatory of all businesses, payday and title loan companies. As Muller notes:

> A gift is like a seed. It is not an impressive thing. It is what can grow from the seed that is impressive. If we wait until our seed becomes a tree before we offer it, we will wait and wait, and the seed will die from lack of planting in the warm, moist earth. The miracle is not just the gift; the miracle is in the offering, for if we do not offer it, who will?[19]

Your particular gift need not be related to offering legal service, but since you are studying to be lawyer, or perhaps are already a lawyer, looking at ways to give legal gifts is a place to start. With over 80 percent of the population unable to hire an attorney when they need one, your gift may be providing legal services. Whatever your gift is, don't worry that it won't be enough. Just have the courage to give it.

LAW PAUSE

Complete these sentences:

- A good life is _____.
- A useful life is _____.
- A successful life is _____.
- A happy life is _____.

[19] Wayne Muller, How Then Shall We Live? 242 (Bantam Books 1994).

EXAMPLES OF WORK IN LEGAL NON-PROFITS
OR EVEN AT SCHOOL

At my school, I learn every day from the activities, goals, dreams, and motivations of my students. Time and time again, they show the resolve to take on whatever problems they see, even while still in law school. From these experiences, I can see their unique individual gifts and imagine their future place in the legal community. I can readily recommend them for whatever paying jobs come along, due to their drive, determination, and commitment, not to mention organizing skills.

For one example of a huge effort undertaken by many students, look at this one event announcement that asked all students and faculty to spend a day at our state legislature fighting for causes we care about. The event was organized not by faculty but by a very engaged 2L student, Zachary Quintero. This sort of student organizing is not unusual, but I think you'll agree that it is extraordinary.

Fellow Students and Faculty!
After much coordination and anticipation, we are excited to announce **Feb. 17th as a Coordinated Legislative Day of Action**. Students from various organizations have come together to create a targeted day of action at the Roundhouse focusing on various topics and issues that they feel will define New Mexico for generations to come. Join your fellow students, organizations, and faculty on Friday Feb. 17th for a day of advocacy.

Details:
The day of action will involve a morning and afternoon session, with the morning one starting at 10:00 am and going to 12:00 pm. Can't make the morning session? That's fine! The afternoon session starts at 1:30 pm and goes until 4:30 pm.

For those traveling up in the morning and looking for lunch, there are various cafes, restaurants, and food trucks adjacent to the Roundhouse. Organizations that focus on New Mexicans getting involved will also be hosting lunch-ins so be sure to check out who is hosting what once you arrive. There will be speakers in the afternoon session starting at 2:30 pm.

Please consider helping save gas and world resources by carpooling for the day of the event. Some students already travel up to Santa Fe most Fridays and have expressed interest in giving people rides.

Captains and Areas of Interest:
With multiple issues circulating this legislative session, students have stepped up to be captains for various issues on the big day. These captains will be your persons of contact and relay key information such as: which elected officials to speak with at the legislature, bills related to the topic, and guide your group at the Roundhouse. Please review the list of interests and if you find something that you would like to team up on, email the captains!

Working list:

- **Women's Rights and Domestic Violence** – Erin Phillips & Ben Osborn
- **Environment Policy and Public Lands** – Ashley Cook
- **Native American Public Policy** – John Morseau
- **DACA/Human Rights/Immigration Topics** – Verenice Peregrino Pompa & Phil Davies
- **LGTBQ Issues** – Reyes De La Cruz
- **Animal Rights Public Policy** – Ann Brethour, Bianca Duran, and Katie Rose Marion
- **Economic Development/Jobs/Business** – Zackary Quintero

Something missing from the list? If you have an issue you are passionate about advocating for during the day of action send an email and we will add it to the list for students to join in on.

Additional cool stuff to participate in before or after advocating:

- Attorney General Hector Balderas has asked for students who are interested in visiting the office and speaking with staff to stop by (located right next to the Roundhouse). Please send an email in response if you are interested so that we may have a head count.
- You can tour the New Mexico Supreme Court and Court of Appeals (again located right next to Roundhouse).
- Meet up with fellow students, faculty, and legislators after the afternoon session for drinks and food.

Location: 490 Old Santa Fe Trail, Santa Fe, NM 87501.

Here is another example from a staff member taking on community hunger:

Dear Professors, Students and Colleagues:

As you know, food insecurity is a large and growing problem across our country, and in particular, on college campuses. Recent studies indicate that as many as 48% of college students experienced food insecurity in the thirty-days prior to the survey (Dec. 2016). It is a problem that our own community struggles with but one that is rarely addressed. In recognition of this need, our students are launching a program to provide a food pantry for law students.

In planning this program, one of the goals was to allow privacy for those who may wish to access this resource anonymously. The student organization leaders have agreed to allow us to use some of their space to provide storage for the food that is donated, and they will allow us to provide access to students during specific hours.

Beginning next week we will accept non-perishable food donations in the Office of Student & Career Services. Our students will coordinate transferring the donations to their offices for organization and distribution. We will also gratefully accept gift cards that can be used at grocery stores which will allow students to purchase the perishable or non-perishable food items that we won't be able to provide.

It is a testament to the character of our community that the support for our students who are in need has been swift and strong. Thank you for your consideration. Please let me know if you have questions.

Best regards,

Nancy Huffstutler, Career Service Office

You can do many similar things to help your community, whether they involve sharing legal expertise or not. For example, you can join your city council or the school board, run for office, put together a neighborhood association. There are no limits to how you can help. We all have a gift, or perhaps a few gifts. Plan how you can make the choices necessary to share your gift, either at work, or in your free time. Keep in mind that connections are the lifeblood of happiness. What kinds of communities would you like to be part of in your life, and what would you like your own role in these communities to be?

DREAM BIG, NOT SMALL

Your power to change the world is vast. Millennials in particular are defining their professional roles and responsibilities differently than previous generations. Many young people today think they can do anything, and in many ways, they can. Today's twenty- and thirty-somethings are making societal changes on their own terms. These influences are occurring in all fields, but to demonstrate, consider these young tech professionals.

Amazon's Alexa was created by three young, female, liberal arts majors, Michelle Riggen-Ransom, who has an MFA in creative writing, Farah Houston, a psychology grad specializing in personality science, and Beth Holmes, a mathematician. For another example, thirty-four-year-old Parisa Tabriz, the head of security at Google Chrome,[20] has made the web safer for all of us by using machine-learning tools to find insecure sites, rather than relying on information from users. As Tabriz explains, two billion people use the Google Chrome server and many do not know how the internet works. Her goal is to keep humans safe. While most engineers, she explains, act as if "humanity" does not exist, her goal is to make humanity her focus by keeping people safe.

Similarly, young Stanford bioengineer Manu Prakash invented a cheap, lightweight, microscope that magnifies objects up to 2,000 times but costs less than $1 to produce. While visiting rabies clinics in India and Thailand, Prakash learned that traditional microscopes are useless in remote villages. Within a year, his lab had shipped 50,000 of them to users in 135 countries, from Mongolia to rural Montana.

---

[20] *Next List 2017: 20 People Who Are Creating the Future*, WIRED MAGAZINE, 63, May 2017.

John Brooks, a 25-year-old middle school dropout, created an app that hides not just words but also the social graph of your connections. Unlike other messaging apps, Ricochet allows conversations to travel from the sender's computer to the recipient's without ever passing through a central server. The cloud never sees these messages, making this app totally unique. Another young millennial, Latina entrepreneur Laura Gómez founded Atipica, a recruiting software company that sorts job applicants solely by skills sets. She created this hard-data, judgment-free tool to increase diversity through reduced cronyism, and it is working.

Young entrepreneur Leslie Miley, President of Venture for America, created an executive in residence program to build tech businesses and talent in challenging cities such as Detroit and Baltimore. He claims that Silicon Valley generates astronomical wealth, but that this wealth never extends beyond the Bay Area, a situation he wants to change. He claims that anxiety following the 2016 US presidential election has caused some companies in the tech industry to examine their own role in overlooking large swathes of talent in the rest of the country. This start-up is Miley's way of building that talent and wealth outside the Silicon Valley.

Young people often question why the world cannot be more collaborative. It can, actually. Due to the influences of young adults, collaborative approaches have even hit the most capitalistic bastion of society, Wall Street. Typically, it is every man or woman against the next, and data scientists compete to make more money than all their peers through their investment choices. South African Richard Craib, who is 29, is the founder of Numerai,[21] a San Francisco-based hedge fund that makes market trades through collaboration rather than competition. Market scientists make investment choices anonymously. These trade suggestions are combined into an algorithm (through crowdsourcing) that is used to choose Numerai's investments. Craib rewards collaboration by compensating those who collaborate best. He obviously believes that the best investments result from collaboration, the "two heads are better than one" theory in practice. When the fund does well, all collaborators benefit. As Craib explains, "I don't want to build a company or a start-up or even a hedge fund. I want to build a country – a place where everyone is working openly toward the same end."

As these examples show, times are changing. You are part of that change, so make sure the change you are part of is something you want to see.

A DISRUPTIVE MOVEMENT IN LEGAL EDUCATION

As we discussed in Chapter 5, legal education experienced a major paradigm shift in the 1870s when Harvard Law School's Dean, Christopher Columbus Langdell,

---

[21] Numerai is a hedge fund, which means that it is an investment vehicle used only by the wealthy (those with income of over $200,000 and net assets of over a million dollars, excluding equity in the primary home. Hedge funds are limited partnerships of investors that use high risk methods, such as investing with borrowed money, in the hopes of realizing large capital gains.

moved legal education from a law school as "trade school" model, to a more analytical and academic model. Before Langdell completely disrupted legal education with these controversial innovations, lawyers were trained by practicing lawyers in the technicalities of legal practice. Langdell took the training of future legal professionals out of the hands of the practicing bar and bench, at least at Harvard, by hiring academics – not practitioners – to teach law. In so doing, he transformed teaching methods in law school from traditional lectures to a teaching method using real cases and hypothetical problem-solving techniques.

This innovation was thought to increase academic rigor and improve the thinking and analytical skills of lawyers. Soon this trend moved beyond Harvard to other law schools around the country. The skills of the resulting law graduates were thought to better match the needs of many legal employers, including large law firms, which wanted attorneys trained in more complex analytical skills, particularly written communication skills. This change in legal education completely altered and redefined American legal education. This change was a disruptive movement in legal education because it changed everything for everyone involved. While we will never return to the law school as trade school model, there is evidence that another disruptive movement in law is afoot.[22] Recall that law school changed in Langdell's day in large part because society demanded the change.

Society is now demanding another revolution, one in which lawyers respond to society's needs on a more gestalt or holistic level. Professions are more like the arts than the purely intellectual disciplines. Systematic rigor has contributed greatly to legal education, but it can't be the final goal of legal education, particularly given that interpersonal skills are so deeply valued in lawyers.

UNM School of Law Dean of Inclusion, Christine Zuni Cruz, has written extensively about many of the topics covered in this book. While her teaching and scholarly emphasis is on teaching the law of indigenous peoples, teaching law students to practice law within tribal communities, and teaching the world at large about the uniqueness of tribal communities, her advice is relevant in any setting. She notes that "how something is approached is often more important than the result."[23] She further notes that lawyers are not typically taught to work internally within communities but rather to be legal warriors, fighting the enemy.[24] We typically do not train lawyers to help build community consensus, for example, but just imagine how society could benefit from that type of training. Society needs lawyers that can fight, but also make peace within communities and among communities, as Dean Zuni Cruz explains:

> In preparing law students for lawyering, we must also prepare them for law/lawyering internally within the community or "peace leadership", as well as preparing them to be

[22] William M. Sullivan, *Professional Formation as Social Movement*, 23 ABA Center for Professional Responsibility The Professional Lawyer 1, 1 (2017).

[23] Christine Zuni Cruz, *Toward a Pedagogy and Ethic of Law/Lawyering for Indigenous Peoples*, 82 N. D. L. Rev. 863, 896 (2006).

[24] *Ibid.* at 880–81.

"legal warriors" or "war leaders" when they are operating against threats to sovereignty external to the community. The peace chief exercises leadership differently than the war chief. Internally, lawyers are dealing with people and must adapt their style of lawyering, much like the peace chief exercised a different type of leadership. During peace time decision-making is handled differently. There is more time to focus on process rather than a need to make immediate and quick life-or-death decisions. A shift must occur because the lawyer is not at war with people internally.[25]

As lawyers, we need to be bigger than the proverbial hired gun. We need to provide professional assistance that is analytical, but also flexible, innovative, and responsive to society's needs. We also must provide this help in a way that is emotionally intelligent. To do this, we must internalize our service role in society. As explained by William M. Sullivan, in *Professional Formation as Social Movement*:

> [Legal education] cannot be entirely reduced to procedure because it is performative expertise, inseparable from the person who internalizes it. Studies suggest that this is, if anything, even more true for professional education, at least for the most lasting and important parts of it. It is the formation of identity that guides and finally controls what is learned and how it is understood, an insight that has now begun to gain traction in the education of both physicians and lawyers.[26]

In this new legal education world, professional purpose or meaning trumps knowledge of substantive legal rules as well as analytical skills. The skills learned in this book, and through interpersonal interactions with professors, mentors, peers, and clients, are the ones that will be most critical to you as you develop your career. Lawyers trained in these essential professional skills will have a leg up in the profession. They will flourish and thrive.

When I started practicing bankruptcy law, there was a new bankruptcy code or statute. The older lawyers were used to the old one and did not really want to learn a whole new system. I knew no other system so I took to the new one, in much the same way that children, new with words, take to a second language. If you take to the professional identity guidelines and the skills described here, you too will be in the enviable position of having what society now wants and needs. These skills will go hand in hand with the successful and meaningful practice of law. We may be on the precipice of another disruptive movement in legal education and the legal profession. You are an integral part of that history in the making.

FINAL LAW PAUSE

This is the last exercise that we will ask you to do. Please sit down and write what you would like people to say about you at your memorial. If that is too grim, write about

---

[25]   *Ibid.* at 881.
[26]   William M. Sullivan, *Professional Formation as Social Movement*, 23 ABA CENTER FOR PROFESSIONAL RESPONSIBILITY THE PROFESSIONAL LAWYER 1, 1 (2017).

what you'd like people to say about you at your retirement party. Be as specific as you can. Keep this piece of paper handy for the rest of your life.

SETTING YOUR OWN COURSE GOING FORWARD

As you go through life, we hope you will periodically stop and reflect on the practices engaged in here, particularly these last few exercises. Always remember that you can choose to make a significant impact on society through your work. You can also do whatever you really want to do. You just need to know what that thing is. That is where most of us fall short. We don't ask the tough questions. We don't get what we want because we don't know what we want.

When seeking out what you want, think big not small, and really focus on the details. Harvard Psychology Professor David McClellan found that he could predict people's future by studying their daydreams about the future.[27] He found that successful people daydreamed about their goals, including how they would achieve these goals and how they would feel once they had achieved them. He found that if people picked challenging goals to dream about, they experienced extra satisfaction upon achieving them.[28] See what you can dream up for yourself!

If you like, you can create more tangible change by writing down your long-term and short-term goals. An author by the elusive name of RHJ wrote a little red book in 1926 called *It Works*, which is still available.[29] Though twenty-eight pages long, the heart of the book is contained in one simple idea, with three follow-up steps, which the author swears can create seismic shifts in thinking and thus in lives.

The author simply asks that we write down on a piece of paper the things we really want in life, in their order of importance to us. He then asks that we change the list daily, adding and subtracting until we get it right, and then adding and subtracting as things change. He asks that we not hold back and write out what we want in excruciating detail. He says the list can and will change over time, as our desires shift. He then asks us to do these three things each day:

1. Read the list morning, noon, and night.
2. Think of what we want as often as possible.
3. Do not talk to anyone about the plan except to the great power within you, which he says "will unfold to your objective mind the method of accomplishment."[30]

I will not ask that you do this, but I am certain that the technique works. Put all the energy you have into your dreams and you will accomplish them. You have the power to do so. I hope you will use that power wisely.

---

[27] BARNET BAIN, THE BOOK OF DOING AND BEING: REDISCOVERING CREATIVITY IN LIFE, LOVE, AND WORK 121 (ATRIA 2015).
[28] *Ibid.*   [29] R. H. JARRETT, IT WORKS (DEVORSS & CO. 1991).   [30] *Ibid.* at 13–15.

18

Gratitude

Nathalie Martin

Think back to Chapter 1, when we learned how to improve our lives by planning the perfect day. We hope you're still at it! The next time you plan the ideal day, start by expressing gratitude for all the wonderful things you have in life. In his book *The Upward Spiral*, neuroscientist Alex Korb cites dozens of empirical studies showing that gratitude practice activates a gratitude circuit in the brain. This circuit elevates physical and mental health, boosts happiness, improves sleep, and helps one feel more connected to other people.[1]

Gratitude practice is easy. We just write down one or two things we are grateful for each day. I like to do this in a calendar. As you look back, you see all the things you have to be grateful for in one place. As explained by yoga teacher Deborah Joya:

> We lift ourselves and each other when we are grateful in the moment. A gratitude calendar can help remind you to take time to reflect on the abundance in your life. Beginning and ending every day with a gratitude list helps us move into the day and night feeling good, enhancing our experiences. Imagine how uplifting to see on your wall a whole month full of things that made you grateful!
>
> We can choose to be grateful for everything, because even the biggest challenge has a blessing, which may be a valuable lesson. When we look through the sunglasses of gratitude, beauty and generosity show up all around, and peace and joy can be found in anything.
>
> When I know I am going to see a challenging person or be in a difficult position, listing all the things I am grateful for about that person or situation greatly helps me be more calm, present, and gracious. Physiologically, a relaxed state of mind (which can be induced by gratitude) helps the body's nervous system shift into the parasympathetic mode, giving more energy to the normal self-healing functions of the body.

---

[1] ALEX KORB, THE UPWARD SPIRAL: USING NEUROSCIENCE TO REVERSE THE COURSE OF DEPRESSION, ONE SMALL CHANGE AT A TIME 33–34 (NEW HARBINGER PUBLICATIONS 2015).

We've all experienced being affected by the emotions of others, so we can also surmise that our practice of gratitude is good for the happiness and therefore health of those around us.[2]

Many studies have shown the health benefits of spending time in gratitude. The website Heartmath.com describes in detail the process through which gratitude practice evens out heart rate patterns and creates smooth, regular patterns, also known as heart rate coherence. This keeps the cardiovascular system running efficiently and calms the nervous system. As we learned in Chapters 2 and 8, calming the nervous system improves one's overall health.

Gratitude then, like overall attitude about life, changes everything. As you go through each day, law school, and life, remember to be grateful for the positives in life, as well as for the learning that can be achieved only through difficulties. Know that you have the capacity to choose how to react to others as well as the capacity to choose gratitude for what you have. I have deep gratitude for my publisher, my editor Matt Gallagher, my students, and most of all, for my husband Stewart, my true one and only soul mate.

---

[2] Deborah Joya, *Gratitude Calendar*, 2017, available at www.deborahjoya.com/.

Index